Sassy

Sassy

THE LIFE OF SARAH VAUGHAN

LESLIE GOURSE

MAINSTREAM
PUBLISHING

EDINBURGH AND LONDON

Copyright © Leslie Gourse, 1993

First published in Great Britain in 1993 by
MAINSTREAM PUBLISHING COMPANY (EDINBURGH) LTD
7 Albany Street
Edinburgh EH1 3UG

First published in the United States of America by
Charles Scribner's Sons,
Macmillan Publishing Company,
866 Third Avenue
New York, NY 10022

ISBN 1 85158 413 7

A catalogue record for this book is available from the British Library

Phototypeset in Bembo by Intype, London
Printed in Great Britain by Butler & Tanner Ltd, Frome

This book is dedicated to the
wonderful people in the jazz world
who contribute not only their
beautiful music but information and
insights about their experiences.
This book is also dedicated
to my mother, Zelda Fisher Gourse,
and pays tribute to the memory
of the well-loved bassist
Major Holley

Contents

Acknowledgments

First of all I would like to thank my agent, Madeleine Morel, of 2 M Communications, for her enthusiasm and persistence in representing my books on jazz. Also thanks to Bill Goldstein, my editor, for his clarity, sensitivity, and his genius for organisation; without him, this book would have been immeasurably the less. Thanks to my special friend, John Parker, trumpeter and comedian, the veteran entertainer at New York's Chelsea Place, for his encouragement and advice. I'm also grateful to Ray Ross, jazz photographer and videographer and my friend, for insisting that I get a computer this time around and for putting me in touch with Gil Fuller, the arranger.

Thanks to Dan Morgenstern of the Institute of Jazz Studies, Rutgers University, for the resources of his library, and to Robert Medina of the *New York Times* morgue for his reference material. Special thanks to Larry Clothier, Sarah's friend and staffer, for his memories of incidents and the chronology of Sarah's career, to Robert Richards, Sarah Vaughan's friend, for the depth of his understanding, and to Phil Schaap for sharing his knowledge of Sarah's discography.

This book would also not exist without the inestimable help of Johnnie Garry, Modina Davis, Roy Haynes, Brooks Kerr, Doris Robinson Thomas, Maude Crews, Earlene Rodgers Scott, Evelyn Greene, Carmen McRae, Clyde B. 'Pumpkin' Golden Jr, Annie Ross, Dizzy Gillespie with his lead to Howard Scott, who is now Mohammed Sadiq, and John Williams, Clifton Smalls, Harold Mitchell, Mundell Lowe, Grady Tate, Joe Williams, Carl Schroeder, Jimmy Cobb, Walter Booker, Michael Tilson Thomas, Nat Hentoff, Norman Simmons, Ronnell Bright (Dr Ron L. Bright), Chris Colombo, lawyer Andrew J. Feinman, James Harper, George Wein, Dr Edward Holtzman, Dr

Fred Alofsin, Aretha Landrum, Buster Williams, Mike Wofford, Harold Jones, George Kanzler Jr, Thomas C. Guy Jr, Bob James, Frank Rio, Charlie Lake, Bill Mays, Jimmy Rowles, Molly Shad, Ron McClure, Dori Cyammi, Roy McCurdy, Andy Simpkins, Kay Simpkins, Pee Wee Ellis, Greta Reed, Hank Crawford, Ralph Lalama, Leonard Feather, Stanley Dance, Sarah's discographer Denis Brown, Andy Bey, and Katie Neubauer.

Also for their contributions, thanks to the Reverend Granville Seward, Joe Muranyi, the late Jabbo Smith, Ted Sturgis, Gary Stevens, Vivie Brown, Bobby Durham, Roger 'Ram' Ramirez, Bobby Tucker, Larry Willis, Stan Britt, Sonny Canterino, Bertha Hope, John Levy, Buddy Collette, John 'Preacher' Wells, Don and Johnny Pate for their efforts, Lionel Hampton, Little Jimmy Scott, Maurice Prince for references to people among her wide-ranging clientele at Maurice's Snack 'n Chat in Los Angeles, and those of the record companies for whom Sassy directly recorded and who provided me with music and references, and the countless people who led me to other people for bits of enlightenment.

And the photographers, whose works grace this book, deserve special attention.

Author's Note

Sassy gave innumerable performances, many of them celebrated concerts in the 1970s and 1980s. People who remember her concert with Henry Mancini, for example, for which she sang 'Mr Lucky', among other songs, may be dismayed to find that I haven't examined that concert in depth but have focused on other performances. I apologise for omitting some of her stunning performances, such as her dates at the Village Gate, and for confining to the discographical survey mention of some records which may be your favourites. It wasn't possible to include everything in this book.

Introduction

Evelyn Greene was reading a church bulletin from the Mount Zion Baptist Church in Newark, when an item about her old friend Sarah Vaughan caught her eye. Sarah was sick in the hospital. 'What?' Evelyn Greene asked herself. So she called Sarah's mother, Ada, who was then living in Sarah's sprawling ranch house protected behind the entrance gates to the private community of Hidden Hills, California, and asked how Sarah was. Mrs Vaughan confirmed that Sarah was sick and added: 'Pray for her.' Evelyn took the phone number of Cedar Sinai Hospital and called Sarah. Sarah's adopted daughter Debra Lois, by then using the name Paris Vaughan for her acting career, answered the phone; Paris was always with Sarah during those days in the hospital early in 1990. When she told Sarah that Evelyn Greene was calling, Sarah cleared her throat. So Evelyn thought Sarah's soft voice sounded smooth and fine.

Evelyn said, 'Hi. What's going on? You know we don't lay around here.'

Sarah didn't say what was wrong with her. She didn't sound very concerned.

'You know I love you,' Evelyn said.

Sarah said, 'I love you, too. You should come on.'

'I'm calling you from New Jersey.'

'Oh, I forgot,' Sarah said.

'Anyway, I'll pray and hope,' Evelyn said and hung up.

She was left with the impression that Sarah wasn't seriously ill. Not very much later, Evelyn heard the news. Sarah had died from lung cancer. Lung cancer! Sarah had always smoked a lot – about two packs a day, most of her friends remembered. Evelyn thought about all the

· *13*

smoke-filled clubs that Sarah had sung in, surrounded by smokers for so many years. Smoking had never bothered her voice, which had always sounded wonderful, although it had become lower and more resonant as time went on. John S. Wilson, jazz critic of the *New York Times*, once wrote that when she showed off her glorious voice, swooping around in her baritone register, she could sound as if she had fallen down a well. But most people adored that richness. Few people had thought about her smoking, only her age. All singers' voices lowered as the years passed. She had always had an affecting contralto, and she could still perform so many tricks in her soprano register; few coloratura sopranos could sing as well or communicate as much feeling as Sarah Vaughan. In her twenties and thirties, her voice had been as light and brilliant as fine wine; by her sixties it was as robust as cognac.

She had sung nearly every style of music except for opera – and even then she had come close, singing Handel's *Messiah* for the soundtrack of the 1969 film *Bob & Carol & Ted & Alice*. Some of her music had been hard to categorise as pop, jazz, spiritual, or contemporary classical. She had been such a great technician as a musician and an improviser that she could transform popular songs into arias. Under her care, 'Danny Boy' became art music.

'God had given Sarah that magnificent voice. She must have been able to ignore any of the effects of smoking,' Evelyn thought. 'God had also blessed Sarah with an exquisitely astute ear. From her childhood, she had known how to listen to instruments. And then she had just begin to sing.'

Evelyn had never known Sarah to study singing. Sarah had taught herself how to manipulate her voice from the low notes to her high range with lightning speed. The beauty of her sound gave people chills. Some of her recordings and videos had the force of her live performances; her Columbia album, *Gershwin Live*, with her exquisite scatting, was one of the best examples. Her vocal duet with Louis Bellson on drums for the Pablo album, *How Long Has This Been Going On?*, had the impact of a full orchestra. Musicians who had worked with her night after night for years reacted during each performance with strong rushes of emotion. Right after Sarah died, Evelyn turned on the radio and heard a jazz station playing Sarah's records for days. The continuous sound of her friend's voice reminded Evelyn of what made Sarah a wonderful singer.

Within the week, Evelyn was getting dressed to go to an old stone Gothic church, the Mount Zion Baptist Church at 208 Broadway in Newark, not the church to which she and Sarah had gone throughout their entire girlhood friendship, but anyway a hometown Baptist church from which Sarah would be buried. A coloratura soprano who had sung professionally for a time, Evelyn wanted to sing 'The Lord's Prayer' for Sarah at the church but was told that Leontyne Price, the opera diva whom Sarah had said many times she admired most in the world, was going to arrive to sing it. In the end, Leontyne Price did not show up but sent a message saying Sarah was now where the music came from, and Sarah's recording of 'Ave Maria' was played instead. Evelyn thought that Sarah might have preferred 'The Lord's Prayer'. But it was not Evelyn's choice. Other people involved with Sarah's illustrious career had done the planning. A horse-drawn chariot took Sarah's coffin from the church to the graveyard. After the funeral, Evelyn and several others of Sarah's childhood friends, most of whom had sung with her in a church choir, and who had not moved far away from the Newark area, were left with their private memories of her, after singer Billy Eckstine and a collection of other musicians and friends behind the scenes in her life had left town.

Perhaps no man felt sadder that Billy Eckstine, who had championed Sarah from the moment he heard her sing; he had enjoyed her respectful friendship for the next forty-seven years. Now he wasn't well himself. Of all the men behind the scenes, Marshall Fisher may have had the most painful and poignant memories. Fisher, like John 'Preacher' Wells, also at the funeral, had usually been referred to as one of Sarah's five husbands. Sarah had never legally married either Marshall or Preacher. Fisher had already grieved about a dozen years earlier when his relationship with Sarah had ended; he had rarely mentioned her to anyone since then. Or perhaps loyal fans of her voice and of that 'secret music' – saxophonist Clifford Jordan had called jazz 'that secret music' because nobody knows exactly what the musicians, all of them improvisers, are doing except for themselves – cared the most, or in the purest way, about her death, and knew the least about her life.

Modina Davis, a beautician and friend of Sarah's since childhood, cried at the funeral as if she had lost a sister. Modina recalled how she and Sarah once had watched a funeral in Kingston, Jamaica, when they had been touring in the 1950s. They saw a coffin being borne on a chariot drawn by two white horses away from a church. Sarah, then in her twenties, was in awe of the spectacle. 'I'd like that myself,' she said to Modina. Sarah had rarely dwelled on such ideas. She had loved to laugh. When she had become ill, she hadn't mentioned what her disease was to Modina. 'Sarah had never been a crybaby,' Modina mused.

Sarah had known exactly what the story was; it had been tough, and she had been tough, one of her best friends, Clyde Golden Jr, could testify. He and singer Annie Ross and others sometimes tried to pretend for a while that Sarah wasn't dead; she was simply back on the road. Others had reasons to take a more sanguine, measured view. But all of them focused on the wealth of recorded music she had left behind.

ONE

'Let's Go Pick Some Dillies'

Sometimes the regular organist at the First Mount Zion Baptist Church in the Ironbound, or Down Neck, section of Newark, New Jersey, wasn't able to play for Sunday church services, so Sarah Lois Vaughan took over the job. By October 1942, Sarah, who was then eighteen years old, had been playing the organ for years for choir rehearsals on Saturday mornings and services the next day. She could play the hymns in her sleep. She also played at events during the week for the children in the congregation; she was never too busy to play for any church event. Sarah grew up hearing her mother sing in the choir there, so it was a natural step for Sarah to follow her mother's example and become involved with the musical life of the church. Some people would always remember Sarah's pretty, ripe voice. By her early teens she was elevated to soloist in the choir.

The old church building at 186 Thomas Street stood in a decidedly unglamorous section of town, near the railroad station. When Sarah's parents, Asbury and Ada Vaughan, had migrated to Newark from Virginia during World War I, they found the church growing because of waves of migration from the South. Arranger, composer, and musician Gil Fuller had been born to a righteous Baptist family in Newark. As his famiy had done, Sarah's parents fitted snugly into the community of straightlaced, hardworking Baptists. 'They were the sort of people who didn't even want their children to go to dances,' Fuller recalled.

Yet everyone knew that Sarah, born 27 March 1924, was very talented. They passed along the word, so that even people who never went to that church began to hear about the gifts of this only child of the Vaughan family.* Newark's Little Jimmy Scott, who became a jazz singer, heard that Sarah was a soulful singer; the gossip he remembered was that Sarah could become another Marian Anderson – or so he reflected many years after Sarah became a famous singer.

'Sarah had a strong, alto voice,' her friend Evelyn Greene said, but Evelyn says she never heard Sarah sing a solo; when they were children, Evelyn, herself a soloist in church, had no idea how remarkable Sarah's voice was. But Maude Crews recognised Sarah's talents. Mrs Crews, a close friend of the Vaughan family, had been born and brought up in Newark; she worked as the choirmaster and an organist for the First Mount Zion Baptist Church from which vantage point she observed closely which children in her choir were talented and interesting. And Sarah was an 'outstanding' musician even as a child, Mrs Crews thought. Sarah apparently even then had a mighty desire to sing; later she told people she had always preferred singing to playing piano or organ.

A humble church with a poor congregation, the First Mount Zion Baptist Church had been built, stone by stone from its cement foundation, by its founding members in the late nineteenth century. And the congregants felt passionately attached to it. Evelyn Greene was proud that her family had helped with the construction. Doris Robinson, like Evelyn a close friend of Sarah's, was attached to the church, too, and the three girls sang in the choir together. Sarah, Doris, Evelyn, and a few more girls loved to get together after school at Sarah's house on Brunswick Street. (Sarah transferred from her neighbourhood high school, East Side High School, to Arts High for Newark's gifted students.) Sarah played her family's upright piano, while the others sang – usually sentimental love songs popular at the time, Doris remembered.

Evelyn noticed that Sarah ran home every day to hear the 5.15 p.m. broadcasts of singer and pianist Bob Howard, who during the 1930s and into the 1940s had a regular show on the CBS station in New York City. He was an exuberant musician who copied Fats Waller's style but was not especially talented, according to jazz historians. Sarah imitated the chords Howard played and showed off what she learned from the radio at the girls' afternoon musicales, playing everything from Ella Fitzgerald's 'Oh, Rock It For Me' to 'The Bluebird of Happiness', 'Danny Boy', and 'Ave Maria'.

---

*Evelyn Greene later heard from her mother that a son had died at birth, but the Vaughans seem never to have discussed this, and no corroborating evidence of such a birth is available.

Sarah's mother, Ada, had decorated the Vaughans' apartment in the two-family house where the family lived with bright floral-printed wallpaper. There was always music in the house. Either the radio was playing, or Sarah or her mother played the upright. At dinner time, Asbury Vaughan, whom most people, even Sarah, called 'Jake', sat down to pick his guitar and sing simple, bluesy country songs. Evelyn remembered a Victrola in the apartment, at a time when records cost thirty-seven cents each. Ada, who supported and nurtured her daughter's talent, set aside whatever little money she could to give to Sarah. She always seemed to have enough money to buy a few records. So the girls were able to listen to Count Basie, the Savoy Sultans, and Erskine Hawkins, and it was through records that they discovered Coleman Hawkins's classic rendition of 'Body and Soul'.

Ada Vaughan worked as a laundress. Paid by the piece, she earned between fifteen and eighteen dollars at most in a week, Sarah's girlfriends estimated; they thought that Asbury Vaughan, a carpenter, earned as much as his wife and perhaps more. With only three people in the family, the Vaughans got by, living frugally in an era when a month's rent was eight to ten dollars.

A short, dark-skinned man with sharp features, Jake Vaughan believed in his religion devoutly and attended church punctiliously. Asbury liked mainly to hear Sarah play church songs, though he seems to have tolerated the pop music she insisted on copying from the radio. Yet one of her girlfriends, Modina Davis, would remember how much he disdained Sarah's taste for pop music. He worried about the direction it led her in. 'He believed that Sarah would never be anything,' Modina recalled. But Ada Vaughan would always defend Sarah's right to play any music she liked. Mrs Vaughan even set aside twenty-five cents a week to give Sarah piano lessons with Josephine King, a church member. These lessons began when Sarah was about seven, she later said.

Sarah's love for popular music soon began to shape her social life. The Court Street YMCA sponsored afternoon sports events that were followed by dances, where the kids learned the lindy hop. And Sarah and her friends also liked to go to the skating rink on Montgomery Street, a short walk from Sarah's house on Brunswick Street. It cost a little money, which Sarah rarely had, to get into the rink. Whoever had some money helped the other kids pay the admission fees. Lionel Hampton and his band played at the skating rink; so did Buddy Johnson's band. Sarah's favourite place was the Laurel Garden which featured big bands. And when a local group played anywhere in the neighbourhood, Sarah would occasionally sit in and sing a song. Jake Vaughan minded most that pop music was taking his daughter away from home. To Sarah's father, her attraction to dances, pop music, and show business was anathema. 'He didn't even approve of her going out the door,' Sarah's mother recollected for a documentary tribute to Sarah aired on the Public Broadcasting Service on 29 July 1991.

Modina's mother allowed her daughter to go to dances, provided that she return home to meet a midnight curfew. But Modina never left the dances until the last song was played. 'I knew I was going to get it when I got home, but it didn't matter,' Modina recalled. Sarah's parents were more strict than Modina's and forbade her to attend dances. So Sarah, Modina remembered, simply climbed out a bedroom window and headed where she pleased at night. This way, according to Modina, Sarah didn't get into an argument with her parents, who would never permit her to go out. Later, she returned home by sneaking back in through the window. Her parents didn't find out about this scheme right away. They certainly didn't know that Sarah often cut classes at school, because Modina says it was something Sarah would definitely have been punished for. Sarah apparently had little fear of her parents, even though friends remember that she was sometimes punished for whatever wild behaviour her parents did know about.

'We weren't bad kids,' Modina says. 'We wanted to go to dances, but if the older people didn't give you permission to go, and you went, you were considered a "bad" kid. And Sarah qualified as a bad kid.'

Nevertheless, Sarah managed to get around. If she and her girl-friends had the price of tickets, they went to the Adams Theatre, where they heard the Erskine Hawkins band and Billy Eckstine with Earl Hines's band among others. The Adams was so popular that it lured New Yorkers across the river to see the stars there. At Newark's Proctor's Theatre one day, Doris Robinson and Sarah were thrilled to watch Josephine Baker perform. Afterwards they followed La Baker as she walked down the street, but they were too shy to approach the glamorous star. This was 1936, when Sarah was only twelve. Josephine Baker didn't return to the United States until 1948. By then Sarah was becoming a star herself.

Sarah met aspiring musicians in a downtown Newark record store, where they gathered to buy records and hang out. Sarah listened to their conversations. and her own ears helped her form opinions about the music everyone was discovering on records; in those days, record stores allowed people to listen to the music without buying records. While many of her girlfriends, Modina and Evelyn among them, stayed in school and earned high school diplomas, Sarah dropped out in her junior year. To Sarah, it didn't make any sense to go to school when she could learn the latest songs by day in the record store and play piano in the evening – even for no pay, as she began doing by her mid-teens – at such places as the USO near Newark Airport. Her friends remembered that at the request of people in her audiences, she even began to sing there. 'There might be something I didn't know how to play on the piano, but I could sing it,' she later reminisced to pianist Marian McPartland for her 'Piano Jazz' radio show on National Public Radio. Sarah probably earned a little money in tips at the USO.

Newark had over sixty vaudeville, burlesque, and first-run movie theatres – quite a trove of all kinds of entertainers, Gil Fuller recalled about his hometown. Fuller, who would write arrangements for Dizzy Gillespie in the 1940s, was playing piano and learning about music as Sarah was beginning to make her way around the music scene in Newark. He was aware of Sarah, who was a few years younger than he; she was one of the people whom he knew was becoming interested in the busy music scene, where he was already earning money as a professional.

Newark's musicians made up a lively, talented subculture. Every-one liked the Mosque, a reasonably nice ballroom, which later became Symphony Hall. In later years, Sarah sang at the Mosque and then starred at Symphony Hall. For her, Newark was always a clean, thriv-ing place filled with talented, hopeful youngsters who constantly trav-elled across the river to New York in search of fame and fortune in the Wednesday amateur night contests at the Apollo Theatre. As Gil Fuller remembered it, 'Musicians were always buttonholing each other and saying, "Let me show you this", or "Listen to this, my new song". Entertainment was the thing. Everybody wanted to become a star.' Sarah was caught up in the excitement. She made sure that she knew who everybody was and what they were playing, and she was friendly and polite to musicians.

Babs Gonzalez, who would later become a popular bebop singer, lived on Prince Street for a while. James Moody, who learned to play tenor sax and flute about as well and inventively as any jazz musician who ever lived, even though he was hearing-impaired and couldn't hear the high notes he was playing on flute, met Dizzy Gillespie through a Newark trumpeter, David Burns. Dizzy hired Moody, who soon wrote 'Moody's Mood for Love'. Many aspiring musicians played music for dances at the Y and hung out to talk about their music and their dreams at Pete's restaurant on Spruce Street, where they bought hot-dogs for ten cents apiece. A poolroom on Montgomery Street was another favourite spot. So was the Nest, a club on Warren Street. Sarah went to all these places to be among musicians.

The drummer Cozy Coles's brothers Teddy and June, both pianists, worked around town. Erskine Butterfield and Melba Moore's father, Clem Morman, among many other pianists, played in town and on WHBI, a station featuring local musicians. Hal Mitchell, a trumpeter in the leading local band, the Savoy Dictators, caught Sarah's attention, though Mitchell, who left town with a band in 1941, didn't meet Sarah until he made a record with her in Manhattan in 1947. By the early 1940s, Sarah had few close friends who weren't taking part in Newark's musical life at least to some degree. If they weren't entertainers, then they were kids who liked to go to dances, says Modina, who by 1947 was taking care of Ada Vaughan's hair and then Sarah's. Later Modina, as a hairdresser and Girl Friday, joined Sarah on her tours.

One of the first clubs that Sarah ventured into was the Piccadilly. The club had no cover charge, and its sympathetic manager let Sarah, Doris, and other youngsters step in to hear the music in the afternoons, even though the girls were far below the legal age limit, then twenty-one. Soon Sarah started going to the Piccadilly at night, and there she took her turn at the piano. By singing and playing, Sarah made an impression on the night people. Sometimes they tipped the girl in the wrinkled, plain clothes with chaste-looking necklines. A 'skinny minny', as Evelyn Green described the teenage Sarah, she lacked glamour from head to toe. The rich Southern foods her mother cooked never put an ounce of fat on Sarah, and her figure was raillike; her waist and chest measurements were about the same. She was five feet three and a half inches (not five feet five, as articles would later say). And she wore her hair in a nondescript style that Evelyn called 'a fuzz'. Sarah gave her friends the impression that she was slight and vulnerable. But she quickly discovered she could overcome the stigma of being considered unattractive from the moment she sat down to play or sing. As a musician, she would never be overlooked.

After Sarah's death, Ada Vaughan would recall that a club owner had told her about Sarah's fledgling professional life. Mrs Vaughan was shocked to hear that Sarah was playing in a club, because Sarah was only fifteen at the time. Furthermore, the man wanted to hire Sarah; that's how talented she was. Mrs Vaughan was proud of the compliment, but her daughter's life-style worried and amazed her. The characters whom Sarah met in the clubs didn't bother her, however. They could be slick if they wanted to be, and she could be herself, a musician.

Often, the slicker they were, the more amusing they were – and the less they might remind her of the plain routine of a quiet, church-centred life-style. It was lovely to be the centre of attention when she sang and played piano. In fact, her slight figure and sloppy style of dress probably helped her attain her musical goals. She wanted to develop as a musician and to be treated as one of the boys, as an equal who didn't require special coddling. Musicians felt at ease around her; they accepted her. At the same time, because she kept up her church work devotedly, her parents seemed to overlook her transgressions. To Sarah's way of thinking, both worlds revolved around music. 'That's why she felt no conflict at all in travelling between the two places,' says Robert Richards, in later life a close friend and confidant of Sarah's. Another friend, Larry Clothier, who would work in her road company on and off for years, said, 'It didn't seem strange to her at all.'

Maude Crews reminisced, 'I thought there was some hope for Sarah in show business, even though it was very risky.' Mrs Crews also knew that Sarah's father disagreed about Sarah's prospects. And, although Sarah loved her quiet father very much, the atmosphere between Sarah and him remained heated for as long as Sarah lived under his roof in Newark, because 'he did not want her to go on the stage. He was protective,' Mrs Crews explained. But Sarah told her father, 'I want to. I like it! And I'm going to hit!' Mrs Crews reflected, 'That was Sarah's attitude, and her father couldn't do anything about it.'

Modina Davis knew that Asbury and Sarah argued often. Years later, Maude Crews laughed about the tension in the Vaughan family. It was simply a dusty family scandal that turned out not to be serious. Modina recalled that Jake Vaughan challenged Sarah all the time and often about the simplest things. 'You never saw that,' Modina heard him say. 'If he said that salt was black, you could never prove to him that it was white. He could be very provocative, and he could make Sarah very angry.' So Sarah's reassurances that she would become a success didn't impress him. All Sarah could offer as proof was a few dollars she earned at times as a musician and the obvious truth, which even he had always acknowledged, that she played piano and sang beautifully.

Yet Sarah's own character was patterned somewhat after his despite the differences of their ideas. As he did, she disliked being fawned over and didn't expect to be. She disliked clinging vines, and sooner or later she disentangled herself from them, though she could become emotionally dependent upon the most unsuitable people. Her dedication to music was as strong as her father's devotion to the church. And sometimes, like him, she dabbled in painting, although she liked landscapes, and he was an amateur portraitist. At the same time, apparently unlike her father or mother, she could be guilelessly open on first meeting people. And in some ways, completely unlike them, she adored excess – noise, commotion, and staying up late. As a thin and angular young woman, Sarah resembled her father more than she did her mother; in later life, when Sarah gained weight, she began to look like her short, plump, energetic mother. Sarah was never exactly like either of her parents, however. Her great musical gifts differentiated her from everyone she knew as a girl. Maude Crews remembered with amusement how independent Sarah was and thought Sarah's nickname, 'Sassy', was apt. 'She was quite impertinent, very pointed. Whatever she had to say, she would say it right out. She didn't hold things back; she was a very forward girl. If there was anything she wanted to do, she would keep that in mind and go forth and try to do it. And that's why she was so successful.'

By the time Sarah had been an aspiring musician for a while in Newark, the fellows were calling her 'No 'Count Sarah'. From the musician's grapevine, an informal communications system that could get a message around the world in a few days, Gil Fuller heard about the nickname, a usual bit of slang in her circles. Eventually one of her albums would have that title. It didn't mean that musicians thought she was a hustler but rather the opposite. Unadorned as a woman, she was a musician who looked out for herself, hung out with musicians, and did as she pleased.

It would be a long time before she developed any interests aside from music. Not until the 1960s would a friend from Newark teach her to sew, which Sarah came to love. She would become so handy with a sewing-machine that she could quickly put together gowns to wear on stage and design suits and caftans for friends. Sewing, which Sarah called 'meditating', became one of her favourite ways to pass the time in hotel rooms when she toured. Eventually she started cutting and styling her friends' hair, too, after watching Modina for a long time. Sarah would occasionally say she had once toyed with the idea of becoming a hairdresser. As she began to struggle to establish a career, she focused only on music.

In her teens, she couldn't imagine that she would ever have complicated business affairs. She never became a businesswoman, and that naïveté would cost her a lot. 'She never thought about any of those [money-oriented] things,' Modina Davis recalled. Sarah had a simple answer when anyone told her to pay more attention to the nonmusical details of her career. 'I sing, I just sing,' she said. She didn't want to think about anything else. Sarah knew that her mother wanted her to pursue a concert career, and Sarah always seemed to keep that in the back of her mind. But that venture was exceptionally difficult for anyone to launch without powerful backers. Negroes were essentially barred from the world of classical music. Marian Anderson not only had a great gift, but her supporters and teachers had influential connections. Sarah was virtually on her own, slightly educated and very naïve, sophisticated only in her ability to play and sing the music she was drawn to under the conditions that prevailed.

In Newark, in her late teens, she had the stamina to hang out all night. Then she slept late and began all over in the afternoon. By dusk, she was circulating among musicians someplace, immersing herself in music in clubs and in repartee with her friends until dawn. The lifestyle was paradise for her. If she had some spare money, she liked to spend it on fried bacon. That was her idea of a great treat. Smoking didn't bother her voice at all. 'Nothing bothered her throat,' her friend Robert Richards reminisced. 'Once she saw that she could smoke without affecting her voice, she must have simply felt relieved, and she kept smoking. She didn't worry about it.' Around this time, Modina remembers, Sarah would drink gin with a dash of water and a twist of lemon. Smoking and drinking were just part of the initiation rites into the nightlife.

Everyone noticed that nothing, not even a cold, bothered her throat. In fact, all her friends testify that she sang at her best when she was tired or troubled in some way. For Sarah, music was the core of joy. 'God is good,' she would begin to explain in a soft, shy voice to people who complimented her backstage after performances.

Earlene Rodgers, who was a few years younger than Sarah, was in awe of the older girl. A mischievous girl herself, with a pretty soprano voice, Earlene was a stagestruck kid in her own way. She used to go to hear musicians, including Sarah, play in a variety of clubs, primarily in the afternoons, in the early 1940s. The managers at the Piccadilly Club and at a small club called the Alcazar knew how much Earlene liked to hear music, so they let her in, even though, like Sarah, she was under age. Earlene followed Sarah to a little place called Our Club and to a second-floor club on Kinney Street. Earlene, who had occasionally joined Sarah and her friends at their musical afternoons in Sarah's apartment, was impressed by how outgoing and friendly Sarah was in those places. Everybody – the older musicians and other people hanging around – had time for Sarah, and she had a bright if buck-toothed smile for everyone. Sarah confided to her that when she sang, she liked it best if the club's management let her play the piano for herself. Most times nobody could give the kind of instrumental support she wanted. In one of her earliest interviews, in *Ebony* magazine in 1949, she said that ideas came to her through continual practice. She played around with gliding passages on a piano or an organ. 'Then when I'm singing I close my eyes and picture my voice following the piano or organ runs.'

Trombonist Howard Scott moved to Newark from Irvington when he got married and was soon playing trombone professionally in town. One sunny afternoon, he passed the Alcazar and heard a beautiful voice emanating from the club. A woman was singing 'Skylark'. He had never heard anyone sing like that before in his life. He went in, sat down, and was hypnotised by Sarah's sound. Afterward he applauded wildly, introduced himself, and told her how marvellous she was.

Sarah was eighteen and a woman by then, even though she never thought of herself as good-looking. 'I wasn't much to look at,' she didn't mind saying about her appearance. Dark, with bright eyes, a broad nose, a large, mobile mouth, and a forthright, strong chin, she was actually an adorable, at times bubbly, young woman with no idea of how to accentuate her best features. Her low hairline tended to exaggerate the thrust of her large jaw and its residual baby fat. Though she was generally unsure of herself as a woman, she had only one real physical blemish – her buck front teeth and the gap between them. In those days, the measure of a black woman's attractiveness was the degree to which she resembled Lena Horne. Sarah, with her crooked teeth, didn't count for very much. Perhaps for that reason, none of the slick men whom she inevitably hung around with had offered to help her try to build a career beyond Newark. Doris Robinson says she never heard Sarah talk about men or romance. Doris thought Sarah's dream of a career captured all her attention. Earlene later recalled that Sarah had confided she also dreamed of falling in love and having a happy marriage and children. But she didn't develop a special attachment to any of the men whom she knew in Newark. Music was her connection to them. Jabbo Smith, a trumpet player, remembered encouraging Sarah to try to win an amateur night contest at the Apollo. It was perfectly natural for Sarah to try. Many of the professional musicians she knew in Newark had tried for prizes there, and many had won.

One day in 1942 during choir practice at the First Mount Zion

Baptist Church, Sarah passed Doris a note, which said, 'Let's go pick some dillies'. Doris knew very well that Sarah meant they should spend the afternoon in the Piccadilly. There Sarah suggested, 'You should go to the Apollo contest. Give it a try. I bet you'll win.'

'You think so?'

'Sure,' Sarah said.

'Okay, you play for me,' Doris said.

'Sure,' Sarah said.

It would be like the time in 1939 that Sarah had played accompaniment for Doris on WHBI, when they substituted for a friend of Doris's taking a three-week vacation from his show.

'What will I sing?' Doris asked Sarah.

'"The Bluebird of Happiness". You should do that. I'll arrange it for you.'

'Oh, I don't know, Sarah,' Doris said, having second thoughts about the whole idea.

'Yes, we'll do that. You know you can do it.'

'It makes me nervous to think about that.'

Doris's fiancé didn't want her to sing professionally so he didn't encourage her to enter the Apollo contest. But the young women decided to try. If they lost, even if they were booed off the stage, they would have had an adventure and survived it together.

On many occasions, Doris and Sarah had set out from Newark's Pennsylvania Railroad Station to Manhattan. They bypassed Fifty-second Street, which had many clubs on two West Side blocks, and ducked into the subway and hurried straight uptown. In Harlem, they usually went to the Savoy Ballroom to hear the big bands. That always constituted an exciting night for them, even though they noticed that at midnight, as they were leaving to go home, the crowds were just starting to arrive at the Savoy. The only other place they went to in Harlem was the Apollo Theatre, which had shows all day long.

This night in 1942 when they set out to compete in New York City, Doris made sure to dress prettily in a clean, well-pressed dress. Sarah showed up in a nondescript outfit as usual. That was Sarah. Before going on the Apollo's stage, Doris kissed the symbolic 'tree of hope' that all amateurs kissed for luck, and then stepped forward to sing 'The Bluebird of Happiness', with Sarah playing the piano. To her joy, Doris won second prize – ten dollars; she split the money with Sarah fifty-fifty.

It didn't take Sarah long to decide that she wanted to go back on the Apollo's stage and try to compete as the star. Sarah told some of her friends that she thought she could probably win a prize there, too, as so many aspiring entertainers from Newark had done. Someone said she couldn't win. So 'I went on a dare,' she later recalled in an article she wrote as a guest columnist for the National Negro Press Association, a news service. 'I entered the amateur show at the Apollo Theatre in New York City on the condition that friends would be in the audience to cheer me on.' Her mother remembered that Sarah went three times. Certainly she went one night in October 1942, with a group of friends accompanying her. 'They paid her way,' Modina Davis later said Sarah told her, 'because she didn't have any money to pay her fare.'

Sarah arrived at the Apollo so late that night that Ralph Cooper Sr, the master of ceremonies, didn't want to let her sing. He recalled how flustered she was; she could barely tell him what she wanted to do, and she projected how crestfallen she felt when it appeared that he wasn't going to let her go onstage. So he changed his mind and gave her a chance. She forgot to kiss the 'tree of hope'. But when she sang 'Body and Soul', everyone cheered for her.

In his own book, *Amateur Night at the Apollo*, Cooper said he had felt protective toward Sarah. She looked so small, and he knew how menacing the audience could seem when it didn't like a performance. He thought 'the roar of the crowd would knock her off her feet'; instead the audience succumbed to her bravura interpretation of a song they knew so well from the same Coleman Hawkins record that Sarah knew. Billie Holiday's heartfelt rendition of the ballad was the stuff that her stardom was made of, too. Sarah's glorious voice, its range and the creativity of her embellishments, surprised Ralph Cooper. 'I was so impressed by her in-depth soul and her ability to vocalise changes around the melody . . . Sarah Vaughan was a superstar in the making . . . She jumped octaves like she owned them . . .' Sarah went home with the first prize – 'ten dollars', Sarah recalled in a bright voice forty-four years later in a radio interview with pianist Marian McPartland on 'Piano Jazz' – plus the promise of a week's engagement at the theatre sometime in the near future. Sarah decided to make singing her business.

All she could think about was the phone call to summon her for a week's work with a big band at the Apollo Theatre. The days dragged on. By Christmas, it appeared as if the Apollo's management had forgotten about her. Winter passed; the war was still being fought in Europe; life went on in the usual way in Newark. Sarah was caught up in her routine of singing, playing, hanging out, laughing, joking, and passing the time. Maybe she would be on the Newark scene forever.

The call came in the early spring of 1943. Crowds arrived at the Apollo to see Ella Fitzgerald, the headliner. Billy Eckstine, who had an apartment on 125th Street near the Apollo, decided to drop in for Ella and the whole show. And when Eckstine heard Sarah sing, he couldn't believe his ears. How lovely her voice was! 'It was just something different. Something you hadn't heard before,' Eckstine later explained. Ella Fitzgerald heard Sarah's quality, too, and noticed a number of agents crowding around her. Later Sarah reminisced gratefully, 'She stopped me from signing myself away to all the agents hanging around.' She and Ella became friends later, not right away, because on the night she won the contest, Sarah was so 'very very very very very very very very shy', she told Marian McPartland.

Eckstine told his boss, bandleader Earl Hines, but the information may not have registered on Hines right away. In any case, Eckstine was often credited with introducing Sarah to 'Fatha' Hines; Sarah herself said that 'B', as Eckstine's friends always called him, did it. But Hines told Stanley Dance for publication in his book, *The World of Earl Hines*, that he and a friend, June Clark, a trumpeter and a valet, discovered Sarah on their own. By this account, Earl and June Clark had spent a day drinking and, very high, had gone to the Apollo to hear Ella. When Sarah sang, Hines reminisced, he said, 'Is that girl singing, or am I drunk or what?' A wizard at stagecraft by then, leading one of the best bands of his career in the 1940s, Hines trusted his eyes completely to tell him that Sarah looked like 'homemade sin', he said – an unkind and extreme evaluation of her looks which Sarah would encounter often and spend the rest of her life trying to overcome. Her dress and stage demeanour proved Sarah's lack of sophistication on the day Hines heard her for the first time. But if her hairline was too low, her voice was highbrow.

Ralph Cooper wrote in his book, 'Earl Hines was so amazed when he heard her. It took three weeks to get his mouth closed.' Hines immediately decided to replace his girl singer, Madeline Green, with Sarah.

'Would you like to come to work with my band?' he asked Sarah after introducing himself backstage.

She was sitting down alone on a Coca-Cola crate. 'Eey-uh', he remembered her saying in her customary no-frills style, perhaps shocked and certainly timid. But she was not so afraid that she failed to seize the opportunity instantly.

Hines was delighted that Sarah could play the piano very well. That meant he could list her as a musician, a member of the musicians' union, and avoid any pressure from the American Guild of Variety Artists, to which performers who didn't play instruments belonged. The union's authority took precedence over the guild's. Hines instructed Sarah to play 'second piano' for him – to sit at a second piano set on the Apollo stage, where she played a few measures, supplied embellishment for his work, and enhanced his image. She was primarily asked to sing songs with Billy Eckstine and also a solo toward the end of each show. Hines played for her and Billy.

The men in Earl's band, who were used to the sophistication of Hines's previous girl singer, Madeline Green, thought that Hines had lost his mind. But once Hines's men heard Sarah sing, they were as delighted as Billy and Hines. Furthermore, nothing shocked or alarmed Sarah. She had heard all the cursing and seen all the hustling in Newark. No one needed to treat her with kid gloves. When Earl's men discovered she could swear as handily as any of them, they started to call her 'Sailor'. Most important of all, she made sure that nobody deluded himself that he was harder working or more talented than she.

Jake Vaughan was beside himself when he learned that his nineteen-year-old daughter planned to travel in buses and on trains packed with hard-drinking, fast-living musicians on the road. But the most artistically adventurous among them would adopt Sarah as a virtual mascot of the fledgling new jazz style called bebop and a fellow explorer of the new harmonies in jazz composition. She had a voice of fascinating quality, which enveloped any group that she sang with. And she could sing any kind of music, because she knew harmony from her piano playing, and she understood the unusual harmonies that the accompanists were playing for her. She could sing in tune with the most complex figures; she could change keys with ease. Dizzy Gillespie, who was playing in the Hines band when Sarah joined, told people, 'Sarah can sing notes that other people can't even hear'. It was the same thing he said about Charlie 'Bird' Parker, who was also playing in the Hines band then and was inventing bebop with Dizzy. Dizzy never said that about anybody else. Sarah was beside herself, too – with happiness. 'She was just so glad to get into that band,' recalled John Williams, the group's baritone saxophonist. 'From then on, it was shocksville,' Sarah later said about her start in show business. 'I haven't gotten out of it yet.'

TWO

Portrait of the Artiste as a Young Songbird

Earl 'Fatha' Hines had a reputation as a great connoisseur of talent. He knew exactly what he was doing when he hired Sarah. As musician and jazz historian Gunther Schuller recalled about Hines's band★ at the time Sarah joined it, performing with Bird in it, 'They were playing all the flatted fifth chords and all the modern harmonies and substitutions and Dizzy Gillespie runs in the trumpet section work . . . what was so exciting about the Hines band was that they were playing harmonies and complex rhythms and textures that I already knew from classical music. Although what was new in jazz was forty years old in classical music, they discovered it on their own route. Imagine how bored I was with Dixieland music, which was all one-four-five, and if you got a seventh chord you were in heaven already! These guys were coming out with bitonal chords (though Ellington had been doing it ten years before that); this was a whole new age of discovery in jazz.' Sarah was suddenly learning how to polish her singing style from some of the best players of the big-band era and the adventurous Young Turks of bebop, especially the horn players. Later she would reflect with modesty, 'I thought Bird and Diz were the end. I still do. At that time I was singing more off-key than on. I think their playing influenced

★Band members during Sarah's tenure with Hines were Dizzy Gillespie, Shorty McConnell, Jesse Miller, trumpeters; Gail Brockman, lead trumpeter; Charlie Parker, Thomas Crump, tenor saxophonists; Andrew 'Goon' Gardner, George 'Scoops' Carey, alto saxophonists, with Carey the band's 'straw boss', in charge of the band after Earl; John Williams, baritone saxophonist; Cliff Smalls, who joined after Sarah did, trombonist and pianist; Gus Chappell, Benny Green and Howard 'Scotty' Scott, who later changed his name to Mohammed Sadiq, trombonists; Rossiere 'Shadow' Wilson, drummer; Connie Wainwright, guitarist; and Paul O. Simpson, bassist, who would be replaced by Ted 'Mohawk' Sturgis. Alto saxophonist John Jackson may have played in the Hines band while Sarah was with it.

my singing. Horns always influenced me more than voices. All of them – Bird, Diz, Pres, Tatum, J.J., Benny Green, Thad Jones – listening to them and others like them, listening to good jazz, inspired me.'*

Sarah and trombonist Howard Scott had joined the Hines band nearly on the same day. 'We walked hand in hand into the band,' Scotty recalled. Leonard Feather, the jazz critic, wrote an item in *Metronome* about seeing Sarah perform during the few days of her tryout period with the Hines band at the Apollo Theatre before she joined the band officially on 4 April 1943. He watched the Apollo curtains part to reveal Hines at one piano and 'a shy young girl from Newark' at another piano. When she came forward to sing 'Body and Soul', Feather knew instantly about her bright talent. *Down Beat*'s reviewer John S. Wilson (who signed his name 'Wil') said Sarah was handling her first band assignment well. (In Feather's book, *Inside Bebop*, later reprinted as *Inside Jazz*, about the birth of the new music, Feather would reflect, 'Sarah's own influence as a musician is not to be discounted.' And in his *Encyclopedia of Jazz* [published in the 1950s], he repeated Dizzy and Bird's comment that Sarah was 'a new development in jazz.') The sound of that Earl Hines band was lost for posterity because of a recording ban during the American Federation of Musicians strike called by James Petrillo against the record companies in a successful bid for better working conditions for musicians. Billy Eckstine had heard about Scotty and, when the Hines band was playing in Newark, Eckstine approached the trombonist about joining. Scotty, of course, was delighted.

The men in the Hines band had to look immaculate. That was Hines's edict. He provided one uniform for his men, who usually bought a second themselves; Hines also bought accessories for those men who had none, and he deducted the cost from their salaries. Each man had a wardrobe trunk and a small piece of hand luggage. When the band arrived at a destination, the trunks came out of the baggage car; the men, who usually stayed with black families, since hotels didn't accept black guests, had a chance to clean their clothes. They always found someone available to do laundry overnight. Black bands did a great number of one-night stands, playing for dances around the country. It was a luxury for a band to have a week's engagement or

---

*Pres was tenor saxophonist Lester Young; the others were pianist Art Tatum, and trumpeter Thad Jones. J.J. was either alto saxophonist John Jackson or more likely influential trombonist J.J. Johnson, who won *Esquire*'s New Star Award in 1946. Jackson played in Earl's band.

more at a theatre, the baritone saxophonist John Williams recalled. So the men really had to organise their clothes to keep them at all fresh.

Ready for her first professional trip with the band, Sarah showed up at Pennsylvania Station, carrying all her belongings in a paper bag. Billy Eckstine and Scoops Carey, who would later become a lawyer in Chicago, took the bag from her and tossed it back and forth as if it were a ball. 'They tore it up,' John Williams recalled. 'She took it in good humour.' The paper bag was soon a thing of the past. Scoops and B bought her a good suitcase.

Earl picked out a very pretty, long white dress for Sarah to wear on stage. Photographs of her taken in 1943 show her as a slip of a girl with a sparkling, sincere, guileless smile. She placed a sprig of white flowers in her upswept hair, which made a shiny ring above her forehead in a tasteful version of the 1940s fashion for piling up hair and exaggerating a coiffeur with combs, feathers, and fruit. Sarah's hairstyle was achieved with a wig – perhaps Hines's idea. Sarah's white dress had a peplum and a squared-off neckline. Since the men in the band and her close girlfriends recalled that Sarah had no noticeable bosom, she probably stuffed the bodice to make herself look fetching and feminine. She achieved a dainty, demure look which contrasted suitably with the warmth and power of her mature voice. In photographs taken between 1943 and 1945, the only blemish in her ladylike appearance onstage remained the gap between her buck front teeth.

Offstage Sarah was left to her own devices about her clothes and personal hygiene. 'She didn't know anything about anything, but that child had a terrific voice,' John Williams mused. Because he was about twenty years older than Sarah and the eldest person in the band after Earl, Williams felt responsible for looking after each youngster who came into the band. 'I noticed that Sarah was a little slow about getting her clothes cleaned,' he reminisced. 'She wore one pair of stockings for so long that I bought her a new pair and told her to wash the old ones or throw them away.'

Audiences had no idea about how she fumbled behind the scenes with her appearance. 'She won over the crowds everywhere,' Scotty, the trombonist, noticed, 'and she was such a great artist, everyone in the band looked upon her as a great musician.' Sarah had friendly relations with the Hines musicians, as the few survivors recalled in 1991. She was sweet, agreeable and comradely, Clifton Smalls remembered, without a hint of the temperament or moodiness that he would hear about in connection with her much later in her life.

Sarah had been set at the second piano onstage solely to enhance the band's image before she stood up to sing. She played a few notes at the piano primarily for the Apollo shows, when Hines liked the idea of presenting himself as so prosperous that he could afford a second pianist. After Smalls joined the band, Sarah didn't play the piano during performances with Earl's band anymore. She had become popular as a singer with the band. Reviewers had thought the slender girl looked waiflike at the piano and had marvelled at how she seemed to gain stature once she stood up to sing. The quality of her voice was so seductive.

With her uncanny ability to sing runs, she spent her time improving her control of her voice, learning from the swinging, energetic horn players whenever they played, jammed, or simply talked about what they were trying to do. Dizzy's speed and daring with harmonies impressed her. But Dizzy thought she especially loved Bird's music. 'She didn't want to know about nothing but Bird's music. She was a musician herself,' Dizzy said. He thought highly enough of her as a pianist to ask her to play with his early groups.

In those days, Dizzy, Bird and others headed uptown in Harlem to Minton's and Monroe's Uptown House to practise playing more complex harmonies, and from those experiments came new melodies with unusual, sometimes dissonant-sounding harmonies and poly-rhythms – a more intense, aggressive style of jazz. At first musicians called their contemporary expressions 'progressive jazz'. The music was so new to the world that it didn't even have the name bebop yet. It sounded so strange to most ears that Cab Calloway had called it 'Chinese music' because of its bizarre, exotic harmonies. 'Sarah was crazy about that type of music,' Cliff Smalls noticed. Nobody knows exactly which New York newspaper writer first coined the word *bebop*, but every journalist and musician seized upon it, because it imitated the fast, sometimes choppy rhythmic sound and the unusual sequences of notes of the intense music.

Sarah never accompanied the men to Minton's or Clark Monroe's Uptown House, as Dizzy recalled, though others saw Sarah occasionally hanging out in Minton's. They remembered seeing her more frequently at the grill in the Braddock Hotel, a spot popular with musicians on Eighth Avenue at 126th Street. The hotel's front door faced 126th Street; downstairs was a rehearsal hall – Chick Webb's band, with Ella Fitzgerald, practised there as others did when they passed through town. Everybody in entertainment went to the Braddock Grill sooner or later. It was a favourite hangout for a budding young singer and pianist named Carmen McRae for several years in the 1940s, even before Sarah set eyes on the place. After Sarah started travelling with the Hines band, she discovered the crowd at the Braddock and became friends with Carmen McRae – and with Carmen's husband, drummer Kenny Clarke, who was experimenting with the beboppers at Minton's.

If a man in the Hines band had an idea, as the band travelled around, he would say to someone, especially Sarah, who could play piano, 'Play this tune'. And with the chords of the old song as the foundation, a musician changed the melody lines and invented new bebop songs. The chords gave musicians clues to the appropriate notes to choose for creating contemporary songs. The chord structures of 'I Got Rhythm', 'Cherokee', and 'How High the Moon' for example, inspired musicians to invent hundreds of new melodies. One of the most famous early bebop compositions was Bird's 'Ko Ko'; substitute notes for the melody were inspired by the chords of 'Cherokee'. Dizzy regarded Sarah as a colleague who could wrest as much richness, warmth, and inventiveness from melodies with her voice as the instrumentalists could manage on their horns. Dizzy arranged quite a few songs for her, Smalls recalls; he especially liked a ballad called 'East of the Sun, West of the Moon', which Sarah performed only once or twice, if at all, with the Hines band – Hines thought it was too slow and odd for his fans, who wanted to dance. (Sarah began recording the song soon after she left the Hines band.) Other songs that Smalls loved to hear Sarah sing were 'Sweet and Lovely' and 'He's Funny That Way'. One of Scotty's favourites by Sarah was 'Once in a While'.

Eckstine loved to tease Sarah and sometimes became pretty rough on her, calling her 'a greasy bitch', as one friend of Sarah's remembered B doing playfully. 'In those days, everybody called each other "m.f.",' recalled Gil Fuller, 'or a greasy m.f., if a person was as unkempt as Sarah.' Gil recalled bumping into Sarah in the Braddock Hotel in New York one day and noticing the grease on her suit collar from a cosmetic grease treatment for her hair. 'I told her to clean herself up, and then she could be somebody. But she was a church chick and poor. She didn't have the money to get her suit cleaned,' Gil recalled. It was typical of B's irreverent sense of humour to tease Sarah about her slovenliness. Neither B nor anybody else talked to or treated Sarah 'like some prima donna or a society broad. She was one of the musicians on the road,' Gil added. B, who was known as a 'scrapper', a fighter, could say anything he liked to Sarah. His teasing was affectionate, she felt. And it was. B also called her 'my baby' and 'little sister', friends recall. Sarah was in awe of B as a singer and a man. Though their longtime friends clearly knew that B returned Sarah's respect, the guys in the Hines band liked to tell B: 'Say what you want to say but Sarah is outsinging your ass.'

Sarah could do her share of teasing and bantering, too. She began to call Clifton Smalls 'Clifford', because it sounded 'real coloured', she told him. She knew it annoyed him, he recalled with a laugh, and she never quit it. Years later, Cliff, in his eighties, remembering Sarah after her death, giggled as he told how the playful young Sarah had loved to put some spice in life; on the road, she had even carried a bottle of hot peppers with her. The musicians needed the spice to enliven the dull-tasting food in many of the places where they ate, usually simple restaurants in black neighbourhoods.

'She hung out with everybody,' Cliff observed. Wherever the men in the band went during the day, Sarah went with them. She was never content to sit in the hotel until it was time for the show, as some of the girl singers of the period did. Other girls became involved in romances with musicians in their bands; making the girls stay behind was one way the musicians could curtail the other men from 'hitting on them'. But Sarah went to eat meals, see movies, and drink in the bars with the men. She played cards and dice with them on the buses and trains.

She was also always ready to join the men in a prank, Smalls remembered: 'Once we got on the bus away from the rest of the world, everything changed. We did terrible things. If you bought a hat and the others didn't like it, they would throw it out the window, and no one would say who did it. And it might have been that Sarah threw something out on occasion.' He recognised, too, that by 1943 Sarah was already a fine musician – 'kind of deep', he mused to himself, even when she was only nineteen years old. 'She knew so well about harmonies and exactly what she was doing when she improvised as a singer. She never yelled or screamed, and she never found herself too far out in the water and unable to make her way back. And she never let it go to her head how great she was when she was with the Hines band.' The band was a family, and Sarah was the family jewel, in Smalls's view. Scotty remembered how the band members would knock each other down to congratulate each other if they liked the way something had been played. The men treated Sarah the same way for her singing. 'Everywhere she went, she blew the walls down,' Scotty remembered.

Sarah was paid fourteen dollars for every night that the band worked – usually three or four nights a week. That was not bad pay in those days, Williams mused, when other people were making ten and fifteen dollars a week. 'You could live on it, and in fact [we] did.' A room for a week in a black family's house was likely to cost five dollars. Hines paid for transportation between dates. Soon Sarah had saved a little money, as John Williams had been encouraging her to do. Then Charlie Parker, a notorious borrower, and Thomas Crump began to borrow from her. Despite his cavalier attitude towards other people's possessions, Bird did repay people when he could. 'She was easygoing, and she was taken advantage of, kindhearted and sweet as she could be,' Williams remembered.

The baptismal tour with a band had its lessons. Sarah immediately became aware that Bird was one of the musicians with a heroin habit, although he never used heroin in front of Dizzy; it was unlikely that Sarah ever saw Bird take intravenous drugs. Sarah, the band members say, never had anything to do with heroin herself, though undoubtedly she smoked marijuana with Bird and some of the other men on the road. It's not clear exactly when Sarah smoked her first joint; if she did it while working with the Hines band, Hines himself didn't know about it. Much later he raved to friends visiting him in a dressing room about how innocent Sarah had been when they travelled together. But marijuana and other refreshments, legal and illegal, came with the territory, if you wanted them to. Eventually, though probably not while in the Hines band, Sarah discovered cocaine. A taste for cocaine stayed with her for the rest of her life.

The popular band travelled all over the United States year-round. The only days that the musicians had off were the ones for which they had no bookings. At a dance in Jacksonville, Florida, they played to thirty thousand; in Camden, New Jersey, to ten thousand; to six thousand in New York, and to other large crowds in a handful of Southern cities along the tour route between 21 November and 4 December 1943, Stanley Dance wrote in his book about Hines. The band covered thousands of miles through a mine-field of segregation laws to play music. In Mississippi and Alabama, they played for some white dances, but mostly they played for black ones there. With segregation in force in the South, the band played a job, then often had no place to eat or sleep; nor did every town have a hotel for blacks, and musicians couldn't always find black families who rented out rooms. Before the war, the musicians had simply gotten into their cars or back on to the bus and slept there, while the drivers went two hundred or three hundred miles or even more to the next job. Sometimes when the men found a hotel or a house to sleep in, there wasn't a separate room for Sarah, recalled bassist Ted Sturgis; sometimes it wasn't practical to rent a whole room for one woman. 'Sarah would bunk with the boys,' he remembered; she found a little space for herself without much ado. Sarah didn't require any coddling, B always said admiringly. A woman who needed coddling couldn't survive the hardships of the road life. By the time Sarah joined the Hines band during the war, musicians travelled primarily by trains, which were invariably crowded. 'Sometimes you couldn't get a seat for eight hours. But when you're young and making money, you can stand a whole lot. And Sarah was strong,' Williams remembered.

The band stood as a family, a buffer, against the scarring incidents of racial discrimination in the North, too. Tagging along with the Hines men on a shopping trip for new uniforms in Philadelphia, Sarah watched them being shown to a stockroom upstairs. Because they were black, they weren't allowed to try the uniforms on. Dizzy Gillespie's memoirs, *To Be or Not to Bop*, has Sarah's accounts of other similar incidents. One time in Wilmington, Delaware, a young white man refused to shine B's shoes. 'So B walked back there and said [to the men in the band], "Hey, guys, young kid back there said he don't shine no nigger's shoes," Sarah said. 'So everybody said, "Oh, damn, that sure is a shame," started stretching, and walked off to get their shoes shined. We left town by foot. Everybody spread out and said, "I'll see you at the next gig." Well, he shouldn't have said that.' Memories of prejudice were deeply etched into her spirit.

Whenever the band stopped in Newark, Sarah's parents offered their apartment as an oasis. Her success had impressed Jake and confirmed Ada's hopes. The whole band would come to dinner when in the area. Though Sarah always seemed to embrace Newark as a reminder of her roots and a place to rest and touch base with her old friends and her perhaps overprotective parents, she no longer thought of Newark exclusively as home, friends say. Home was with the band. She was establishing herself as a trouper and a champion at staying up all night to listen to music, talk, eat, smoke and drink. She didn't seem to need any sleep.

The nightlife she loved was simply part of the ambience of the music for her. She associated smoking and drinking with work. 'The minute she stepped into a nightclub, she started smoking. It was like a buzz,' said Robert Richards, whom she would meet in a nightclub. 'Work, smoke. They automatically went together for her. Smoking calmed her down. She would usually stand in the wings, smoking. And she refused to put out a cigarette on the floor. She'd hand it to anyone standing close to her just before she went onstage.' In the clubs, she always liked to join everyone in having a few drinks, too.

Hibbie and Vivie Brown, entertainers who danced as the Brown Twins at the Cotton Club, used to go to the Shalimar, a popular bar that, Vivie remembered, Sarah frequented along with the Braddock Hotel and Grill. Gil Fuller noticed that Sarah hadn't changed much when he met her again at the Braddock Grill. She was still Sarah, 'No 'Count Sarah', having a good time, sounding like a horn when she sang, learning from the horn players, and all the while looking dishevelled offstage. 'Press your clothes,' he coached her. (Onstage she didn't worry that the white dress Hines had selected for her to wear had a cigarette burn – a real hole – in the back. It had been damaged by a customer somewhere along the way. She coped with it by always keeping her back to the stage, so the audience wouldn't see the hole.

Of much greater importance to her was her profound friendship and musical collaboration with B. On the road with the Hines band, Sarah looked up to the seasoned Eckstine, ten years older than she, as a role model; he was as famous for his sangfroid offstage as he was for his warm, thrilling baritone onstage. She learned taste in choosing songs from B. And critics and some of Sarah's close friends later theorised that Eckstine's style influenced her phrasing and her dramatic style. There are no recordings by Sarah in her pre-Hines days, so it is of course impossible to know how Sarah sounded *before* she sang with Hines and B. One has Scotty's testimony about the beauty of her voice singing 'Skylark' in the Alcazar in Newark. But by the time she had her first recording contract for Musicraft in the mid-1940s, she knew how to unfurl her voice slowly and use the shimmering little ripples of her vibrato for dramatic purpose. The richness of her timbre led people to describe her sound as smoky. Waving the word 'me' up and down in the song 'Once in a While', she brought the intimacy and softness of a jazz singer to what could simply have been a big-band belt. She luxuriated in the drawn-out words *once*, *I*, *you*, *two*, and *apart* with such lushness that with those words alone, she imparts the seductive message of the song completely. Even as a novice in the early 1940s, she embellished the melody, rising to a high note no one else could think of hitting, and, with her unique vocal quality, holding the beautiful note, changing keys, and finishing the song on a pure, higher note, while another singer would look to the written music for guidance. She sang 'Sometimes I Feel like a Motherless Child' in a pure, haunting coloratura soprano and employed a mature-sounding contralto for her one recording of 'The Lord's Prayer', skilfully changing octaves

• *39*

until she joyfully crowned the prayer with a glowing soprano at the end.

One of Eckstine's hallmarks was the way he drew out the ballads with his rich baritone. Undoubtedly his style affected Sarah's approach enormously; a generation of male singers, too, came under the spell of his love songs just as much as his female fans did. He was a charismatic romantic hero of pop music, the first black male sex symbol among popular singers; his power of communication with audiences was magical. White women clamoured as readily as black women to get in line in front of their friends to meet him at his public performances and offstage; in the 1950s, photographs showed him being mobbed by white bobby-soxers. Sarah's mere appearance onstage couldn't generate the same sexual excitement, but what Sarah learned from Eckstine made itself clear in the intoxicating romantic duets they recorded together. 'They were connected souls,' her friend Robert Richards feels.

It's possible that B also learned from Sarah's musicality. In his early days, Eckstine sang in a higher register and with much less vibrato. The deepening of his voice and the new warmth it radiated made him famous. Sarah never sang without vibrato; young as she was, the strength of her musical instincts, natural artistry, and beautiful voice must have inspired B the way his suaveness impressed her. Earl Hines thought Sarah was more versatile and told critic Stanley Dance: 'Billy Eckstine was a balladeer and never good on uptempo songs. Sarah Vaughan could do something a little faster than the average tempo.' And Sarah played an instrument well; in those days, Eckstine didn't. Her instinctive grasp of the structure of a song made it easy for her to sing an uptempo version of 'I'm Gonna Sit Right Down and Write Myself a Letter' and careen so far away from the written melody that, in the best spirit of bebop, she created a new gleeful message from the heart.

Both B and Sarah, in interviews later in life, typified themselves as unemotional singers, for whom singing was a business. To A. James Liska writing for *Down Beat* in May 1982, Sarah would say that her mind sometimes wandered to household matters while she was performing. 'I never think about singing . . . I never think about the how or the why of it. It's just according to how I feel and it's never the same . . . Sometimes I'm wondering if they fixed the fence, or I wonder if my dog got well. That's why I forget lyrics sometimes.' By then she was speaking from the vantage point of a singer with forty years of experience. Technique could keep her buoyant, but it was impossible to say where her technique ended and her genius began; the fusion of the two created powerful music even in her earliest days.

B would recall that, as Sarah did, he learned many aspects of technique – phrasing, intonation, an independent imagination and improvisation, the power of vibrato, plus the basics of music, rhythm and harmony – from the horn players, at a time when music was becoming more complicated. As a singer, he focused upon marrying what he considered to be a wonderful lyric with beautiful music that made harmonic sense. 'I believe in the song if it's believable . . . Anything that is good and musical, something that's harmonically good . . . I don't sing a lyric if I don't like it . . . With "My Foolish Heart", I was given a great lyric and great music, and I married them and tried to cover the song for MGM at the time. But if you have fifty songs, you can't change feelings from a ballad to uptempo just like that. The techniques come with experience. And fundamentally it's a part of you, the way you play or sing a thing. That's why there are so many different styles,' B said in 1982 for the book *Louis' Children*, about jazz singing.

The songs on Sarah's recordings show that she sometimes compromised her sense of what was good; she sang many songs that she didn't like, because she was still learning what was best for her in her early years and also because she simply didn't have B's willpower to refuse to sing a bad song. She claimed to dislike her first million-seller hit, 'Broken Hearted Melody', because she couldn't find anything harmonically interesting in it. But she sang it often, calling it 'corny' and all the while feeling that she must seem silly when she sang it, she confided to a girlfriend. Sarah, unlike Eckstine, compartmentalised her repertoire; she sang pop songs for financial reward and jazz songs for spiritual satisfaction. She also enjoyed creating an aria eventually from the song 'Feelings', a song B detested. If she was more broad-minded than B about accepting the songs that came her way, she also knew she could make anything sound pretty. 'She knew how good she was,' Robert Richards says.

When Earl hired Sarah, B was thrilled. His good taste was confirmed. Sarah would always remain uncritical of B. She never forgot his immediate appreciation of her talent. 'Throughout her life, whenever he telephoned her, she metamorphosed into a giggling schoolgirl, thrilled at his attention,' according to Robert Richards. Many of Sarah's friends observed that when she looked at him, or talked to or about him, something soft and respectful crept into her manner.

The public knew only that Sarah's and B's voices, in duets during their days in the Hines band, then with B's band and on records, blended magically. B married two glamorous-looking women; both marriages ended in divorce (although the second marriage lasted from 1953 to 1978). In the long run, B and Sarah might have made an ideal couple. They shared an enduring personal affection and professional respect and attachment. But theirs was not a 'steamy love affair', says Robert Richards, but an expression of affection that lasted 'forever', unlike any of their marriages. 'She always loved B,' Richards said.

Behind the scenes, the young progressive musicians in the Hines band became restless to try out their experiments in front of audiences. In love with bebop, a more aggressive, often undanceable style of jazz, with many songs played at breakneck speeds, B decided to throw his support behind his talented friends. Dizzy Gillespie may have been the one to urge Eckstine, who already had a loyal following for his popular jazz style, to start his own band in late 1943. Dizzy became its first musical director. Bird went along, too, playing the alto saxophone, the instrument he had put aside so he could fill an empty tenor chair in the Hines band. How sorry and angry Earl Hines was to see them go is debatable. When they left, all of them were unknown youngsters, except for B. Hines had already tried to fire Bird, because he was an exquisitely unreliable employee. It was as a musician and a virtuosic altoist, and not as a tenor player imitating himself on alto, that he would later ignite a fiery jazz revolution with Dizzy Gillespie.

Jerry Valentine and Budd Johnson, whom B had met in earlier years with Hines, joined the new band, too. Johnson became the new band's 'straw boss', in charge of the logistics of the band's day-to-day operations; Valentine's arranging talents were important for the new venture. Trombonist Howard Scott, drummer Art Blakey, trumpeters Miles Davis, Fats Navarro, Howard McGhee, and Kenny Dorham, and saxophonists Lucky Thompson, Gene Ammons, and Dexter Gordon, among others – a startling assemblage of bright lights attracted to each other – played in Eckstine's band at various times. Scotty, who left Hines late in 1943 and went to play with a bandleader from Boston, joined Eckstine's band in 1944 and stayed with it until 1947. Guitarist Connie Wainwright from the Hines band also played with Eckstine's new group. So did Shorty McConnell.

According to Leonard Feather in his book, *Inside Bebop*, Eckstine and many of the musicians in the new band first left Hines and went their separate ways – Eckstine as a soloist in the clubs on Fifty-second Street, where he performed under the management of Billy Shaw at the William Morris Agency. But B, who had been an important part of the Hines band's popularity, didn't cause the great stir he had expected on his own. And his management decided that he should try leading a big band. So he called his former colleagues from the Hines band to join him. Dizzy was playing with some important groups. Bird had joined another band. They came together again under B's leadership as Billy Eckstine and His Orchestra. 'Nearly the whole (Hines) band joined B's band,' Sarah later reminisced. She stayed with Hines for a while after B started his band.

Hines hired Wardell Gray on reeds as one of the replacements for his personnel and added violinists and a harpist. Leonard Feather later wrote that Hines had really been miffed with Eckstine for leaving and tried to overcompensate with replacements. But the Hines band didn't remain commercially viable at its new size for long. Hines said he was harried by trying to accommodate the string players, all of them women, on the road. He never complained about Sarah, however, and regarded her as a comrade. One cold night on a street in Chicago, when a taxi wouldn't stop for them, she told him she was going to throw a rock through a window to call the police's attention to them. 'They'll take us to the station, and we'll be able to get warm,' he quoted her as saying when he repeated the story to Stanley Dance. Hines said, 'She meant it, too, but luckily a cab came by just about that time.' Another night, Hines, dressed in beautiful, formal evening clothes, stood up in front of his band at a college dance. An orchestra pit, which Hines didn't know about, lay in front of him; decorations covered it. As Sarah opened her mouth to sing, Hines tumbled down into the pit. 'It seemed as though I was going down for half an hour, but when I landed, there was Sarah, looking down with her poker face, and several of the guys clustered around her,' Hines told Dance. Sarah didn't panic. Hines reminisced to Stanley Dance that it was wonderful to have Sarah in the band. 'She was a big asset . . . she was so nonchalant.'

Scotty recalled that Earl managed to perform wonderful shows after the Progressives went away. Eckstine's first replacement didn't stay with Hines very long and left Sarah as the band's only singer. One night, as she was getting set to sing 'Sunday, Monday, and Always', Hines told Scotty to hurry up and go to the front of the bandstand to sing a duet with her. Scotty, who did sing occasionally, felt he had 'no business standing next to Sarah, because she's such a great singer'. He also thought that he shouldn't stand next to her because, in her high-heeled shoes, she stood much taller than he (he was probably shorter than Sarah even without her shoes on). Gazing into each other's eyes, he looking up, she down, they started to laugh and couldn't stop themselves. 'We fell out in the middle of the act,' he recalled. 'It won the crowd. Hines was a great showman. He had known exactly what he was doing.' Hines later hired Johnny Hartman, a mild-mannered, sweet-natured Chicagoan with one of the most beautiful baritones in popular music, as the 'boy singer'.

In 1944, Eckstine invited Sarah to join his group of virtual unknowns. And she did. Later she would come to regard those days with B as an idyllic time for her musical development. With B, she was at home again with her friends – a band of ragtag bebop revolution-aries, for the most part. Even so, she battled the pandemonium of stage fright every time she went onstage. 'I was sitting up there shaking in my boots,' she reminisced to writer Rory O'Connor for a *Down Beat* article. Years earlier she had said the same thing to another writer about the way she felt when she simply played piano with the men as they tried to work out ideas on their own time offstage. But she felt unequivocally committed to the young beboppers. She later explained that she had never regarded the Eckstine band as an experiment; all the musicians had known exactly what they were doing, and they tried to educate the public. 'We didn't care whether anybody really, actually, enjoyed it or not. We were [enjoying it], you know,' she said.

She also recalled that if the men in the band didn't like something she was doing musically, they disciplined her. She tended toward flam-boyance, and they tried to tone her down. 'I'm telling you they used to beat me to death if I got out of line. I mean, literally . . .' As for the musical challenge, she said, 'You had to sing within whatever the chords were they were playing. You had to know a little about music or have a hell of a good ear to stand before that band. I loved it, loved it!' . . . Roger 'Ram' Ramirez, the composer of 'Lover Man', recalled being introduced to Sarah by tenor saxophonist Ike Quebec, when Billy's band played in a San Diego hotel sometime in 1944 or 1945. The instant Ram heard the quality of her voice, he understood why the bebop instrumentalists latched on to her. 'They needed a creative singer like Sass to make them sound appealing,' he said.

So they stood up for each other against segregation and insults, made each other laugh, and helped each other learn, stretch, improve, and survive before they went their separate ways with what they had learned. The band played in tobacco warehouses in the South, travel-ling, still performing under the onus of segregation. She faced up valiantly to the hardships, cussing her way through them, reinforcing her nickname 'Sailor'. With a pointed comment, Sarah could make people stand back at a respectful distance when she wanted to. ('She could be cranky,' her friend Robert Richards knew. 'It made her a whole person, someone for you to deal with.') Comparing her with Ella Fitzgerald, who had already had the number one song in the country, 'A Tisket A Tasket', on the show 'Hit Parade' in 1938, Richards sensitively perceived Ella as 'girlish' in her style and aura, while 'Sarah was independent, unpredictable – and darker things'. John Malachi, the band's pianist, caught the spirit of the young singer adroitly when he started calling her 'Sassy'. She liked that playful description of her tough, fresh, chin-up façade so well that she let everyone start calling her 'Sassy' and 'Sass'. Her friends called her 'Sass', the press called her 'Sassy', and she spelled it 'Sassie' because she thought that had a more feminine air. Occasionally a close friend preferred the formal 'Sarah'.

On 5 December 1944, without Bird on the bandstand, Billy Eckstine led his orchestra in a recording date for which Sassy sang 'I'll Wait and Pray', one of the many arrangements by Jerry Valentine. Sassy's first recording, the song began circulating nationally, bringing her some notoriety – especially in the black communities and among musicians; at the time records by blacks were still pigeonholed as 'race records'. However, in the 1940s, even before he became a star with white audiences, B's records had white fans; his national reputation was growing, and his celebrity attracted bookings for the band. Sassy benefited immeasurably from her connection with B. 'I'll Wait and Pray' has since become a collector's item and part of the Smithsonian Institution's collection of important jazz recordings.

By 1944, Dizzy left the Eckstine band to start his own group. Sassy left B around the same time; B didn't hire a replacement and became his band's only star. Once Sassy left B's band in 1944, she never sought a steady job with another band. She wanted to try to establish herself as a star in her own right, so she tried her luck as a soloist, singing and playing piano for herself in several clubs on Fifty-second Street with a variety of backup groups and musicians such as Charlie Parker. Ram Ramirez heard her sing at the Three Deuces, when Erroll Garner was an intermission pianist there. Sylvia Syms recalled hearing Sassy sing at the Famous Door. B, 'a gorgeous guy', as Sylvia called him, was working at the Onyx Club across the street when he bumped into Sylvia, who also had a gig in a club near his. He asked her: 'Have you ever heard of Sarah Vaughan?' Sylvia said, 'No.' B said, 'Go. It will do your heart good,' Sylvia recalled at a memorial service for Sassy at St Peter's Church in New York. Sylvia went to the Famous Door. 'To the piano came a magical child who played and sang and who blew everyone away. And it was because she knew Billy Eckstine

well, and I wanted to know him better, that we became good friends
– not because I didn't think she was spectacular; she was – but because
she knew Billy Eckstine,' Sylvia said. Sassy also worked at the Down-
beat and the Onyx clubs for seventy-five dollars a week. Quickly it
became known that nobody else in jazz had such a gorgeous voice.

Sassy took whatever club jobs, out-of-town dates, and tours she
could find. When money was scarce, she went home to Newark for a
little relief. But it never occurred to her to do anything other than see
how far she could go on her own. She had promised herself to become
a hit. That meant she had to learn to survive, as every musician had to
decide to do. John Williams recalled returning to the Apollo with the
Hines band and meeting Sassy near the Braddock Hotel. She wasn't
working on a regular basis; she was freelancing – always viewed as a
precarious position. 'I asked her to come to my room and sing a song
for me, and I paid her five dollars to do it.'

Through Dizzy she met Leonard Feather, who was becoming an
important critic and jazz record producer; he was so impressed by her
singing at the 'I'll Wait and Pray' recording session that he gave a tape
of her singing to the owner of a little label, Continental. Feather had
to cajole the owner into letting Sassy record. But the owner did agree,
and, for a small sum, about twenty dollars a side, he hired Sassy to
record four tunes produced by Feather – 'Signing Off', written by
Feather, 'Interlude', 'No Smokes Blues', and 'East of the Sun, West of
the Moon', with Aaron Sachs on clarinet, Georgie Auld on tenor
saxophone, Feather on piano for his own song, Chuck Wayne on guitar,
Jack Lesberg, bass, Morey Feld, drums, and Dizzy playing trumpet on
the first song and piano on one other. It was 31 December 1944, both
the eve of a new year and of a new, post-war era of jazz. Record
producer Teddy Reig listened to Sassy in the studio that night, according to jazz historian Phil Schaap. That meeting would be important for
Sassy's recording career later in her life. Not many years later, in his
Encyclopedia of Jazz, Feather published one of the early, flattering, and
even prophetic analyses of Sassy's style: 'Sarah Vaughan's voice . . .
brought to jazz an unprecedented combination of attractive characteristics: a rich, beautifully controlled tone and vibrato; an ear for the chord
structure of songs . . . [and] a coy, sometimes archly naïve quality
alternating with a sense of great sophistication.'

On 11 May 1945, for the little Guild label, Sassy recorded 'Lover
Man' with a quintet led by Dizzy improvising in his favoured high
register, with Bird on alto sax sounding mellifluous and adventurous.
Also playing are pianist Al Haig, bassist Curly Russell, and drummer

Big Sid Catlett. Here was the genuine sound of young instrumentalists with a contemporary feeling; even forty-five years later, their yearning for greater musical freedom rises out of the grooves. The record helped alert the world to the changing of the guard in the jazz leadership. Dizzy could play in a higher register than his most famous predecessors, trumpeters Roy Eldridge and Louis Armstrong, and Dizzy played more complicated rhythms and convoluted, exotic melodies than either of those greats. Sassy's elegant voice both enveloped and encouraged her fellow musicians to explore new harmonies and improvise complicated accompaniments. Unlike any other singer, she was emphasising sound, sometimes syllables, not just words, to communicate emotions and moods; she could communicate the meaning of a song simply through her treatment of the 'oooo' sounds in words. Recording for small labels, she was reaching some fans in both black and white communities.

Years later, when revolution settled into routine, her approach to songs would begin to sound more mellow than it originally had, and so would the accompaniment. But at the time of their first release, the unusual harmonies sounded strange to listeners. In the early 1950s, when publications ranging from *Ebony* to *Time* began to write about her, they suggested her embellishments were eccentric. But Marian Anderson sent Sassy a congratulatory message for her 1947 recording of 'The Lord's Prayer', made for the Musicraft label. 'The Lord's Prayer' was released in time for Christmas late in her Musicraft contract. Backing Sassy is Ted Dale and a large orchestra with strings. The single shows off, all in one song, the richness of Sassy's contralto range, the sweetness of her soprano, and the spiritual power of her elemental sound. A *tour de force* for Sassy, 'The Lord's Prayer' went 'straight up to heaven', Robert Richards would say. Speaking about the recording in 1950 for *Down Beat*'s 'My Best on Wax' column, Sassy, who was already recording for Columbia by then, said, '"The Lord's Prayer" is both my favourite of the records I've made and the one I consider my best. It's the only record of mine I ever play . . . I'd always wanted to record it, but I thought I had no business doing it. Marian Anderson had recorded "The Lord's Prayer", you know.' Of course 'The Lord's Prayer' was the song her father always loved her to sing. The song overrode any quarrels her father or even her mother could have had with Sassy about her jazz and pop career.

Sassy knew the quality of that recording and its importance to her parents. In an interview with *Ebony* magazine in 1949, she said, 'I'll not be satisfied until I'm singing on the concert stage.' It was, however, a goal she seemed to forget about for a long time. For her, life after B's band usually focused on the music developing in Harlem, on Fifty-second Street, and in Birdland, from which everything that was exciting in jazz was radiating to the rest of the world.

THREE

Enter George Treadwell

In October 1945, Sassy landed herself a recording contract with a small label called Musicraft – with a little help from her friend Stuff Smith; a well-known jazz violinist, he invited Sassy to sing with him during his recording date for the label. Smith and Albert Marx, the owner of Musicraft, haggled for a while about whether Marx would pay Sassy ten or fifteen dollars. Then Marx became so excited about her singing that he offered her a contract. Ironically, Stuff Smith didn't get one.

Recording for little labels, she was hired to sing by Barney Josephson, who owned Cafe Society Downtown in Sheridan Square in Greenwich Village. Barney was proud of establishing the first downtown club in Manhattan with integrated audiences. There Sassy would meet two of the people who would become important to her career development for the next decade. One was Johnnie Garry, a strong, gregarious young man with a wide smile, who supported his wife and daughters with his job as a jack-of-all-trades in Manhattan's garment district. One day in 1946, his Harlem neighbour, folksinger Josh White Sr, asked Johnnie to go to Cafe Society Downtown to help move a piano, working as a stagehand during a show at night.

Lena Horne was appearing at the club at the time, along with a roster of other well-known performers. Johnnie didn't think he had the presence of mind to move a piano in front of all those people and an audience, too. Barney Josephson told him, 'Take your time, do it slowly.' Johnnie said, 'Mr Josephson, if I go out there, I'll move it fast.' And he recounted the tale of doing that job quickly by describing a few hand motions he went through as neatly as if he was flicking a handkerchief at a fly. 'And I put the chair under (pianist) Mary Lou Williams,' he recalled. A columnist from *The New Yorker* was sitting at a table in the audience. She wrote: 'Who was that young man who moved that piano so beautifully and in rhythm?' as Johnnie recalled.

Barney Josephson read her remark and told Johnnie, 'You can work here all the time.' Johnnie asked, 'What would you pay me?' Barney said, 'Eighteen dollars a week, and at the end of the week, the musicians tip you.' Johnnie tried it for a while. He met Canada Lee, the actor, and basso profundo and actor Paul Robeson. He saw comedian Jackie Gleason open and close in one night, because he wasn't funny that time. In short order, Johnnie decided, 'This is for me.' He loved the ambience, the music, the excitement, the musicians and comedians, even the colourful murals on the walls, and he was fascinated by the technical jobs that made the glamorous shows run smoothly. He started 'messing with lights', teaching himself lighting engineering, he recalled.

One Sunday night in 1946, he saw Sarah Vaughan arrive for a rehearsal. Johnnie thought, 'She looks fine.' A *Life* magazine photographer, who happened to be at the club, took a picture of her in her turtleneck sweater. By then, Johnnie, who had been born and brought up in Charlotte, North Carolina, was accustomed to the fast pace of life in Harlem, where the trumpeter George Treadwell was also living. George, a good-looking, well-built, mustachioed man, was playing in J. C. Heard's band – he also played with Cootie Williams's and Lucky Millinder's bands – when Sassy arrived to sing with the band for two weeks. She also sometimes sang with Cliff Jackson, the intermission pianist and singer entertaining between the shows.

George had long been fascinated by Sassy's voice; he always said he had heard her sing the night she had won the Apollo amateur night contest. Through the years he had heard her occasionally. But Treadwell was about to become the most important person in her life then. Audiences responded to Sassy, and Barney Josephson extended her engagement (to six months, according to a *Time* magazine story in 1950, or a year, according to Johnnie Garry). She earned ninety dollars a week as the intermission entertainment.

Pictures show that at this time Sassy wore very simple dresses that emphasised her stick-straight figure; one dress had cap sleeves that made her look like an adolescent farm girl. She was extending her hair with a weaving technique but still wasn't satisfied with the way it looked, so she wore an ornate wig on stage. The hair piled high did nothing to flatter the contours of her face. Her buck teeth stuck out as prominently as ever. When she wasn't onstage, she often sat backstage, playing solitaire. Sassy, who didn't even have a booking agent or manager to negotiate her fee, was pleased to have a steady job in a well-known jazz club. But she wanted someone to help her find even better bookings. She knew a good manager could bring her to the attention of important people in the music business. One night she had an unsettling experience, she later confided to Robert Richards. An influential record producer sat at a ringside table intended for four people and read a newspaper while she sang. Later she discovered that he was mainly interested in big-band musicians and blues singers. But that night the rudeness alarmed Sassy. 'I became afraid about what the future might hold for me,' she told Richards.

Often she went back to Newark to sleep in her family's apartment; for Sassy, her parents' house was a place to rest between gigs. Sometimes she stayed with friends in New York. In Newark, she liked to get in touch with her old friends whenever she had a chance. Doris Robinson had stayed in Newark and married her boyfriend; although she had won a prize at the Apollo, she never sang professionally. But she frequently asked Sassy about how her career was going. About travelling with a band, Sassy said, 'Try it. It's the greatest experience in the world. But it's also a very hard life.' And she told Doris details about the gypsy life-style, the segregation, the financial insecurity. She had often moved so fast from city to city that she lost what little jewellery and possessions she had; she just forgot to pack them. 'You simply have to love show business to make the risk worthwhile,' she summed up.

At the time Sassy joined the Hines band, Evelyn Greene was working in a factory so she could pay for vocal lessons. The two old friends lost touch. Sarah was making a name for herself in the jazz world, and Evelyn still wanted to become a classical artist. Then Evelyn won a scholarship to study music in Philadelphia. There, she bumped into Sassy when Sassy was singing with the Eckstine band (on the same bill with Nat King Cole). Evelyn went to hear her and was struck by how beautifully Sassy was singing; it was a far cry from their days in the choir in Newark. A few months later, Evelyn was appearing in the musical *Carousel* in Cleveland, and again she went to see Sassy, who was passing through town with the Eckstine band.

'Evie, what are you doing in Cleveland?' Sassy wanted to know. Evelyn explained that she was appearing in a show; it was usually very difficult for her to find work – blacks were virtually shut out of the classical music business in those days. But in the jazz world, the situation was different. Although racial politics in jazz were enormously complex, in no other part of society did blacks and whites mix as freely.

· *51*

Whatever obstacles stood in the way of black musicians' success in the marketplace and kept them from getting the lucrative recording and performing dates, Sassy was never in danger of being unable to find work in jazz, an art created by blacks, and developed by blacks and whites together.

The Vaughans still belonged to the First Mount Zion Baptist Church, which in the late 1940s had moved to new quarters in an old stone Gothic church that had been built at 208 Broadway by a Presbyterian congregation in the late nineteenth century. The new church was supposed to be a step up for the congregation. The chance appealed to Ada Vaughan; she influenced Sarah, as Mrs Vaughan always called her daughter, to attend the new church, too. Asbury Vaughan, however, opposed the move, which he thought was just a ploy by which the minister might bring in more revenue. Many members of the First Mount Zion Baptist Church agreed with Asbury and decided to stay in the old church. The move caused a rift in many families. In Sassy's family, it was symbolic of Asbury's austere, old-fashioned attitudes. The only time Sassy ever went to her father's church again was for his funeral in 1973, Evelyn remembered. Then Sassy showed up to sing the hymn he loved, 'The Lord's Prayer'.

Evelyn Green recalled the division of the congregation as a milestone in her community's life. She saw Asbury Vaughan often in the old church, where she and her mother remained members. Asbury attended concerts that Evelyn sang in the church. Her mother's youngest brother went to the new church. Evelyn was somewhat vindicated in her loyalty, she thought, when the neighbourhood of the Broadway church began a slow decline. After World War II, new immigrants moved into the neighbourhood's apartment buildings, which were converted into rooming houses to accommodate the new numbers of people. But Sassy's attention was focused on her career. She rarely went to church anymore, even though she regarded the church as her roots and would soon tell the *New York Post* that she loved to sing hymns. 'Choir singing's a wonderful thing for what ails you. There's a lot of meaning in a hymn if you think about it when you're singing it. And the music is there, just about as beautiful as it can be.'

But Sassy was more deeply concerned with what was going on in Manhattan's jazz scene. Even before she worked at Cafe Society, she had become a familiar figure in the Braddock Grill around the corner from the Apollo Theatre. Musicians later recalled often seeing Sassy hanging out at the Braddock with Carmen McRae, an attractive, rather exotic-looking young woman with chiselled features who, like Sassy, played piano and sang. 'They were laughing and giggling together,' Gil Fuller would recall. (Carmen would have more difficulty establishing herself in clubs and on records than Sassy.) Carmen was married to Kenny Clarke, a pivotal bebop drummer whose nickname, 'Klook', stood for the sound of the rhythmic figures he played at Minton's, a popular uptown club. Carmen loved Sassy's early recordings with B, Dizzy and Bird, though at first she thought that Sassy didn't even know who she was. But one day, Sassy said, 'Hi, Carmen.' Carmen recalled, 'That really knocked me out.' From that moment on, Carmen and Sassy became friends, hanging out together 'against the law, honey', until 'six, seven, even eight in the morning. When I got tired, I split and went home. Sass never got tired.' Gil Fuller thought that Sassy sometimes found a corner for herself in a room rented by one instrumentalist or another in the Braddock, so that she didn't have to go too far away from the music. Even in one of the Braddock's basement rooms, musicians often rehearsed. Or she could walk to the Alhambra Theatre or the Harlem Opera House, which were nearby, too, and where other musicians from the Braddock went to pass the time. At the Shalimar Club, people passed a microphone down along the bar; Sassy sometimes sang there with the jukebox. And Sassy also went to Small's Paradise at 135th Street and Seventh Avenue, where Count Basie and saxophonist Eddie 'Lockjaw' Davis played.

Sassy would eventually write a little reminiscence of her early relationship with George for *Tan Confessions*, a magazine about the private lives of prominent blacks, in November 1950. 'He gave me a great deal of encouragement,' she wrote about the night she won the Apollo contest. 'We later saw each other a number of times, but it was nothing serious until three years later when we played at Cafe Society together.' He saw the vulnerable-looking young singer every night there; though he thought she lacked glamour and was still as plain as when he had seen her at the Apollo contest, he explained that he fell deeply in love with her singing and then with the woman.

The couple became friends with Johnnie Garry. After work at Cafe Society, the three of them often took the A train up to West Fifty-second Street, where they spent the rest of the night going from one tiny jazz club to another, listening to the musicians they loved. The club crowds spilled out onto the neon-lit street, as the musicians, on their breaks, went to other clubs to hear their friends. Some nights, George, Sassy and Johnnie went to Harlem, where they also found music they liked.

One night, Sassy and George were attacked by a group of neighbourhood kids who wanted to harass some blacks. A story about the attack was printed in *Down Beat* magazine. Sassy and George had been trying to get into the West Fourth Street subway station at 4.00 a.m. when a gang of about twenty-five boys 'started pushing and shouting epithets and in a few seconds had thoroughly manhandled the pair'. Both Sassy and George 'suffered minor injuries, including bruises and contusions', wrote the *Down Beat* man, who happened to be on Sixth Avenue at the time and soon saw about fifteen of the gang members throwing rocks at a Negro bootblack. Police said the gang of hoodlums was well known to them; two of the leaders were arrested. Johnnie Garry remembered the attack on Sassy and George clearly, because he and J. C. Heard were with them. Six kids attacked them. 'We were all in the station. J.C. and I pushed one guy on the tracks. Sarah was biting and fighting the guy. She got the worst of it,' Johnnie recalled. The other kids ran away. Sassy and George were very shaken up. They and J.C. and Johnnie took the subway to a club on Forty-seventh Street, where they told some members of the Count Basie band what had happened. With some of Basie's men, Sassy's group went back to the subway station in the Village, but the kids were gone by then. After that Sassy, George, Johnnie and J.C. kept taking the A train; it was their only choice. 'None of us had any money in those days to take a taxi,' Johnnie Garry recalled. And they didn't dream of quitting their nightly rounds of the clubs.

Johnnie watched the love affair begin between Sassy and George. They confided in each other their hopes for their own futures. George kept telling her what a beautiful voice she had and how she needed a great manager to book her into the right clubs. Sassy agreed with him; that was exactly what she needed. And that was what George really wanted to be: an artist's manager. He loved music and show business, but he didn't want to play trumpet as a sideman in groups forever. If he could become a businessman in the music world, he would be happy. 'I think they fell in love on the A train,' Johnnie later reflected. 'They were drawn together by their shared love of music.' And they needed companionship, too.

In her piece for *Tan Confessions*, Sassy wrote, under her own byline: 'One night we went out after finishing work . . . George told me again what a great singer he thought I was and that I should have a manager to see that I got the right breaks. So I said to George, "Why don't you manage me?" He looked at me, a little surprised. Then he replied, "Sure, Sass, I'll manage you, but it would be even better if we managed each other." The next morning we got our marriage licence at the court. I guess the only trouble was that George was very slow in getting around to proposing. Several times I almost proposed to him.' Johnnie Garry thought they decided that George should be her manager 'because they didn't trust anybody else to do the job'. When George began working as her manager, he told Johnnie, 'If we ever make any money, we want to hire you to come to work for Sassy.'

Sassy's and George's relationship gave rise to some gossip. Cliff Smalls heard some musicians say that George was stupid to give up his horn to take care of Sassy. Other musicians had the opposite impression; they thought that George latched on to Sassy because he was a hustler, not because he loved and admired her. But Gil Fuller, the arranger, who knew George fairly well, thought George was the ideal fellow for Sassy; he was street-smart and loved the girl and her talent.

Although Sassy was ambitious, she lacked George's focus and business acumen. 'I sing, I just sing,' she was fond of telling people. And when she wasn't singing, she could hang out longer and harder than George and most other people. George's emphasis on promotion, whether of Sassy or himself, irritated some people, Sassy among them. She tired of the way he always corrected her grammar and told her whom to speak to and to avoid. Over a period of time, he would try to direct every aspect of her personal life. But when George and Sassy started out together, everything was smooth. Never before had anyone paid so much attention to her. It was exciting for her to have George as an ally.

In May 1946, Sassy made her first recording as a leader for Music-raft. She was still appearing at Cafe Society when she recorded such songs as Tadd Dameron's haunting 'If You Could See Me Now', done in her rich, musical style, and 'You're Not the Kind', a soft but jaunty, upbeat tune. Dameron, a brilliant arranger, had hired the instrumentalists for that record date. Sassy loved trumpeter Freddie Webster's bright, high-register introduction to 'If You Could See Me Now'. Treadwell was nowhere in sight in the recording studio and probably had nothing to do with that session, recalled Ted 'Mohawk' Sturgis, the bassist Dameron had hired. But by June 1946, when she made her next records, George was everywhere. She recorded 'Don't Blame Me' with tenor player Eddie 'Lockjaw' Davis's quartet at the Spotlite Club, and later that month she made 'Body and Soul' with George leading the group. He managed her career from then on.

Her recordings from this period became jazz classics. In July, a fine Tennessee-born pianist, Jimmy Jones, went into a studio with Sassy to record 'I've Got a Crush on You', 'I'm Through with Love', and

'Everything I Have Is Yours', all with George as leader. Jones plays piano on 'Body and Soul'. These records made her even more popular with musicians, jazz music fans, and the jazz press. Celebrating and confirming their little bit of progress together, Sassy and George married on 16 September 1946.

A year later, on 2 July 1947, with George leading and Jimmy Jones, Sassy's favourite accompanist, at the piano again, Sassy recorded four more tunes – 'I Cover the Waterfront', 'Ghost of a Chance', 'Tenderly', and 'Don't Blame Me'. The trumpeter, Hal Mitchell, who had met George Treadwell through trombonist Bennie Green and then played with George in the trumpet section of Benny Carter's band, was hired by George for that recording date. In the studio, all the musicians thought that 'Tenderly' would be the dud. But it became the most popular of all the cuts and a notable hit for Sassy – her first record to rank in the pop music charts. It rose to its peak position, number 27, during the week of 15 November 1947. For the first time, *Down Beat* magazine gave her an award as the most popular female singer. She won the *Esquire* New Star Award for 1947, too. Her success didn't seem to make her at all conceited or arrogant. Hal Mitchell noticed how shy she was; she found it very difficult to have a conversation and sat by herself in a corner. She let George take charge of the group in the studio, while she dealt only with the music.

Sassy's next popular record was 'Nature Boy', which she made on 8 April 1948 for Musicraft. It went to number 9 the week of 3 July 1948,* shortly after Nat King Cole had become a folk legend in the country with his hit recording of the tune. In those days several artists recorded and had hits with the same song, though usually one artist was the most successful, and the others had mild successes. 'Nature Boy' was such a popular, haunting song that anybody who recorded it achieved at least a moment's notoriety. Then came the biggest hit of all, 'It's Magic', which she recorded with Richard Maltby and his orchestra for Musicraft on 27 December 1947. The song focused more attention on Sassy than she had ever had before. In a press release George circulated for Sassy at the time, he took credit for arranging 'an audition' for Sassy to sing 'It's Magic'. Actually it was just another day in the studio with Sassy recording a pretty song that she liked. The record peaked at number 11 and stayed in the charts for eleven weeks.

*All chart rankings come from *Pop Memories, 1890–1954*, *Top R&B Singles, 1942–1988*, and *Top Pop Singles, 1955–1986*, by Joel Whitburn (Menomonee Falls, Wisconsin: Record Research, Inc.).

Taken from the movie *Romance on the High Seas*, in which Doris Day made her début, the song earned Sassy more money than she had ever made before with a recording. But Modina Davis and others among Sassy's friends thought she may never have known exactly how much. For one thing, George was in charge of all the money Sassy earned and spent. He knew how much money she could run through when she had it in her pocket. 'She knew it, too,' Modina recalled. So George put Sassy on an allowance to keep her from spending too much, an arrangement Sassy liked.

Sassy not only left the bookkeeping to George; she never examined the books for information about her earnings. George took in whatever amount Musicraft paid him. In the late 1940s, jukebox owners needed multiple copies of popular records because they wore out very quickly. Profits reported in the press ran the gamut from twenty-five thousand to fifty thousand and more. Modina Davis, who would come to see that Sassy paid no attention to income and expenses, thought that Sassy was simply negligent. Sassy knew instinctively that she couldn't manage her money and music simultaneously. That's why she had a manager. And the division of labour suited her outlook on life. Furthermore, she trusted George; a revelation about the way he had handled her money would come to her later as the first setback in her professional life. But in 1948 she was still too busy singing and doing what George advised her about her image to bother checking the accounts. She was winning important awards in the critics' polls – *Down Beat* magazine awards for every year from 1947 through 1952 and *Metronome* awards from 1948 through 1953. She was too happy to worry about money.

On 8 April 1948, she made the last of her thirty-three recordings for Musicraft. Most of the musicians she played with came from the ranks of young, struggling, talented fellows in Manhattan, among them Thelonious Monk, drummer Kenny Clarke, Freddie Webster, Leroy Harris, Leo Parker, pianist Bud Powell, and bassist Ted Sturgis, an old friend from the Hines band. Everything about Sassy's records for Musicraft, from the songs themselves to the arrangers and players who helped them come alive, showed impeccable taste. George and Sassy agreed on such matters. Musicians remembered that she was learning about recording sound quality by listening to the takes intently.

Of all the musicians who played for her early records, Sassy adored Jimmy Jones above all. He had migrated first from Memphis to Chicago and then, at about age twenty-five, had travelled from Chicago with Stuff Smith's group, which included bassist John Levy. Sassy's recording with Stuff Smith for Musicraft in 1945 had given her the opportunity to meet Jimmy Jones, although he didn't play for that record. Eventually he decided to concentrate on arranging and wrote for Duke Ellington among others. But Jones spent the late 1940s and much of the 1950s with Sassy. In the 1950s and 1960s he became the favourite accompanist and arranger for many singers, because of his understanding of harmonies, as well as his ideas for arrangements and the subtlety of his performing style. For Sassy he extended the influence of Dizzy and Bird. Jones knew exactly which chords to play for her; she heard his interesting choices of notes and took inspiration from them for her own embellishments.

In 1947 a reporter asked Sassy about whether her married life was happy. Sassy, true to her nickname, glibly summed up George's gift and their common interest in enjoying life by saying that she thought her marriage was perfect, because 'he can count good, and he likes chilli and so do I'. Sassy meant what she said.

George took care of every aspect of Sassy's promotion with a flair and attention to practical details she could never have organised by herself. The couple never signed a written contract to work together; their marriage licence was it. George would go into a club and simply tell the owner, 'I'm Sarah's manager.' Soon he arranged for her to sign with the booking agency of Tim and Moe Gale at 48 West Forty-eighth Street. 'Tim was her personal agent,' Johnnie Garry recalled.

And Sassy, George, and Jimmy Jones set out in a well-worn car to tour the country. In the late 1940s, she would appear at the Blue Angel in New York, the Rhumboogie and Sherman in Chicago, the Bocage in Hollywood, and Ciro's and the Casbah in Los Angeles. Added to her *Down Beat* and *Metronome* victories, *Orchestra World*, a magazine emphasising the big bands, and *Billboard* also picked her as a top vocalist in the period. In 1948 *Metronome* magazine called her 'Influence of the Year', too. A review in that magazine said: 'Her bent notes and her twisting of musical phrases have been the envy of and basis for the styles of a good many singers . . . many of them were mimicking her every vocal stance and prance; not since . . . Billie Holiday has a singer hit other singers so hard . . .'

The acclaim was by no means universal. Some writers were still misspelling her name *Vaughn*. Dale Harrison of the *Chicago Sun* disliked the 'Vaughn' singing style. 'Her tempo drags unconscionably – the boys in the rhythm section have time to yawn between every beat – and her wandering around notes, which I assume is what the disc jockeys would call "style", struck me as annoying and amateurish.'

Don C. Haynes, an assistant editor at *Down Beat*, went to war for Vaughan. 'You might as well say Benny Goodman is amateurish,' he countered. 'How wrong can these square nincompoops get and still write for newspapers? . . . Anyway, Mr Harrison's taste to the contrary, Sarah tied up this town like no other singer has done for a long time. Eight great weeks at the Rhumboogie, three packed concerts, two King Cole air shots (Nat wouldn't settle for one), and three weeks at the College Inn – and would all who know nothing about art be good boys and desist from vilifying it?' Harrison came charging again to excoriate jazz in general, saying Sarah had done no such thing as tie up the town, 'and for [Haynes's] information, no singer in that medium has tied up Chicago or any other place.' The sophistication of bebop still sounded eccentric to many people. More than forty years later, it was easy to see who had been right and who had been wrong about Sassy.

Time magazine published an article in its 20 December 1948 issue, saying that Sarah Vaughan sang 'in a style like a kazoo'. Writer and editor George Hoefer, on behalf of *Down Beat* magazine, wrote a letter of protest to *Time*. *Time* begged off from squabbling with a letter saying: 'The editors have read your comments on *Time*'s reporting of jazz, and in particular Be-Bop, with interest. Some explanation is in order on our saying that Sarah Vaughan's voice sounded like a kazoo. One of the things about her singing which most struck our reviewer is her ability to sing half and quarter tones with astounding accuracy. The best method of describing this accomplishment seemed to be to compare her singing with some musical instrument, especially since be-boppers use voice as another instrument. One of the few pieces which can reproduce this variety in tone is the kazoo, so that the simile was meant neither unkindly nor inaccurately.'

In 1952 jazz writer Nat Hentoff asked Sassy whether she was bothered by critics who claimed her singing was overstylised, a criticism that had actually always been levelled at her. 'I don't pay them any mind,' she told Hentoff for an article in *Down Beat*. 'They have a right to say what they think, but I always sing the best way I know how.' Hentoff wrote, ' . . . as vocally important as Sarah's best is to music, equally vital is her integrity, for her greatness is an extricable compound of the two.'

Despite controversy over her style and how to describe it, by the end of the 1940s, Sassy had many bookings and only six to eight weeks of the year to rest in. In mid-1949, she starred in a concert at Robin Hood Dell in Philadelphia, singing with both the Duke Ellington band

and the Philadelphia Symphony Orchestra. The show, a benefit to raise funds for the Philadelphia orchestra, was billed as '100 Men and a Girl'; Sassy was the girl. The audience overflowed the Robin Dell amphitheatre; many people sat on tombstones in a cemetery far from the bandstand. (Five years later, Sassy described that performance as one of the high points of her career in an interview with Sidney Fields, a columnist for the *Daily Mirror*.) She still didn't have a great deal of money left after expenses, but she and George had earned enough to buy a three-storey house at 21 Avon Avenue in Newark. George renovated the first two floors for an apartment for Sassy's parents there, and he also designed and built a charming little apartment for Sassy and himself to stay in on the top floor. The floor was decorated in brightly coloured tiles forming a G clef, Sassy's autograph, and a trumpet. Sassy loved it and showed it off by inviting friends to the apartment to see it. It made a lifelong impression on Evelyn Greene.

Sassy would soon tell a reporter for the *Sunday News Magazine* that her parents were retired. 'They've worked enough. I'm taking care of them now,' she said. Evelyn Greene remembered calling once when Sassy was asleep. Ada Vaughan was screening calls and wouldn't awaken Sassy, asking, 'Is there anything I can do for you?' Evelyn never got used to the new, protective arrangement.

The press was writing of Sassy's success, promulgating George's claim that he had given up his dream of having his own band so he could put his life savings (eight thousand dollars) into elocution lessons for Sassy. He also paid for her new wardrobe, he said.

'The truth was that George had never had any life savings,' Modina Davis said with a smile, 'but he might have had enough money for a two-dollar marriage licence. George might have put his horn in a pawn shop and spent the money for material to give to his mother. She was an expert seamstress, and she sewed gowns for Sassy.' Tailored for her, they had nipped-in waistlines and extra material in the bodices to accentuate her figure. George's fine and fussy taste in clothes extended to his own extensive and fastidiously maintained wardrobe. Modina admired George's mighty influence on Sassy's stage bearing. 'He had many ideas of his own [about how] to create an image for her,' Modina knew. It's unlikely he spent any money on formal classes. Modina remembered that George usually went along with Sassy when she bought clothes; he couldn't find a way to teach her how to choose the right style for herself. When George couldn't go for some reason, he asked Modina to go in his place. He paid a dentist to cap Sassy's buck teeth. The noticeable gap between them disappeared.

Sassy's looks further metamorphosed as Modina trimmed Sassy's top-heavy wig. Then Modina decided that Sassy shouldn't wear a wig at all. So Modina trimmed Sassy's hair very short in back and cut it in a fluffy style on top.

And George not only negotiated Sassy's fees adroitly; he made sure she earned a percentage of the door charges. *Down Beat* reported that she earned $200 a week when George booked her into Cafe Society in 1947 and then $2,250 a week plus a percentage in the same club in 1950, more than twenty-five times her salary there in 1946. George had Modina stand at the door to check the number of people coming into clubs.

During off-hours, at home in Newark, Sassy had time to wonder about why she wasn't becoming pregnant. 'She never told me exactly what the doctor gave as the reason she couldn't have children,' Modina says. 'She could be vague and even totally close-mouthed about some personal matters.' All that Sassy conveyed was that she was probably never going to be able to have a baby. Her inability preyed on her mind. She and George very much wanted to have a child, she told Modina. Sassy knew that her parents, particularly her mother, wanted grandchildren.

Sassy especially doted on her mother and liked to buy her gifts. A catty but touching tale circulated in the community. One day Ada Vaughan showed up in church wearing a fashionable hat that Sassy had apparently bought, but it wasn't the sort of hat that a conservative-style, churchgoing, middle-aged woman would buy for herself. And it still had the price tag hanging from it. Apocryphal or not, the tale symbolised the community's respect laced with envy for the Vaughans and the successful daughter who took care of them.

By 1950 she was earning enough money for George to hire Johnnie Garry as the road manager for the group. For Johnnie, who would later manage the internationally known club Birdland and then work for Jazzmobile in Harlem, the job with Sassy became a joy with spiritual as well as financial rewards. Sassy still hadn't made any 'real money' at the time he started working for her. Life was still rough, Johnnie recalled. 'We all suffered together. She stayed with us, if we stayed in a place that wasn't a good place. The first time we played the Fontaine-bleau Hotel in Miami Beach, which was segregated, the owner offered her a room there. But the rest of us couldn't stay at that hotel. We had to stay in the Sir John in Miami near Second Street. That's where the musicians stayed. It had a pool.' So Sassy stayed there and cooked for the group in her suite's kitchen. She liked macaroni and cheese, she loved to cook pork chops, and she made a great potato salad. Johnnie felt that her cooking helped make up for the insults of segregation that surrounded them in Miami. They even needed police passes to cross from Miami into Miami Beach, where she was performing at night. Right after the job, her group had to leave Miami Beach and go back to Miami. Restaurants were restricted; signs on water fountains in department stores stated: 'For Whites Only' and 'For Coloreds'. Train stations, buses, everything was still as segregated as it had been during Sassy's days with Hines.

One time Sassy worked in Miami at the Celebrity Club owned by Alan Gale, who also owned the Martinique on Fifty-second Street in New York. Business was so good while Sassy worked in his Miami club that he told her, 'I sure would like to do something nice for you.' She said to him, 'I'd like you to let my own people in.' 'Okay,' he said, and he did. Extremely happy, she invited some local friends from Liberty City to hear her performance. That was the first time Johnnie Garry heard her sing 'The Lord's Prayer' a cappella. People not only clapped, they cried.

Johnnie always liked to reflect on the early days of road-managing for Sassy. He liked driving the couple to their house on Avon Avenue in Newark when they finished their tours. He went to sleep himself in a room on the second floor and returned home to his own family in New York in the morning. Johnnie loved to be around the music; Sassy's voice especially held him in thrall. He loved Ada Vaughan's cooking. He loved Sassy and George and musicians in general; they were his people.

When all of them were struggling in concert, they had taken heart from every little upward turn in their fortunes. During one engagement in the old Chicago Theater, Sassy wasn't attracting big audiences. 'She's dying in there,' Johnnie Garry said to George, who arranged for some men to throw things at her from the balcony, turning the engagement into a racial incident to catch the attention of the media. The newspapers publicised the story. 'Headlines!' Johnnie reminisced years later.

Dave Garroway, whose midnight radio show, 'The 11:60 Club', was broadcast from a studio in the Hotel Sherman in Chicago, started playing Sassy's records on the air all the time, using the eerily atmospheric 'Don't Blame Me', with its long-held final note, as a virtual theme song. He played 'Mean to Me', 'Tenderly', and 'East of the Sun' repeatedly; he loved 'Tenderly' so much that he had Sassy sing it over the telephone to his wife. Garroway began calling Sassy 'the Divine One'. It was one of the signal moments of her career, something that altered her status, just as joining Earl Hines's band, and meeting B, Dizzy and Bird, and finding George Treadwell to manage her had been. Garroway began making sure Sassy met the right people and had broadcast exposure. As early as 1947, Garroway had made his support for Sassy well known. On 13 April he had presented an '11:60 Club' jazz concert featuring 'The Crystalline Sarah Vaughan and the Fabulous Slam Stewart, the bassist', advertised by way of the three Hudson-Ross record stores near the Loop. On 12 September of that year, Hudson-Ross advertised in the *Chicago Daily Tribune* that Sarah Vaughan would appear in person to sign autographs that day at the store at 8 East Randolph Street. Dave Garroway added his praise to the ad: 'Come and meet Sarah Vaughan, the crystalline, iridescent singing star . . . I'll be there, too!' Her Musicraft records, including latest releases, 'I Cover the Waterfront' and 'Ghost of a Chance', were in stock at seventy-nine cents each, along with 'Lover Man', 'If You Could See Me Now', 'My Kinda Love', 'Tenderly', and at least ten other recordings.

Johnnie measured their progress after that by the cars. At first the group toured in a car so rundown that its motor fell out after a trip from New York to California. Luckily the car was parked in a friend's driveway when the accident occurred; Sassy's group was staying with her friend anyway, and her commodious house could accommodate the group for the long period until the car was fixed. Eventually George and Sassy were able to buy a second car, which meant the group could travel without being cramped with luggage and props. It was a Chevrolet with a standard shift; Johnnie only knew how to drive an automatic. Sassy told him, 'You like music. Count one, two, three, four. Change gears, one and two and three and four, and follow me all the way to Chicago.' By the time he got to the Pennsylvania Turnpike, Johnnie was swinging.

Among the myriad ways Treadwell helped Sassy, Johnnie noticed, was the way he taught her what makeup could do for her. So she never underplayed or overdid makeup. She just put a little emphasis on her eyes; for her face, she had a sponge and a small bottle of Max Factor foundation in her pocketbook. 'And that's how we got through those one-night stands, with four gowns and a little makeup in her pocket-book,' Johnnie recalled. Treadwell was such a perfectionist about every aspect of Sassy's performances that he even made Johnnie wear a tie when he carried the bags.

Johnnie recalled a day when their little group, still consisting only of George, Johnnie, and Jimmy Jones, had a vision of what the future might hold. Carlos Gastel, then Nat King Cole's manager, took them on a boat ride to Catalina Island. Gastel took George aside for a talk. Afterward George whispered to Johnnie, 'Can you believe that Carlos just offered me a hundred thousand dollars for Sarah's contract?' Treadwell and Sassy didn't even have a contract, of course. That technicality notwithstanding, George might have been able to put her career in Carlos Gastel's hands for a hundred thousand dollars payable to *George*. Johnnie told George, 'If he's offering you that, she must be worth millions. Hold on to it. At least you've got me and Jimmy Jones.'

However unformed and naïve Sassy may have appeared at the start of her solo career, she had nevertheless managed to find a niche for herself with a three-year contract with Musicraft – apparently without George's help. Under his guidance, she had recorded her first big hit, 'It's Magic'. (Whether he had chosen the song for her is unknown; in a publicity release he wrote for Sassy, George claimed credit.) But by September 1948, Musicraft was facing bankruptcy. The company claimed in court that Sassy wasn't honouring her contract. Treadwell countercharged that Musicraft wasn't paying Sassy any of the royalties she was due. In 1948 the Treadwells hired Andrew J. Feinman, a lawyer specialising in the music industry, who helped them break her contract with Musicraft. Her case was based 'on the theory that her contract with Musicraft had been nullified due to that company's failure to meet its 1948 royalty payments to her', according to the black newspaper, the *Pittsburgh Courier*, which had chosen her the best singer of the year for its 1947–48 poll.

Sassy left the legalities in the hands of Treadwell and Feinman and, anticipating the dissolution of her contract with Musicraft, jumped labels to Columbia. In early January 1949, she recorded 'Black Coffee', 'As You Desire Me', and 'Bianca' for the company, and later in the month recorded 'While You Are Gone', 'That Lucky Old Sun', and 'Tonight I Shall Sleep'. She was now presenting herself as a pop singer who could do popular ballads in a straightforward style, the soft, sultry sound of her voice unfurling with hypnotic effect, moving with ease between her soprano and contralto registers.

On 29 January 1949 the trade papers reported that Musicraft contemplated releasing her if 'the singer waiv[ed] all claims to money owed her' and 'any claims to her Musicraft masters – both those released and those in the bin – and for the chirp to cut two more sides for the firm at her or Columbia's expense'. When the lawsuits ended, Columbia Records was free to release recordings she had already made for the company. 'Black Coffee', an affecting, moody dirge about women's lonely fate, made it to number 13 on *Billboard*'s popular song list for four weeks in June 1949.

Fresh from this success, she went back into Columbia's studio in July to record more ballads, some delightful, others forgettable, but all of them showcases for the quality of her voice. Jimmy Jones played a subtle piano accompaniment on such tunes as 'Just Friends', recorded with the Joe Lippman orchestra. The song didn't make a great showing on the charts, but it presented Sassy luxuriating in haunting, atmospheric improvisations. 'That Lucky Old Sun', recorded in the summer and released in September, did nearly as well as 'Black Coffee', and a month later, 'Make Believe (You Are Glad When You're Sorry)' hit the charts for five weeks. Through October 1953, Sassy's records showed up in the pop charts with great frequency – 'I'm Crazy to Love You', 'Our Very Own', 'I Love the Guy', 'Thinking of You' (with Bud Powell on piano), 'These Things I Offer You', 'Vanity', 'I Ran All the Way Home', 'Saint or Sinner', 'My Tormented Heart', 'A Lover's Quarrel', and 'Time' all scored high.

'I Cried for You', a song she recorded in September, showed how Sassy blended jazz and pop feeling in her best records. 'Being a very old man,' one critic wrote, 'I especially like "I Cried for You" . . . She does it in a straight rhythm pattern, although her vocal tricks seem more obvious than they do on some of her more recent platters. The reverse side ("You Say You Care") has a choral background, and I generally don't care for that. However, Sarah handles it well and gets a good antiphonal effect now and then.'

Nearly all of Sassy's songs for Columbia were ballads with a popular, commercial orientation. 'I wanted to prove that I could sing the pops as well as anybody could,' Sassy would say about her Columbia sides. 'Black Coffee', for one, is a Vaughan classic, no matter what category a listener decides it falls into. But in January 1950, when *Time* magazine ran a story about her, the writer ignored her commercially successful Columbia songs and concentrated on her Musicraft recordings of 'Don't Blame Me' and 'I Cover the Waterfront'. Praising her version of 'The Lord's Prayer', the story mentioned Marian Anderson's congratulatory telegram to Sassy for the recording. For Sarah Vaughan, 'Anything might happen on the waterfront,' the *Time* writer predicted.

At the end of the year, much of which she spent travelling as usual, she returned to Cafe Society Downtown for a three-week engagement. John S. Wilson, writing for *Down Beat*, published his review in the 10 February 1950 issue, affirming that Treadwell's Pygmalion role had been completely successful. 'Although she has won *Down Beat*'s poll for the last three years as the top girl singer not with a band, it was 1949 which saw Sarah develop into a finished entertainer who was really worth the large wads of cash being tossed at her. Just a year ago, when she played at the Clique [Club, which she opened] in New York, Sarah was an interesting singer with a lot of distressing characteristics. She lacked presence, she was overdoing her stylistic gesturing and facial expressions as well as her vocal calisthenics, and she looked – to put it bluntly – somewhat in the neighbourhood of a mess. The changes that have been wrought on her in one year's time are little short of a miracle. At Cafe Society, she was dressed tastefully; her hair and makeup had been worked out to give her a pleasantly glamorous touch, and she handled herself on the floor extremely well. She was in command of the situation at all times, and there [were] no jarring notes to detract attention from her superb voice or the individual way in which she uses it . . . It was in this last year that she achieved the polish which transformed her from a relatively esoterically appreciated singer into a showman who can hold her own with those select few who roost up on the top rung. This very process of acquiring this polish has made her a better singer, one who gives the impression of having complete confidence in her abilities, who knows what she can do and does it without straining, with complete ease, and wonderfully well.'

In 1951 Sassy asked Modina Davis to start travelling, too, as hairdresser and Girl Friday. As Johnnie Garry had done, Modina fell in love with the music, the mechanics of the whole production, and the high-spirited personality of the entire group. Modina noticed that George and Sassy sometimes clashed a little; the fights always seemed to be about how and when and with whom Sassy should socialise and what, in general, she should do with her leisure time. Everyone in the group liked to hang out at night, all night, after work.

The road job was a perpetual education. George consulted Johnnie about lighting because Johnnie had become so well self-taught about it. They decided to buy only white gowns for Sassy, 'so we could two-tone her', Johnnie recalled. 'Her face was flesh pink, and for a ballad, her dress was bathed in blue- or magenta-coloured light. For an uptempo song, we used a full body light from toe to face. We had little signals about what to do if the light was too hot. She could signal me with her hands. And I'd flutter the lights when it was time for her to come off. We never wrote light cues; we stayed on our toes instead. We reversed things; we gave her full body light for the verse, and then we tightened up, dimmed the lights, for the melody. Other singers did just the opposite.'

Modina was at first unnerved by the terrors and the joys of living constantly on unfamiliar terrain and by the responsibility of trying to keep things running smoothly for the group. She learned on the job how to handle the packing so that Sassy's gowns wouldn't be crushed during months of moving around. Sassy had gowns for different seasons and climates; periodically Modina brought them home to Ada Vaughan for refurbishing. Now and again, Modina restyled Sassy's hair, and George ordered a new set of publicity photographs. Modina learned to book hotel rooms and airline and train tickets. The transportation plans were always a headache.

In 1951 Sassy went to Europe for the first time – crossing on the SS *Liberte* and landing in Plymouth, according to Johnnie Garry, and by another ship, as Modina recalled, that docked at Southampton. (There would be so many trips to Europe and so many performances in various cities in the 1950s that it was easy for them to forget exactly what ship they had taken where or when. In 1952, though, they actually travelled on the SS *Liberte*.) Modina was always surprised at how they managed to miss so many meals, get so little sleep, and still arrive where they were going on time – and in once piece. Sassy's metabolism kept racing at girlhood speed; no matter how much she ate and drank, she remained slender throughout her twenties and into her thirties. And her voice remained unscathed by an exhausting schedule, constant use, cigarettes and drinks.

For her first performance overseas, Sassy sang in a concert at Royal Albert Hall, where the audience cheered. Harold Davison, the agent who was working for the tour, sent her to the north of England and Scotland, too. Modina soon found herself drinking gin with water and a twist of lemon, the drink which Sassy liked. The Coca-Cola Modina preferred was too expensive. The others in the group told Modina, 'We don't mind buying your drinks, but we hate to spend a dollar to get you a dime Coke.' So Modina followed the leader. In Europe in 1951, when gin was hard to come by, Sassy discovered she loved Cognac. Modina switched along with everybody else. Cognac remained one of Sassy's favourite drinks for the rest of her life.

From time to time, Modina would ask Sassy about money; she seemed to spend a lot without counting what came in. But she kept telling Modina what she had always told her and anybody else who asked: 'I just sing.' When practical questions arose, Sassy seemed puzzled and naïve about the world at times.

In Germany, Modina recalled, both she and Sassy were quite frightened by their first audience. The people sat quietly while Sassy sang;

afterward they yelled a word that she had never heard before and didn't understand. The shouting sounded fierce. Sassy left the stage and kicked off the high-heeled shoes that always hurt her feet. She told Modina apprehensively, 'I don't think they like me. What are they saying?' Modina didn't know. But somebody translated the rumbling, ominous-sounding word for them; the women relaxed when they understood it was flattery.

Modina was particularly unnerved about travelling between small European cities that had only one train connecting them every day. Johnnie Garry was responsible for waking the group members and shepherding them to the train on time. Modina recalled being responsible for helping with that duty. If the group missed the train, everyone would arrive late for the job in the next town. Restaurants in small cities usually closed before Sassy finished her performances. Often the group would simply arrive in a town just in time for the gig. When they had to leave a town very early, breakfast would become another problem, especially if the group hadn't found a restaurant open after work the previous night. But that was life on the road.

It seemed to Johnnie Garry that Sassy and George were happy together; they had their differences, as any married couple had, but Johnnie never thought any of their fights were out of the ordinary. Modina, too, perceived that George and Sassy loved each other, although Modina soon became aware that George was jealous and possessive and had what Modina viewed as a macho personality. She thought it might have been one of the major reasons that the Treadwell marriage became increasingly tense. More and more, Sassy didn't like to be told what was right and wrong for her to do. And especially when she became more popular as the 1950s wore on, she wanted to test her wings more than ever and live in a very free style, not tied down to George. Modina thought both George's jealousy and Sassy's increasing resistance worked in tandem to make them very angry with each other. Neither Modina nor Johnnie Garry talked about it, but a number of other people believed that George hit Sassy. Their marriage difficulties were made more complex by their business relationship.

George Wein, then a young man in love with his Boston jazz club, Storyville, would soon come to diagnose the problem between managers and their clients as a kind of syndrome. The manager began by saying, 'I'll ask her.' Eventually he graduated to saying, 'We'll think about it.' At last he said, 'I don't want it.' And the relationship ended in acrimony, with the manager trying to usurp the prerogatives of the star. Wein saw it happen innumerable times, and to the Treadwells, too, as he progressed from Storyville to found the Newport Jazz Festival in 1954 and then Festival Productions with its many jazz festivals in the United States and Europe.

As early as their 1951 trip to Europe, Modina recalled, Sassy and George fought in a peculiar way about who was going to rule the roost. Modina had just unpacked Sassy's bags in a London hotel room and was on her way to her own room when George stopped her in the hallway. He told her that Sassy didn't want Modina working for her anymore; Sassy was going to rehire a woman who had worked for her before. Modina was thousands of miles from home for the first time in her life. Why had Sassy waited for her to cross an ocean before firing her? Stunned, Modina went to Sassy's room and asked her what was wrong. Sassy laughed and said, 'Of course you're not fired. Don't pay any attention to that. George is angry with me, so he said that to you.'

Modina soon saw it was a pattern with George; occasionally he would do 'spiteful little things like that', as she regarded them. She didn't hold a grudge because he more than made up for his faults by being sweet and generous. When he was going out to shop, or eat, or drink, he always asked Modina along to share in some way what he was going to enjoy.

Modina also saw that Sassy could sometimes be capricious and provocative. When she and George had a fight, she occasionally threatened not to go onstage. Modina would remind her that she wasn't singing for George. 'You're singing for yourself. And if something goes wrong, the people are looking at you.' Sassy always went onstage. Once, when they arrived in a hotel, Modina unpacked Sassy's most important bag first – the one that Modina had organised so that Sassy would have everything she needed at her fingertips upon arrival. Then Modina decided to unpack one of her own bags and finish Sassy's unpacking later. But without a trace of warmth, Sassy commanded, 'Unpack both bags.' Modina did as she was told. Although it was unlike Sassy to treat Modina so much like an employee, and that sort of confrontation didn't happen very often, it was a disturbing glimpse of how Sassy could treat people.

Modina had a husband back in Newark, but she stayed on the road even when she was nine months pregnant in 1954. Sassy was performing in California when Modina's doctor telephoned and told her she should go back to Newark right away. So Modina went home and waited a few weeks; the baby still didn't come. When Sassy arrived in New York to play at Birdland, Modina, who wasn't happy at home, went back to work, taking care of Sassy's clothes and hair. On the last night of Sassy's engagement, the group decided to head to an after-hours spot in Harlem to unwind. It was always the same for the group. The amount of excitement Sassy generated when she performed electrified her and the people around her so much that they had to go someplace and calm down. For Sassy that could take days. All the while she knew she was going to go onstage again soon; she alternated between happiness and stage fright.

Modina wanted to go along to Harlem, but Sassy's group wouldn't let her. Disappointed, she went across the street to Sassy's hotel and started packing Sassy's bags; the group was going to Washington the next morning for another gig. While she was packing, Modina went into labour. Nevertheless she decided to finish packing everything. Then she hurried to a hospital to deliver the baby, a little girl whom she named Mikki.* Three weeks later, Modina left Mikki in the care of her own mother, who now lived with Modina in an apartment in a second building on Avon Avenue that Sassy had bought. And Modina drove alone all the way to Chicago to rejoin Sassy's group. Though Modina's marriage wasn't happy and soon ended in divorce, the job with Sassy wasn't just a diversion. Modina loved the challenge. And she loved being part of what Johnnie Garry would call a veritable family on the road. But Sassy and George found it increasingly difficult to get along with each other. The strain between them affected everyone else.

One time, when Sassy was appearing in Chicago, Sassy and George had a fight. After the run, Sassy decided to stay behind in Chicago at the Manor House, a homey little hotel on the South Side, rather than return to Newark right away. 'She had a friend there,' Modina recalled about the Manor House. On the train trip back to Newark, Modina recalled, George sat up drinking in the parlour car all night, insisting that Modina and others in the group sit up with him; he never liked being alone. Modina sat with him all the way to their front doors.

Sassy, too, liked to have people with her 100 per cent of the time, Modina came to notice. Every night, whether she was working or not, Sassy liked to get out of whatever hotel she was in, go to a bar for a drink, move on to the next one, listen to the music, all the while eating and talking with people about anything at all, music of course, old times, gossip, the news. Then when the sun came up, they would move on to a place for breakfast, and set off to whatever Sassy wanted to do – shop, play golf – as soon as she had changed her clothes.

---

*Mikki grew up to be Mikki Garth Taylor, the beauty editor in charge of covers for *Essence* magazine at the time this biography was written.

Some afternoons, she stayed in her hotel room, watching television and reading comic books; she especially liked the 'weird ones about ghouls', she told the press. But all night long, she liked to have a party, either in her room, or in Johnnie Garry's, or at some place in town. Sometimes the party was a marathon, with Sassy hanging out for three days at a time, never going to sleep, taking part in every kind of refreshment available – cigarettes, drinks, food, marijuana, maybe cocaine if there was any. She would come to love cocaine. Nothing made her sick. Every place she went, her group had an extravagantly good time, living the entertainer's life-style to the hilt.

In Detroit, after she finished performing, she liked to go to Fred Guinyard's after-hours club, where musicians went to hang out and hear good music. On 11 July 1951 the police raided the club and arrested twenty patrons, among them Sassy, and held her pending an investigation for violation of the state liquor law. A United Press story that day said she spent twelve hours in a Detroit jail. Police told the press that Miss Vaughan 'was very pleasant about the whole thing for a few hours. She sang a few songs, but then she got tired of us and wanted out.' When she lit a cigarette, a matron told her smoking privileges were given only to prisoners who mopped the floor. Sassy put out her cigarette.

Even when Sassy alighted for a while in Newark, she celebrated life in her usual way and always with company. Nobody ever saw her vocalise or warm up for a performance, though on occasion she rehearsed, and she loved to sit in with musicians.

One night Shirley Horn was playing at the Key Club in Newark when a beautiful voice joined in while Shirley was singing and playing piano. It was Sassy. Drummer Bobby Durham was enthralled by the interlude. That happened with Sassy in countless places with many musicians for the rest of her life. Legend has it that the owner of the Key Club reserved a microphone for Sassy's impromptu visits. Sometimes Sassy would take Modina to nearby Sparky J's (later called the Cadillac Club) or to Len and Len's, a place owned by Lenny Pearson, who had played baseball for the Newark Eagles. Sassy especially liked Len and Len's, where she and her friends warmed up for the night before crossing the river to hear the last set at Birdland. Sassy was a party.

FOUR

'The Bitch is a Genius'

After a while, George opened a management office on West Fifty-seventh Street in Manhattan, partly because he took on other clients who needed his attention, among them the Drifters and singer Ruth Brown, and partly because he and Sassy were fighting so much. He didn't always accompany her on the road anymore. The separation put an extra strain on the Treadwells' marriage. Johnnie Garry reflected that he was quite an authority about that, because his own life on the road taxed his happy family life severely at times. 'With George in the office and Sassy on the road, their love affair cooled,' Johnnie says. But other people thought it was the other way around. Modina noticed that George often showed up at Sassy's out-of-town gigs without calling to say that he would be coming. Sassy usually was not at the hotel, and he often became jealous. He insisted on 'sneaking up on her, to see if he would catch her' in some compromising position, Modina said. Sassy was usually hanging out with Modina and other friends at a bar or a club. But George would accuse Sassy of fooling around. He and Sassy would start to fight. 'He provoked Sassy to make good his accusations,' Modina said, 'and then he became disgusted with the way he thought things were going.' Sometimes Modina and Sassy would sit at the bar in a club where Sassy was working, and George would object if a man talked to his wife.

Years later, Sassy confided to Robert Richards that she and George together with Billy Eckstine and his wife might find themselves in the same city, having a good time out on the town; as soon as they returned to their hotel rooms, the two couples started fighting. They made so much noise that hotel managers knocked on their doors and told them to calm down. 'It got so that the hotel managements hated to see us arriving,' Sassy told Robert. Drummer Jimmy Cobb, who worked for Sassy much later on, recalled being in the Watkins Hotel in Los Angeles in 1951 at the same time Sassy and George were staying there. 'The rap was that [they were] fighting all day up in the room. George used to put her in the closet and kind of smack her around a little, so no one would hear that.'

Not only socially and emotionally but professionally, Sassy found herself relying less on George in the 1950s than she had done when they had first got together.

How well Sassy might have done on her own, without polish or business savvy, is open to speculation. People who knew George Treadwell well thought that he did an important job for Sassy before their relationship deteriorated. Jazz impresario George Wein, who felt that Sassy never had first-rate management, said, 'George Treadwell did the best he could' for Sassy. And Wein himself knew what Treadwell could do. In 1952 Wein paid Sassy twenty-seven hundred dollars a week to appear at Storyville, his Boston club. Ella Fitzgerald earned less from him because Ella didn't have the same kind of protective manager to negotiate for her, and despite her reputation, she wasn't as contemporary as Sassy. Not until Norman Granz began guiding Ella's recording career in 1955 did her popularity really surge.

Sassy was so shy in those days, 'not temperamental but shy', George Wein reminisced, that it was very difficult for him to get her to agree to go back onstage for an encore; her three sets a night lasted only about twenty minutes each. 'To get her to sing twenty-five minutes was like pulling teeth,' he said. 'And she never talked to audiences from the stage' in those days. Wein concedes that Treadwell made a difference for Sassy. But Wein wasn't convinced, as Modina and Johnnie were, that Treadwell played a crucial role in Sassy's success story. 'She survived in spite of her husbands,' Wein says. Without Treadwell, she undoubtedly would have survived on the strength of her voice alone, Wein believed, just as Ella had done in her days between losing her first mentor, bandleader Chick Webb, who died young, and signing with Granz. But Sassy would have suffered from the handicap of being 'a shy woman', wrote Nat Hentoff, who interviewed her at Storyville.

George Wein never forgot how Sassy, bashful as she was, used her voice to help him stymie Boston's police force. During one of its periodic drives to enforce the state's blue laws – clubs were supposed to close by midnight on Saturdays – the police marched into Storyville and made all the customers leave hurriedly. The police would simply cut off the performers in midnote at midnight. So Wein asked Sassy to sing 'The Lord's Prayer' at midnight one Saturday. As the police were getting ready to converge upon her, she started her breathtaking prayer. The police held still. Nobody was rushed out of Storyville that night.

Despite her shyness, Sassy loved the exciting pace of her life. In 1951 she celebrated her twenty-seventh birthday at Birdland, where she had already appeared several times. The glamorous party started at midnight. The bar closed at 4 a.m., but the party went on, with the cake-cutting reserved until 4.30 a.m. *Ebony* magazine photographed her wearing a tasteful, full-skirted dress with a spangled bodice. She looked happy in the company of boxer Joe Louis; she was photographed kissing and holding hands with her husband. Sugar Ray Robinson's sister, Mrs Marie Brewer, showed up, as did dancer Harold Nicholas of the Nicholas Brothers, and Yul Brynner, then starring in *The King and I*, and French actress Denise Darcel, an intimate friend of Billy Eckstine. Dinah Washington was there. (Dinah liked to show up at Sassy's gigs in clubs and sing along. She did it so much, once even singing from the audience while Sassy stood on stage, that Modina thought Dinah was competing with Sassy; Sassy sat in on Dinah's gigs, too, but never tried to upstage her from the audience, Modina recalled.) Bandleader Lucky Millinder, Rose Hardaway, Erroll Garner, pianist Mary Lou Williams, critic Leonard Feather, actress Gloria DeHaven, and soul singer Ruth Brown, who would become George's client, came to the party. So did Eartha Kitt, with her hair bobbed even shorter than Sassy's, in the days before she was well known.

Comedian Nipsey Russell and Birdland's doorman, Pee Wee Marquette, a dwarf whose piping, lusty little voice was as much imitated in the jazz world as Ed Sullivan's was on national television, acted as master of ceremonies, along with Symphony Sid Torin, a popular disc jockey. Torin brought Sassy to a microphone to sing a few songs. Sassy's spirited mother turned up in dangling earrings and a nearly strapless gown with sheer shoulder coverings. Dainty bright jewels shone on Sassy's earlobes; close to one temple, nestled in the short hair tended for her by Modina, Sassy wore a jewel that matched the earrings. Whether they were rhinestones or diamonds is impossible to tell; she lost so much jewellery on the road that she often substituted costume jewellery for the real gems. Here was the Sassy whom fans thought was so adorable, before her dream of a happy romance and a highly charged, lucrative career revealed itself to her as a trap of mixed-up relationships and Byzantine financial dealings.

She kept working in clubs, making records, and appearing on radio and television shows. In the early 1950s, *Ebony* estimated, she earned $150,000 a year. (Other magazines said her income was $200,000 and even $250,000.) *Time* magazine reported she sold three million copies of records a year, but only George Treadwell knew for sure what she earned; he was not only in charge of the money but of the information released to the press. Among her best-known engagements were appearances at Carnegie Hall; the Million Dollar Theatre in Los Angeles; the Apollo, Loew's State, the Strand, and the Paramount in New York; the Regal, the Oriental, and the Chicago theatres in Chicago; the Earle in Philadelphia; and the Howard in Washington DC – many of which she played with the Big Show, a travelling show featuring some of the greatest stars in music and entertainment.

On at least one Big Show tour, in the early 1950s, she travelled with Nat King Cole and his trio, and a crowd of black comedians and dancers – the dance team of Stump and Stumpy, and Marie Bryant among them. The Big Show tours had so many stars in their companies that no matter how exciting and glamorous each act was, Johnnie Garry thought the shows lasted too long. Nat Cole usually closed the first act, Sassy the second act. The road company was as big as a circus, with a spirited lot of troupers living and travelling together. With all the hardships, she loved the entertainment world.

Sassy played in Las Vegas at the Thunderbird and La Frontier. She sang on 'The Perry Como Show', 'The Lucky Strike Show', and 'The Red Robbins Show' on radio, and on television she starred on 'We the People', Ed Sullivan's 'Toast of the Town', and 'So This Is Show Business'. She sang her best-known songs, recorded for Musicraft and Columbia. Working so much, winning polls in the magazines popular in music and show business circles and in the black press, too, Sassy acquired enough prestige to set off little arguments among musicians about who was the better singer, Sassy or Ella Fitzgerald. Ella's quicksilver interpretations and rhythmic genius were weighed against Sassy's indisputably more luxuriant voice. Ella was called 'the First Lady of Song', Sassy 'the Divine One'.

In Minton's in Harlem late one night, Sassy, who rarely went there, and Ella, who almost never hung out, showed up at the same time – but not together. Jazz critic Nat Hentoff had an idea that some interesting musical event was going to happen that night. He didn't know exactly what it was going to be, but a musician had told him to go there. Then Ella and Sassy took turns singing and 'got into a real cutting contest', Hentoff said. 'And Sarah won. She had the instrument, and she really pushed herself.' With or without George Treadwell,

Sassy's competitive spirit was as important for her as any manager could be.

By 1953, Sassy was able to afford travelling with a full-time trio on her payroll. That year, she hired drummer Roy Haynes and bassist Joe Benjamin. Jimmy Jones was on sick leave for two years at the time. John Malachi, Billy Eckstine's former band pianist, had replaced Jones and went to Europe with her for her first trip there.

Roy Haynes recalled his baptismal night with Sassy's trio at the Rendezvous Club in Philadelphia. Malachi had got his calendar mixed up and didn't show up for the first night, so Sassy sat down to play the piano for herself. (Pianist Norman Simmons, a budding accompanist in Chicago, had once been asked by Jimmy Jones to sit in with Sassy's group for a night at the Blue Note. Norman requested the music and was told there wasn't any. 'What do you mean, there's no music?' he said. 'I heard you changing keys.' He heard other complexities in the music, too. Jimmy Jones said, 'Sometimes she leads and you follow, and sometimes you lead and she'll follow anyplace you go.' Astounded and leery, Norman declined the job. Sassy and Jimmy Jones communicated so well that they never had to use music; each one understood exactly what the other was suggesting. With other pianists, Sassy always used written music.) Roy Haynes's confidence carried him through the crisis that first night. Sassy, happy with his remarkable work, took him out on the town afterwards and introduced him to Gordon's Gin. Unusual as it seems, Roy maintained, 'I had never had a drink in my life. Sass could really hang out. I looked at a clock and saw it was ten in the morning.' He recalled how much he suffered with a hangover that day.

At the time Roy joined Sassy's entourage, he thought that Sassy and George were, in effect, separated, and that their relationship was strictly business. During this period, when she sang in New York, she would finish a job on a Saturday night and drive right away to Atlantic City, New Jersey, usually without George. She would head straight for the main street of Atlantic City's black district, Kentucky Avenue. 'There was everything for our people on Kentucky Avenue at the time,' Roy reminisced. Another drummer and a friend of Sassy's, Chris Colombo, spoke affectionately of Kentucky Avenue as 'the most exciting street in America, beginning in the 1930s, continuing through the 1940s and 1950s'. Colombo worked there at the Club Harlem, which hired excellent black entertainers – Willis 'Gatortail' Jackson for one, and Milt Buckner, a pianist who had developed a 'locked hands' style of playing, repeating the same notes with both hands, so that his sound could be distinguished when he played in the Lionel Hampton band. Nat Cole used to stop in and sing at the Club Harlem for no pay – he was too famous to work for the little money the club could have paid him. But he had felt the urge to perform there. Sassy used to sing for no pay at Club Harlem, too.

Across the street stood two restaurants, Sap's Barbecue and Jerry's Barbecue, which kept the night people fed. They bought food and carried it to Club Harlem's bar, where they ate while they drank. Even before gambling came in, Atlantic City was open twenty-four hours a day. Sassy was in her element. She loved Club Harlem's breakfast show. Colombo, who knew Treadwell and other men with whom she went to the club, prided himself on holding on to her cash for her; she asked him to look after it because everyone knew Colombo didn't drink. He also made sure that she returned to her hotel with her bankroll still intact. 'All the guys were trying to take her,' he said. By now she was getting $350 a week pocket money as an allowance.

Sassy became aware that Sonny Payne, Colombo's son, had taught himself every song in Count Basie's book, learning the drum parts by listening to records and by showing up at Basie's gigs and tapping on the table right along with the band's drummer. When Basie was looking for a drummer in 1954, Sassy asked him to audition Sonny. He impressed Basie instantly and went on to become one of the Count's favourite drummers. So Colombo had good reason to be grateful and protective of Sassy; he took a dim view anyway of the hustlers who surrounded her in the club where he saw her hanging out tirelessly. But Sassy loved the nightlife where she was a star, a sought-after woman disproving her earlier reputation as an ugly duckling. She never got tired of hanging out with the pimps, hustlers, gamblers, playboys, all the characters as well as the celebrities: these were her people. Everyone called her 'Sass'; that, to her, was an accolade. Performers also started calling her 'the Divine One', following Dave Garroway's lead. Writers used 'the Divine One' in their stories and headlines. Eventually she would set up her own management company called the Devine One, misspelling it on purpose; it was probably her way of sassing the language, with which she felt immeasurably less comfortable than she did with music.

Although Sassy now had her own men friends, and George had a girlfriend, he still managed her career attentively. He arranged for her to buy her clothes at Wilma's, an expensive store in the neighbourhood of his office on West Fifty-seventh Street. One day, George and Modina went to meet a plane on which Sassy was arriving from Washington.

He and Modina had travelled to New York a little before Sassy did, because he had organised a reception for her at an airport, complete with a crew of photographers from many newspapers. When Sassy stepped off the plane, she was wearing a dark brown suit, with dark brown shoes, a dark brown hat, and she was carrying a dark brown bag. Everything matched, including her dark brown skin. George covered his eyes and sighed, 'Oh, no.' Sassy had gone shopping at Wilma's by herself; a clerk had let Sassy buy anything she liked. There was nothing wrong with the outfit itself, but there wasn't a dash of brightness, and the colour was wrong for her. George went to see Wilma and told her to make sure that Sassy bought flattering clothes for the hundreds of dollars she was spending. He didn't pick a fight with Sassy about the brown outfit. But he told Modina, 'Make sure I never see it again.'

Sassy was unhappy at Columbia Records, because she was singing so many pop ballads; she was drifting away from the improvisatory interpretations that had first brought her to prominence, and she and Columbia hadn't provided each other with the financial success they had hoped for. When her contract with Columbia ended, George signed a deal for her to record for Mercury and its subsidiary, EmArcy. She began recording in 1954 and would stay with the label until 1959.

'There's nothing necessarily wrong with being commercial,' she had told Nat Hentoff for an April 1952 article in *Down Beat*, 'but there's a point beyond which you can't go without being ridiculous.' They were talking at Storyville during 'a characteristically successful return week' for her there, Hentoff wrote. Sassy added, 'People with genuine talent are lowering themselves by continuing to use some of the material that passes for popular songs these days. I just can't. There are some tunes I just won't do. Look, what I want to put over to audiences is music. If I don't, then to me, I'm a failure. So music is always more important to me than getting with each new hit. And that too is why I like to keep on improvising, even on songs I've been doing for years. I keep pretty close to the record versions in theatres, but in nightclubs, I can let myself go . . . Do you know I've never really made a record exactly as I'd like to? It isn't clear yet [exactly what I have in mind], but I'd like to use voices, strings. Oh, a whole lot of things – Stokowski stuff . . .'

Though her contract with Mercury and EmArcy wouldn't include Stokowski stuff, Sassy was happy to leave Columbia. John Hammond had been responsible for bringing earlier blues and jazz legends into the Columbia studios. And a producer at the company had wanted to cast

Sassy in the role of a new Bessie Smith. When he asked Sassy to record gospel and the blues, she replied that she understood nothing of that kind of career. 'I want to sing pretty things,' she told him. She would confide in Robert Richards that she was disappointed in her recordings for Columbia. 'She said that if she ever wrote her autobiography, she would say that she hated' the producer who had wanted her to sing songs that she felt contradicted her goals. But with that behind her, she relished the prospect of working for Mercury and EmArcy, because George had worked out a contract that allowed her to sing both pop songs and jazz. 'My contract with Mercury is for pops, and my contract with EmArcy is for me,' she would tell *Record Whirl* in July 1955. It was her standard line to interviewers. She now had the leeway she wanted.

Whenever she had a recording date on a Monday morning, Sassy still spent her usual Sunday night in Atlantic City. With little or no sleep, she headed back to Mercury's studios in New York, where artists and repertoire man Bob Shad, with whom she worked particularly well, and her trio and studio musicians waited for her. She sang as if she had spent the weekend sipping tea with honey at a cottage by the sea. After days and nights of carousing, she could perform with an air of having been refreshed; her close friends and musical colleagues came to recognise that Sassy sang at her best when she was troubled or tired. She had incredible stamina and physical strength, they learned. Roy Haynes marvelled that 'she could drink anything and sing like a bird'. In those days, her excesses seemed to slake her insatiable appetite and thirst for the good life; she could show up for business in a good frame of mind. Joe Williams, who would become Count Basie's singer in 1954 and start performing duets with her, recalled, 'I used to get a kick out of watching her walk into a studio and ask: 'Where are my notes? She never needed a rehearsal.' Roy Haynes thought, 'The bitch is a genius.'

Whether she was making records or singing in clubs, her performances were exciting, even the moments when Sassy introduced the trio to audiences in clubs, Roy Haynes felt. She sang her pianist's name: 'John Malachi', then went on to 'Crazy Joe Benjamin', a name followed by a taut drumbeat, then 'Roy', then more drumbeats, and 'Haynes' followed by a flurry of drumming showmanship. The ritual developed into a little song called 'Shulie-a-bop', for which Sassy and George shared the composers' rights and which Sassy recorded for EmArcy.

Molly Shad, Bob Shad's widow, remembered, 'I didn't miss any of Sassy's recording sessions, if I could help it. When she recorded

"Poor Butterfly" [in November 1956], it was one of the most exciting recording sessions I ever went to.' Molly found Sassy to be an 'insecure, sweet, acquiescent' woman, and 'she was the most polished performer'. As a singer, Sassy was totally engrossing, because she never sang the same thing in the same way twice. Sometimes Bobby Shad, 'who was one of the worst singers', Molly recalled, would sing a phrase to demonstrate what he was thinking about, and Sassy howled. She had a fine sense of humour and wonderful rapport with Shad and musicians. Molly thought 'Sarah was the most misunderstood of singers, because she didn't achieve the notoriety of Ella Fitzgerald. I think she out-weighed Ella. Sarah sang like an instrument, and her voice, with her highs and her lows, was not accepted by the general public. Its value was not recognised, like jazz is not recognised. Jazz is a hard thing to get people to like. And Sarah was not accepted as the great singer she was. She was the top in her field. Her singing gave me chills,' Molly summed up.

Bobby Shad also produced Dinah Washington's records for Mercury, and Molly believed that Sassy and Dinah felt some rivalry. When Bobby Shad used Hal Mooney to do arrangements for both Sassy and Dinah, the women didn't like having the same arranger, Molly observed. 'But Sarah was not categorised as much [as Dinah was]. Sarah could have been in opera and done well,' Molly thought.

Sassy's career grew in lustre in a way it hadn't before she recorded for Mercury and EmArcy. The song 'Make Yourself Comfortable', recorded on 24 September 1954, became one of her most successful recordings ever, though it was not the million-seller that journalist May Okon reported it to be in an interview with Sassy and George.

Jimmy Jones, the pianist, returned to work with her again just after she signed with Mercury. Connoisseurs of her music would come to think of the Jones-Benjamin-Haynes trio as one of Sassy's best; that trio played for one of her very best albums, recorded on 16 December 1954, with trumpeter Clifford Brown, flutist Herbie Mann, tenor saxophonist Paul Quinichette, and Ernie Wilkins as leader and arranger, with the personnel lined up by Bob Shad. The album had some of Sassy's best material for Mercury – the exquisite, whimsical scatting on 'Lullaby of Birdland', and on other songs, her high, pure soprano with its distinctive vibrato. The rich, intimate mood of the exception-ally pretty 'Embraceable You' also stands out among a group of gems. Clifford Brown, with his easy, bright sound and creative instincts, was one of her favourite trumpeters and one of the best in jazz history. Sassy would tell Len Lyons, author of *The 101 Best Jazz Albums*, published in 1980, that the album with Clifford was her favourite recording. (She would later make another album she liked even better.)

Bassist Joe Benjamin left her group soon after that album with Clifford. Sassy began a search that would last for a couple of years. Finally she discovered Richard Davis, a bassist who satisfied her need for strength and creativity. A successful studio musician, Davis, with his excellent time and true intonation and a thorough knowledge of music, could play anything and inspire her. He made his first record with Sassy on 14 February 1957. With him in the group that Valentine's Day, she recorded a remarkable version of 'Pennies from Heaven', which she tossed out like jazz manna. As good as the Jones-Benjamin-Haynes trio had been, the new trio with Davis in it – dubbed The Trio by many people – was her very best up to then. Davis later became a professor of classical and jazz music at the University of Wisconsin.

Sassy had several hits on the charts in the mid-1950s – 'How Important Can It Be?' with the Count Basie band, 'Whatever Lola Wants' with the Hugo Peretti orchestra, and 'The Banana Boat Song', a whimsical calypso song with David Carroll and his orchestra that was so out of character for Sassy. All her recordings of the period had mass appeal; she could sing a silly song about how nice it was to do the samba and how much better to waltz down the aisle as gracefully as she could swing 'Lullaby of Birdland' with a jazz sextet. Her style was easy, her voice gorgeous. Haynes, working light-years away from the deafening, hard sound of rock drums to come, created masterpieces of loose rhythms that supported and enhanced Sassy. She did a soft-voice pop song, 'You Ought to Have a Wife', recorded with Hugo Peretti's orchestra in March 1955 for Mercury. The famed saxophonist Julian 'Cannonball' Adderley accompanied her on some records for EmArcy. In two takes of 'Over the Rainbow' with Adderley in the group, Sassy sang playfully in one interpretation, dramatically in the other. An emotionally charged version of the song, reminiscent of Judy Garland's classic, was released in the 1950s; the other interpretation by Sassy was put on the shelf. Both showed off Sassy's swinging and improvisatory genius.

Many of her best popular stylings of standard tunes were done with the Hal Mooney orchestra with strings for Mercury. She sang an exceptionally pretty version of 'A Foggy Day', and her rendition of 'He Loves and She Loves' soared. She made 'Lucky in Love' refreshingly lighthearted. Except for the arrangements and instrumentation, with the lush strings playing whole notes on her popular recordings for Mercury, it is at times impossible to say whether Sassy was singing jazz-influenced pop or pop-influenced jazz. She never compromised the quality of her sound.

In 1954 she had major successes at jazz concerts, too. In July she starred at the first Newport Jazz Festival, in Rhode Island, founded by George Wein, who thought a festival held at the summer resort would help make jazz more popular. Wealthy and influential Newport social-ites Louis and Elaine Lorillard helped him organise the first festival in the city's Casino, and the public response heartened Wein enough to plan to stage another festival the next year, this time at Newport's Freebody Park. Sassy would sing in Wein's festival nearly every year for the rest of her life, both in Newport and later when it moved to New York City. In the early days, Sassy, Anita O'Day, Louis Arm-strong, Count Basie, Frank Sinatra, and scores of other jazz artists attracted vacationers from all over the country to Newport during the festival week.

In September 1954, Sassy sang at Carnegie Hall on the same bill with Count Basie, Billie Holiday, Charlie Parker, Lester Young, the Bill Davis Trio, and the Modern Jazz Quartet. She sailed to Europe for the second time in her life that October and lured 14,000 people to hear her at Berlin's Sportspalast; 7,500 showed up at Royal Albert Hall in London twice. Then she returned to New York to star at Birdland for the eighteenth time. Sidney Fields, interviewing her for his 'Only Human' column in the *New York Daily Mirror* on 30 November 1954, asked her where she would be going after her four-week engagement at the most famous jazz club in the world. 'Sarah, who has no sense of time, wasn't quite sure,' he wrote. 'She yelled out to ask George [Treadwell], and was delighted to hear she'd have two weeks' vacation until the first of the year.' She would go 'home', she said, 'with my husband, and mother and father and have a nice Christmas. I'm away so much, home is the best place to come back to.' Her father had also just come home himself; he ahd spent two years having hospital treat-ment for tuberculosis. Sassy said, 'All mother does now is sing in the church choir, the Mount Zion Baptist Church in Newark, where we always go.' Sassy said she was going to sing during the church's anni-versary service on 12 December. She added that her parents were very proud of her, their only child. 'But unspoiled,' she said about herself. 'They were never afraid to give me a good whack when I deserved it. Mother still does. Only not so hard now.'

She would be setting out on a Big Show tour beginning on 11 February 1955, a series of one-night stands in twenty-nine cities with Count Basie, George Shearing, Erroll Garner and Jimmy Rushing, she said. When Fields told her that it sounded 'rough', she answered, 'It's been a lot rougher. In 1951, we did seventy one-night stands. On the sixty-eighth, we got a day off in Detroit and we all went nuts with nothing to do. To break the monotony, I drove our bus.' (Roy Haynes recalls being on tour with her and looking up to see Sassy driving.)

Even though her friends and musicians observed that the Tread-wells were living their separate lives, Sassy and George still maintained the third-floor apartment they shared at 21 Avon Avenue. There they welcomed May Okon, a reporter for the *New York Daily News*; the photographs show them as a happy couple with two dogs – Hansel, a poodle, and Byron, a boxer. Cute talk about Sarah filled the resultant article. 'Sarah . . . has three pet pastimes: golf – she's still trying to break one hundred; shopping for clothes – slacks are her favourite apparel; and reading comic books. She scans the latter by the thousands, she says, especially the weird kind that feature witches and vampires. Occasionally, Sarah likes to recall the comment of the first recording executive who ever auditioned her. "Good heavens," he said to George, "tell her to sing it straight. That stuff will never get her anywhere".'

May Okon called Sassy 'the high priestess of the cool jazz cult. Now that she's gone pop, Sarah Vaughan will probably become queen of the jukeboxes.'

Of course, she had not gone pop all the way and was maintaining two careers as adroitly as she was leading a double life in her show of domesticity with George for the press and her arguments with him behind the scenes. Without mentioning the trouble in her marriage, she let another reporter interviewing her for the *Daily News* in 1955 know that something was bothering her. A friend who knew of Sassy's new prosperity said, 'Now you have a nice piece of change.' Sassy said, 'Yes, but no peace of mind!' She continued working with jazz musicians and in person performed primarily at jazz concerts and clubs. She was featured at the annual New York Jazz Festival held on Randalls Island in 1955. Also on the bill were Dizzy Gillespie's quintet; pianist Dave Brubeck's quintet, featuring the fluid, haunting sound of alto saxophon-ist Paul Desmond; Horace Silver's quintet during the pianist's period of great driving, funky compositional activity, when the public first fell in love with his touching songs such as 'Doodlin', 'Song for My Father', and 'Senor Blues'; the popular organist Jimmy Smith's trio; the Johnny Richards Orchestra; and the soulful, seductive-sounding singer Bill Henderson. Henderson could croon with swing and intimacy in his mood, and his rich vibrato enchanted Sassy. She would return to the Randalls Island festival every year into the mid-1960s, when the festival was discontinued.

In February 1956, the *New York Times*'s John S. Wilson reviewed the Carnegie Hall performance of the Birdland Stars, among them Sassy, pianist Bud Powell, and Sassy's sideman Joe Benjamin, who played for that date, and Roy Haynes, singer Al Hibbler, tenor saxophonist Lester Young, and Count Basie: 'The audience's favourite was quite obviously Mr Basie's singer Joe Williams, who manages to project a quiet charm even while beating out a lusty blues.' The next year, viewing nearly the same line-up of stars, Wilson concentrated on Sassy: 'The voice that Sarah Vaughan has been covering up for the last ten years finally came into the clear at Carnegie Hall this weekend . . . She sang straight and to the point, abandoning almost completely the swoops and swirls, the pointless ornamentation which has constantly marred her work in the past. The result was electrifying.

'Miss Vaughan has a supple voice of unusual range, as has been evident even in her periods of greatest distortion. In fact this very suppleness and range may well have been at the root of her former rococo style. She never seemed to be able to resist doing tricks with it, and these tricks eventually hardened into mannerisms.

'There have been suggestions in her work over the last year that she was moving toward a greater emphasis on a natural projection of her voice. But even with this forewarning, the complete switchover was a revelation.

'She has what may well be the finest voice ever applied to jazz, and she is now using it to drive home the dramatic sense of her songs rather than to fight it. She is, as she always has been, completely at home in the jazz idiom, swinging with a jazz feeling through everything she sings. And, rounding out the picture, she has become an assured performer with an elfin charm that can be quite infectious.'

For the rest of her life, reviewers would echo John Wilson's thoughts. Some never enjoyed the ornamentation of songs that others luxuriated in – and she often decorated songs to the hilt, but the beauty and vitality of her voice always commanded respect. Musicians and other singers listened to her in awe. Working with her many times at Carnegie Hall with the Birdland Stars tours, Joe Williams thought, 'She's simply one of the greatest singers I've ever heard.' Audiences cheered for their duets.

Joe Williams, in those days, shared many backstage moments with Sassy. Once, during a tour with the Birdland Stars, he found her sleeping on a dressing-room table after some all-night parties. 'In the dressing room, she was getting the sleep she needed for the night's performance,' he thought. He chuckled, admiring her stamina. Their paths often crossed on the road. Once during the Birdland Stars of 1957 tour, he visited her in her hotel suite in Louisville, Kentucky. Johnnie Garry, drummer Sonny Payne, and guitarist Freddie Green with the Basie band were there, too. They ordered food from room service; when the waiter brought it to the door and discovered he was serving blacks, the smile disappeared from his face. His expression lingered in Williams's memory forever. 'But there we were,' Joe recalled. 'We were used to playing and staying in those sorts of hotels; we were used to dealing with situations at the top, even if the workers in them weren't used to having blacks in the downtown hotels. There were always some incidents. It was never a smooth road to progress.' As Joe did, Sassy used her talent to help transcend in some way the barriers of segregation and prejudice.

Onstage, when he sang with her, he was always respectful of her power and musicality. The musicians playing behind them thought the two of them were like horns, so complete was their control. Offstage, both learned to play golf so they could get fresh air and exercise. Unlike Sassy, however, Joe also liked to sleep; he often spent the days resting in hotel rooms to get his energy back for the evening performances. But he marvelled at Sassy's ability to go from a stage to a party to a breakfast to a golf game to another party and then back onstage. He didn't have the capacity (or the inclination) to keep up with her. Occasionally Sassy knocked on his door in the middle of the night; she wanted him to hang out with her and whomever she was partying with. 'She could be a little bit of a pest that way, but I forgave that,' he would recall with a chuckle. He was charmed by her earthiness; he could mimic the high-pitched speaking voice she used at times when she prattled quickly about this and that. She always had colourful obscene nicknames for friends. 'Mother' was a favourite. 'She was completely unassuming. She never put on airs,' Joe would recall. 'And she was sexy.'

On records and on stages, her performances wielded legendary influence over other 'girl' singers. Annie Ross, an aspiring young jazz singer from Britain, footloose and free-spirited in Paris beginning in 1948, had fallen in with American expatriate jazz musicians living there. They began educating her about the expanded bebop harmonies, and they introduced her to Sassy's early recordings. 'I Cover the Waterfront' and 'If You Could See Me Now' especially held Annie in thrall. 'I'd love to meet her,' Annie told drummer Kenny Clarke, who was living in Paris at the time. Kenny assured her, 'You'll love each other.' Eventually Annie decided to set sail to the United States and leave the bohemian life of Paris behind. While she was struggling to find a niche for herself as a singer, she met Sassy at Birdland.

'Sass was talking with some people at a table. When I was introduced, she seemed indifferent. She barely acknowledged that I was standing there. She was very, very shy. I took her shyness for aloofness. I was a little hurt, though I was thrilled to meet her.' Annie started working with Dave Lambert and Jon Hendricks around 1957; they formed Lambert, Hendricks and Ross, an innovative, swinging bebop group, which put lyrics to the improvised horn solos of great jazz groups; the trito sang at breakneck speed to the great admiration of critics and jazz fans. Annie had a flexible, pure soprano voice, and – the *sine qua non* for jazz singing – the ability to swing. Sassy and Annie started travelling in the same circles, working in the same places. 'She began to warm [to me],' Annie recalled. 'We had music so much in common, and we could talk about everybody [we knew]. We would want to go to the same places and hang at the same time and stay up all night.' By the time Lambert, Hendricks and Ross were singing at the Apollo Theatre late in the 1950s, 'she and I were like two kids. We would hang between the shows . . . One day she came into my dressing room and said, "Annie, teach me 'Doodlin'"' (a Horace Silver tune to which Lambert, Hendricks and Ross had put lyrics). 'Well, I was thrilled to think Sarah thought I could teach her anything. She knew the song, actually, but she wanted to run through it with me,' Annie recalled. (Sassy would soon record it at an easy swinging tempo with the Basie band.)

As a very young woman, Annie, like Sassy, had enormous energy for a life in the fast lane; together they stayed up all night, drinking and smoking. Sassy liked marijuana and cocaine. Later Annie would switch to herbal tea, but in the 1950s, she too liked getting high. Both of them loved to cook and to eat. Sassy would learn to love to sew, Annie recalled. ('She once made me a red suit,' Annie remembered.) On the road together, she and Sassy stayed in the same places; Annie adapted to the jazz life, staying in segregated places with her black friends. One place which they particularly liked was a house in Washington DC, owned by an elderly man named Pussy. 'He always kept a pot of chicken and dumplings heated on the stove for overnight guests. And it was an after-hours place, too; drinks were served for a price.' Annie and Sassy started a lifelong friendship.

On 24, 25 and 26 August 1957, Sassy recorded a dozen Irving

Berlin songs with her beloved B, backed by Hal Mooney's orchestra. B's voice is deep, ripe with vibrato, his enunciation of words so remarkable that on 'Easter Parade' he makes the word 'rotogravure' sound a very fine place to be found. Sassy begins 'It's a Lovely Day' with a soprano that is the quintessence of romantic femininity. Soon she's joined by B's virile baritone; at the end, he says, 'Wow, what a crazy day, Sass,' and she titters something indecipherable. It's a delightful sound that puts the perfect finishing touch on the record and the day. 'Passing Strangers', a simple, rhapsodic blend of their voices, was the cut the public liked best of all from the sessions, and fans put it on the pop charts.

Completely the trouper, Sassy kept roving for long engagements in clubs and just as readily for one-night stands. There were times in the late 1950s when the continuous grind prompted her to telephone George and ask, 'Hey, what's going on?' Modina and Johnnie Garry went everyplace with her. Modina, who had married a second time and had a second child, didn't see her family very much. Johnnie Garry's wife and daughters had to cope with his long absences.

Sassy let George keep the pressure on because her efforts were paying off in popularity. 'I've been doing pops for Mercury and jazz for EmArcy for the past couple of years, and that system seems to have worked out well for all concerned,' she told Henry Whiston of the *Melody Maker* in England for an article published in the 27 April 1957 issue. 'I know it has certainly opened up a lot of club bookings to me that wouldn't have been possible otherwise.' Her trio was a boon because the men had been with her so long that she never needed to rehearse with them, 'only with big bands' or with groups of musicians who were strangers to her. 'All I need is a group of good jazz musicians, so I don't care if it's a jazz tune or strictly a pop tune that I'm doing,' she told Whiston.

She knew that there was a lot more competition from many more singers in 1957 than she had faced in 1947, at the end of the big-band era. 'I don't think there's any increase in attempt at a hit or a good effort because I'm sure most of them are like myself in that they try their best every time out.' She kept herself abreast of everything that was going on in popular music and jazz, she said. 'I've heard Dizzy Gillespie's band two, three, four, five, six, seven, eight times at Birdland, and it's really a surprise, it's that good. I'm happy for Dizzy because I know his dream has always been to have a band like this one. He had a band a few years ago, but it wasn't anything like this one.' And she simply kept pushing herself. 'My birthday was on March 27,' she reflected about her thirty-third birthday, 'but it wasn't a holiday. Record dates – three or four days solid – Storyville in Boston, Mister Kelly's in Chicago, then back to the Birdland Stars for our West Coast tour once Basie gets back from England.' It was a blessing that she didn't need rehearsals, because they were a luxury she couldn't really afford to fit in often.

She was proud of her progress, even of her wardrobe. 'Did you see my gown tonight? . . . I think it's very important to be dressed just right out there onstage because the women notice those small mistakes and the men aren't only ears, either, you know. They like to look at women attractively dressed.'

Sassy spoke about her hopes for the future to Don Gold for a *Down Beat* article published on 30 May 1957. 'I've thought of playing more piano, but I always get cold feet. It's always in the back of my mind. I dig Tatum so much, and Hank Jones, Jimmy Jones, [Erroll] Garner, and [George] Shearing. I practise at home, backstage, when there's time . . . I'd like to do the kind of piano LP Nat Cole has done.' (She was referring to either *The Piano Style of Nat King Cole* or his *After Midnight* albums, both released in 1956. On the first album he only played piano; on the second, he accompanied himself singing in a small group of jazz musicians. Ordinarily Cole performed pop songs as a stand-up singer with studio orchestras.) And she wanted to include some spirituals in her sets. 'It's a part of my life. Every now and then, when I'm home in Newark, I sing with the church choir. I want so much to do a special album of spirituals, like an Italian wanting to do Italian folk songs. I dig most of the spirituals I know from church, what you'd call the "old standards", not too many of the new. I'd like to give an all-spiritual concert, too, with choir. Do it up right, like Marian Anderson. She's always been an idol of mine.

'You know what else I'd like to do. I'd like to have a crazy TV show, like Rosemary Clooney's show. I'd have a variety of things, not just jazz. Something of musical value for young and old. It would be fun for me.'

She didn't mention how much trouble Nat Cole was experiencing as a black performer looking for a national sponsor for his show, which went off the air in the fall of 1957. A white pianist, Mike Wofford, who would work as her accompanist years later, knew that she had endured the worst of the country's racial prejudice, and yet she rarely talked about it. Molly Shad, who is white, recalled, 'It was a tough world out there for black people. They had to go in the back doors.' For public consumption, Sassy reminisced instead about how Dave

Garroway had given her the support that money couldn't buy. 'He praised me so much, some of his listeners thought we were married,' she told Don Gold. She recalled the highlights of her days with Earl Hines, not the hard conditions of travelling under segregation. 'I never had so much fun in my life . . . Not only did I learn much about stage presence from Billy, but several other members of the Hines band were like fathers to me. It was a beginning. No money, but much fun. I wouldn't mind going through it one more time.'

She broadened her horizons by listening to all kinds of music, she told Gold. 'I've got quite a record collection at home, jazz and semi-classical. I start listening as soon as I walk in the door. I prefer to have good music around me at all times . . . I dig Chico [Hamilton]'s group, the Modern Jazz Quartet, and some of [Gerry] Mulligan's things . . . Mahalia Jackson can sing! If she wanted to, she could sing anything well. I dig Doris Day. And I love the way Jo Stafford reads [a lyric]. Clooney can wail . . . Fitzgerald . . . Nat Cole . . . Billie.

'It's singing with soul that counts. Billie has so much soul. When I sing a tune, the lyrics are important to me. Most of the standard lyrics I know well. And as soon as I hear an arrangement, I get ideas, kind of like blowing a horn. I guess I never sing a tune the same way twice. A recent rehearsal we had in Boston was the first I had in years. My trio – Jimmy Jones, Richard Davis, and Roy Haynes – is always up to tricks onstage. I dig it this way.'

Don Gold wrote his own assessment of her position. 'Those who have known her since the awkward days of the mid-forties, when her voice showed indications of quality and her gowns and stage presence did not, can best appreciate the transformation which has taken place. Today, as one of the most successful singers, she is poised and chic, and is singing more communicatively than she has in the past.'

FIVE

What Happened to the Money?

Jimmy Jones decided to leave Sassy's group and concentrate on writing and arranging; at the end of 1957, he was replaced by pianist Ronnell Bright. Bright had been playing with the Johnny Pate trio at the Streamliner in Chicago in 1956 when he first met Sassy. It wasn't until the next year that she really paid attention to Ronnell. He had gone to New York, where John Hammond had heard him and arranged for him to play at the Embers, a fashionable Upper East Side supper club. Willard Alexander took over Ronnell's bookings and sent him to Storyville in Boston, where he alternated sets with Sassy for two weeks. Four months later, George, who had never met Ronnell Bright, called, at Sassy's request, to ask him to replace Jimmy Jones.

One of Ronnell's first recordings with her was done live at the London House in Chicago, at a time when albums were rarely done live. Sassy began singing 'Thanks for the Memory'; when she came to the word *Parthenon*, she started toying with it. 'Parthenon? Parthenon? Parthenon . . . I don't get this word here . . . Parthenon . . . one more time, and we can go home . . . PartheNON . . .' She also forgot the lyrics at the end of that song and improvised them. On 'I'll String Along with You', she kept singing 'I'll sing along with you'. Critics would begin to remark how much more important the music was to her than the lyrics. Trumpeters Thad Jones, with an open horn, and Wendell Culley, using a mute, both played on the album, improvising all around the melodies and reflecting Sassy's own uncannily artful, swinging embellishments. Her patter was left in the album, 'a fine album', Ronnell recalled. Sassy's giggles, her praise for tenor saxophonist Frank Wess on 'Like Someone In Love' – 'I think Frank Wess sounded pretty good on that' – and many other details conveyed the immediacy of a live performance. 'Speak Low' was an excellent example of how slowly Sassy could sing and require her group to play. Her accompanists often mentioned they felt as if eons were passing between each note, but she was singing ballads at exactly the right tempo to create the atmospheric sound she needed to express the full feeling of the lyrics. She might use her high, pure soprano or her mature, resonant contralto; her varied sounds were often the messages of the songs.

But Sassy had so far never had a record that sold over a million copies. One day in January 1958, George Treadwell discovered that Mitch Miller at Columbia Records was going to have a well-known singer record a song called 'Broken-Hearted Melody' the next day. George was livid. Sassy was supposed to do the song for Mercury. He sensed it would be a very big moment for her. So he immediately called people at Mercury. The company was reluctant to change a schedule, but George insisted. Sassy did the recording on 7 January 1958. George took a dub from the master cut and put it on the radio the next day. It became her first million-copy seller. 'Broken-Hearted Melody', done with the Ray Ellis orchestra early in 1958, arrived in the top pop singles charts on 20 July 1959, and rode a crest of popularity for nineteen weeks with a top rank of number 7; it also rose in the rhythm-and-blues category of the pop charts on 31 August 1959, for a stay of eleven weeks, reaching a top position as the number 5 record in the country. So it was a hit with white and black audiences. And it was her first recording nominated for a Grammy Award. The success didn't stop the Treadwells from fighting, however.

Sassy had been appearing at the Waldorf-Astoria in New York when she decided that she and George Treadwell should get a divorce. She confided in Modina Davis, who had seen the divorce coming. 'The meetings were too unhappy. They were always fighting,' Modina says. Exactly when Sassy filed for divorce isn't generally known. Modina recalled only that Sassy made the decision – or got the divorce itself – before recording the album No 'Count Sarah in 1958 with members of the Basie band. Having made the decision, the Treadwells appeared amicable during that album's sessions.

Ronnell Bright, joining the group in early 1958, was under the impression that Sassy and George were already legally divorced. In 1958, when Sassy was performing on the West Coast, Goerge brought along his girlfriend. 'She cooked a wonderful breakfast for me in a hotel suite's kitchen in Los Angeles,' Roy Haynes could recall. Then everyone went to Miami, where Sassy was booked to appear at the Fontainebleau. After five years with Sassy, Roy now gave two weeks' notice to George. The decision upset Sassy so much that for the next two weeks she was quite sullen. 'She barely talked to me,' Roy recalled. 'I felt very bad about it, because I had loved her. Some people who didn't know us thought that I had been married to her.'

Now Sassy began to wonder what had happened to her money. She knew that she had earned a lot, although widely varying reports had been published about her income during the 1940s and 1950s. A publicity release from her own office in 1954 said she commanded more than $3,000 for a concert, more than $7,500 a week for theatre engagements, and brought in royalties of more than $200,000 annually from record sales. Furthermore, she grossed close to $2 million apart from royalties, according to the publicity literature, which was either written or approved by George Treadwell. *Time* magazine, on 16 January 1950, had reported that she had commanded four-figure fees for her nightclub and theatre engagements, for example, a $2,500 fee for a week at the Apollo in 1949, during which year she had reportedly grossed $125,000; she earned $2,700 per week at Storyville a few years after the *Time* story appeared. The *Sunday News Magazine* in New York would publish a story on 13 March 1960 that said Sassy had sold over two million copies of the Musicraft hit, 'It's Magic' – definitely an overstatement of fact; the *Sunday News Magazine* also noted that during the years she made records, she grossed $1 million exclusive of record royalties, which brought in another $50,000 a year by the time she had her Mercury contract. The source of the sales figures wasn't revealed, but if they were coming from her office, then George Treadwell certainly provided the information. Sassy may have known only what she read in the papers.

George had put the money in several different banks, he told her. All that was left was $16,000. Sassy took $8,000, and he took $8,000. When the gist of the financial settlement circulated, jazz insiders thought it simply confirmed that George Treadwell was a hustler. So they went their separate ways in their fine cars. Sassy drove her Oldsmobile; George had his Cadillac or Lincoln. Modina didn't believe for a instant that only $16,000 had been left for the couple to divide. 'That was just an example of a way George could be spiteful,' she said. She had often urged Sassy, as the marriage turned into a combat zone, to go to the office on West Fifty-seventh Street and look at the books on a regular basis. But Sassy had refused to do so even once, explaining her attitude repeatedly: 'I sing, I just sing. And I pay you people . . .' She expected them to take care of the practicalities with the same love and conscientiousness that she brought to her singing. 'Mainly she wanted to get into the music and live there,' said Bob James, who would become Sassy's pianist and musical director for a while in the mid-1960s.

After the divorce, George married a woman named Fayrene, also an artist's manager, with whom he lived for the rest of his life. Rumours to the contrary, Treadwell did not end as an unhappy, impoverished or obscure man. He remained a successful manager, the role which had always suited him best. He and Fayrene remained friendly enough with the lawyer Andrew Feinman that they visited him and his wife at their home once, and Feinman knew that Treadwell was 'a man of no little means'. Treadwell died young, many years before Sassy.

Sassy soon came to view George with a jaundiced eye, forgetting what she had told Don Gold for a *Down Beat* interview in 1957: 'Good management has helped me find much of the success I've got. George was the one who helped me all along.' She came to feel that he had used her.

Johnnie Garry preferred to concentrate on the good times in the early days. Sassy had taught him to play golf and gave him his first set of golf clubs. Years later, when he looked at a photo he had taken of her on a golf course, he murmured, 'She was so sweet that day.' And he reflected, 'Nobody likes to go to work, but we did. We couldn't wait to go to work. When we were on the road together, it was a family, man. People said she was evil. But anyone can be evil. It depends on who's doing what to you. And what about the music? It was as if God said, 'Here, I'm giving you something'.

SIX

At the Top of the Jazz World

Sassy was already looking for a new manager when the United States Department of State invited her, along with other notable American jazz musicians, to represent the United States at the World's Fair in Brussels, Belgium, during April 1958. Frank Rio of the Associated Booking Corporation was handling her bookings, the Willard Alexander Agency was involved in her management, and the State Department arranged for Sassy to do a four-month-long concert tour of Europe in addition to her performance in Brussels. She began in London. Weary and shielding her eyes with sunglasses, going directly from the airport after a ten-hour, forty-five-minute plane ride, she submitted to an interview at a preperformance press conference with *Melody Maker* writer Maurice Burman. When he asked her why she was called Sassy, she said she didn't know, 'but I'd really like a drink'.

She was handed a glass of gin with a glass of water for a chaser. Inquiring about her favourite singers, Burman asked her what she thought of Billy Eckstine. She said, 'Billy – my favourite. I love him.' 'Love him?' 'Yeah, love him.' She thought Louis Armstrong and Ella Fitzgerald were 'wonderful'. When Burman mentioned Elvis Presley, Sassy seemed to drift away, but she came back into focus when Burman said, 'Marian Anderson'. Sassy said, 'So you do know something about music.' Burman, who had heard a rumour that she found most of her own recordings forgettable, asked how she had liked 'Passing Strangers'. She smiled brightly. 'Oh, that was different.' 'Why?' 'Because Billy was on it . . . With Billy doing it with me, it was twice as beautiful.' Burman asked her to take off her sunglasses so he could see her eyes. She called out to no one in particular: 'He wants to see my eyes.' Then she took off her glasses coquettishly. Touched by his flirting, she confided that her spine hurt from the long trip, and she could hardly wait for the performance to start so she could lose her preperformance jitters. She always had stage fright, she said. She was called away to speak to her musicians, and she excused herself. He waited for half an hour; when she didn't return, he decided to leave. Sassy saw him going out the door and called to him, 'Maurice, ask me another question, honey.'

His story was published in the *Melody Maker* edition of 19 April 1958 – the same one in which Max Jones, a leading British jazz writer, reviewed her performance. 'Each time I hear Sarah Vaughan in person, she seems to have got substantially better,' he wrote. 'At the Leicester Square Odeon last Saturday, she was a living knockout. Always her voice and musicianship have been remarkable. From the first, she sounded like an imaginative instrumentalist, though not always like an emotionally mature singer. Now the most capricious effects have been banished – though the style is still boldly original, and there is deeper feeling for the lyrics. Ear, range and control remain extraordinary, and she executes breathtaking changes, scoops and "power dives" with half-amused ease. On the visual side, too, she has taken several strides forward . . . The combination of ear and eye appeal results in a singing act as near perfect as we have any right to expect in a world where quality seldom counts for much.'

Accompanied by Britain's popular Ted Heath band, Sassy sang fifteen songs, 'beginning with "If This Isn't Love" and ending – after several encores – with an exhibition of wordless virtuosity on "How High the Moon?" This last, the only "screamer", was improvised anew at each of the three shows I caught. But every number carried fresh twists, and one of Heath's musicians told me: "I can't remember ever looking forward so much to a fourth performance of the self-same programme." Six songs from *The Land of Hi Fi* [an album Sassy had recorded for Mercury] had Ernie Wilkins scores. [Wilkins was an important arranger for the Count Basie band.] These were strongly attacked by Heath's men . . . For certain sections, only Ronnell Bright's piano, or piano and rhythm, were used. I haven't adjectives to cope with all the varied treatments. Everything Sarah did she did well. She is an artist to the tips of her expressive fingers.'

Sassy and her rhythm section soon travelled to Belgium. George Wein, who had been booking her for the Newport Jazz Festival since its inception, was also attending the World's Fair on business. A jazz lover who had left behind a career as a schoolteacher to become a jazz club owner and then a jazz festival producer, he loved her glorious voice. 'I wanted to manage her,' he said, and he thought he would be good for her career. The Voice of America had recorded and broadcast the Newport Jazz Festival concerts she had appeared in and he had produced.

At the World's Fair, Wein asked if he could manage her. She said, 'How are you going to manage me when you're going with that girl back in Boston?' George was engaged to his girlfriend, who would become his wife. For Sassy, the notion of separating her professional from her personal life seemed unworkable. If someone wanted to manage her, he would also have to travel with her all the time. She liked the feeling of everything wrapped up in one snug, nurturing package. When a writer had asked her during her marriage if George Treadwell was a good manager, she had replied, 'Yes,' and added, 'He should be. He's my husband.' She wanted that vested interest from a manager, a man who would love her uncritically, unreservedly, and without distraction, travel with her, and make her career the focus of the marriage.

George Wein, who didn't think that kind of arrangement was the best thing for her career, told her so, but she didn't agree. Her methods had worked for her up until then. Only Treadwell had been willing to put himself on the line for her twelve years earlier. Nobody else had offered to do the job. And her work made wrenching demands upon her. Often terrified, she went out onstage, with only a microphone to hold on to. Then she came offstage and tried to plug herself emotionally into the world again. It would have taken a man with an exquisite sensibility to go beyond guiding her career moves from a distant office. She wanted more, not less, than George had given her.

Modina Davis and Johnnie Garry still travelled with her. Their loyalty buoyed her up. 'My right-hand man, John[nie] Garry, has been with me for ten years,' she had told Don Gold for his *Down Beat* magazine article in 1957. 'If he ever left me, I'd be out of business. And with my secretary Modina Davis around, I don't have to worry about a thing. I just have to sing.' If she sounded too effervescent, rather like a cheerleader, Sassy always kept her spirits up by concentrating on the support and satisfactions that she *did* have.

At the World's Fair, she alternated sets with Ella Fitzgerald. Many jazz stars and business people behind the scenes attended the fair – Gerry Mulligan, the baritone saxophonist; Willis Conover, broadcasting for the Voice of America; and Quincy Jones, the arranger and bandleader – all friends by that time. Then Sassy travelled around Belgium, singing to cheering concert audiences in many small cities. Reviews echoed Max Jones in Britain, her pianist, Ronnell Bright, recalled.

But behind the scenes, there were tensions from the pressures of the road life. On the way to Knokke, Belgium, by train, Sassy and Johnnie Garry argued about the way Sassy disregarded the travel schedule. She had nearly missed the train, and so, as the road manager, he scolded her. Sassy said, 'I'm the boss, and you're fired, and you can worry about how you're going to get home.' Johnnie reminded her, 'Are you crazy? I have all the tickets. And when you get to Knokke, you're going to have to sing the finale with Ella Fitzgerald. Don't let her sing an uptempo number, or she'll eat you up alive. Sing a ballad.' The second Sassy stepped onstage, Ella launched the swinging 'How High the Moon'. 'They were taking choruses and scatting,' Johnny recalled. 'Sassy starting singing, "Ella, baby, I'm leaving," and Ella sang, "Sassy, baby, I'm just beginning." Ella won that contest,' Johnnie recalled.

Ronnell noticed how much attention Sassy now paid to her clothes. She became particularly attached to a pink-colored gown with a satin top and a flared skirt that had gradations of brighter and brighter shades of pink from the waist to the hem. The gown fitted her well and looked fine under the lights. She liked to wear it all the time; Modina was always sending it to a cleaner. But Ronnell, Richard Davis and the drummer in Sassy's group became tired of seeing her in it. In Knokke, they got a little box and buried the dress outside the casino. Later they invited her down from her room to the burial site. She took the joke in good humour as they had expected she would, because she always loved a good prank; she left the gown in its grave.

Sassy and her trio performed for Princess Grace of Monaco, too. In Stockholm, Sweden, they played for a month with Stan Getz and Dizzy Gillespie at a festival at the China Theatre, staying at the Foresta Hotel on top of a high hill during the time of the midnight sun. At 8 p.m., the sun shone brightly; the sky became dark between 10 and 11 p.m., and the sun rose at 11.15 p.m. If the musicians drank a few cocktails after work, they felt as if they had been drinking all day; the confusion of day and night disoriented them.

When the trio went to Paris in July for a recording date and an engagement at the Olympia Theatre, they carted so much luggage that they needed four taxis to get everything to the hotel near the Champs-Elysées. Johnnie Garry told everybody, 'Go in, I'll take care of the bags.' Ronnell and Richard Davis, who were sharing a room, sat around, waiting for their bags. But they never arrived, and neither did the drummer's. All their formal clothes, the tuxedos, shirts, everything they had bought and collected during the weeks of touring, had disappeared with one of the taxis. So the men rented clothes to wear onstage. Otherwise, all they had were the clothes on their backs – T-shirts and casual slacks. The hotel workers and people connected with the show at the Olympia 'were very kind and sympathetic', Ronnell remembered. Radio stations and newspapers put out urgent messages to the public to try to help the musicians get their possessions back. But nobody responded. Sassy and her rhythm section made the best of it while they recorded the album *Vaughan and Violins* with arrangements by Quincy Jones. One cut on the album is Sassy's first recording of 'Misty', which became a trademark of her repertoire. Later she would embellish the song, and it would become her *tour de force*, a dialogue in which she swooped from soprano musings to a baritone's response. But in Paris, she sang it as a straightforward, dreamy ballad.

Also in Paris that summer, Ronnell noticed Sassy's friendship with Sacha Distel, the singer, composer and guitarist, whom Ronnell respected as a musician. 'He loved music, and he loved Sarah Vaughan,' Ronnell thought. Distel and Sassy used to drive down Boulevard Saint-Germain in Distel's little convertible, from which Sassy waved to Ronnell. He could see how happily she was smiling, having a wonderful, romantic time. When Ronnell would reflect on the places they performed in and saw in Europe that spring and early summer, and on the attention paid the musicians and the usually excellent conditions for their performances and hotel stays, he would think, 'Oh, a long, exciting trip.'

Arriving at the airport to leave Paris, Ronnell remembered, 'We saw the same taxi driver who had taken us to the hotel. Our suitcases were still locked inside his trunk. He had never opened it and had never heard or read the public announcements.' The men had a joyful reunion with their bags.

Back in New York, Sassy gave a concert with pianist Phineas Newborn Jr at the Ninety-second Street YMCA and she starred in a three-day jazz festival in Ellenville, New York, in July 1958, along with Duke Ellington, pianist Erroll Garner, trumpeter Bobby Hackett, George Shearing, Dave Brubeck, trumpeter Buck Clayton and tenor saxophonist Coleman Hawkins. She was headed for what Joe Williams calls the 'payback period', when an artist left behind the days he or she had to work hard to negotiate the right bookings. Now she was an attraction any club owner or concert producer happily paid a steep price for. Audience demand let her choose the places where she wanted to play.

In the late summer of 1958, she and her group took several weeks' vacation before going into a recording studio near Carnegie Hall on West Fifty-seventh Street in New York with the Basie band to do *No 'Count Sarah*. Sassy told Modina Davis to arrange a private vacation for the two of them in England. Modina made reservations for the trip while Sassy went to Chicago, supposedly for a brief visit. She soon called Modina and surprised her by asking for five hundred dollars from the office in addition to the usual allowance. Sassy also wanted Modina to cancel the trip to England. In Chicago, Sassy had met a man named Clyde B. Atkins; people called him CB. She was bringing him to New York for everyone to meet.

'Well, but who is he?' Modina asked.

'You're going to just love him,' Sassy said. She had fallen madly in love. She was going to marry C. B. Atkins.*

'But none of us has ever heard of him,' Modina said.

'Oh, I know you're going to love him,' Sassy said.

---

* Their marriage licence says they were married in Chicago by Municipal Court Judge Fred W. Slater on 4 September 1958. Sassy gave her legal address as Queens, New York, and her age as thirty-four, while Atkins gave his age as thirty. Exactly when her divorce from Treadwell took effect isn't clear. It's most likely that she started proceedings in New York in 1957, and the divorce became final in 1958.

SEVEN

A Bad Marriage

A couple of weeks later, she arrived in New York City, obviously in love with CB. A big, strongly built man, he soon made a bad impression on her friends and acquaintances. She had met him at the Archway Lounge, a popular South Side restaurant that featured music and was owned by a well-known local figure named 'Killer' Johnson. CB had immediately made a present of a watch to Sassy. That intrigued her right away. He was soon described in the press as the owner of a fleet of taxicabs and a former football player for the San Francisco 49ers and the Green Bay Packers. However, neither team had any record of his ever having played with them.

Sassy and CB arrived in New York in time to keep Sassy's scheduled recording date for *No 'Count Sarah* with Ronnell playing with the Basie band; because of his contract, Basie himself couldn't appear on the Mercury record. Soon after arriving in New York, Sassy telephoned Ronnell Bright and said, 'I just met someone who went to school with you.' It was CB, whom Ronnell had always called Clyde. They had gone to James McCosh grammar school and then Englewood High School in Chicago; CB had lived two blocks away from Ronnell and played with the neighbourhood football teams. Ronnell, who had been born in July 1930, was under the impression that he was several months older than CB. That would have made CB about seven years younger than Sassy, although his marriage licence said he was only four years younger.

Sassy invited herself and CB to dinner at Ronnell's house, and Ronnell found out that the couple had gone sailing that day; they were having a romantic time together and seemed very happy. About two weeks later, George Treadwell, who had already remarried, called Ronnell and asked whether it was true that Sarah had also remarried. George had heard that Sassy had married a man with a fleet of cabs in Chicago. Ronnell was intrigued by the suggestion of jealousy in George's continued interest. After the quick courtship and marriage on 4 September 1958, Sassy rented a new management office in the same West Fifty-seventh Street building where George Treadwell kept his office, and she installed CB in her office a floor above George's – a reminder to George that she, too, had found someone else, Ronnell surmised.

The press always referred to CB as a former professional football player who owned a Chicago taxi fleet. Some people thought that he actually did have at least *one* taxi in Chicago; others heard that he was a contractor. Modina Davis thought that description suited him best of all. 'I could believe that,' Modina said, recalling that when he and Sassy bought a house in Englewood Cliffs in 1959 – on the same street to which Dizzy Gillespie and his wife, Lorraine, eventually moved – CB gutted the inside of the modern ranch house. 'Everything that needed to be done on the inside of that house, he did it,' Modina reminisced. He also impressed Modina immensely by the way he hung a beautiful tabletop by chains from a wall instead of setting it on legs. A creative designer, he exercised every iota of his considerable building talent and spared none of Sassy's money to reconstruct and decorate the house. An *Ebony* magazine story published in 1961 reported that 'the couple bought the house two years ago for $53,000' and 'added $50,000 worth of furnishings and equipment'.

Carmen McRae, whose path often crossed Sassy's, had thought that George Treadwell was 'very good' at managing and 'really started Sarah off'. But, Carmen said, 'CB knew absolutely nothing about music, nothing at all.' Though Sassy called him her manager, she went to her office herself and supervised what CB was doing. For the 1961 article, *Ebony* magazine photographed her in her West Fifty-seventh Street office, examining a telegram inviting her to appear at a jazz festival. 'She respects Atkins,' *Ebony* reporter Allan Morrison wrote, 'but when she disagrees with any of his moves, she makes her displeasure vocal . . .' Morrison also reported that 'Atkins came to the business of managing Sarah without any experience, and he has acquired it the hard way, not without making a few mistakes and enemies. Whoever is responsible, the fact remains that under the Atkins régime the Vaughan organisation has prospered more than heretofore. When they were married in 1958, Sarah was earning $230,000 a year, hardly a paltry income. Last year her income from all sources hit $400,000. For nightclub engagements she commands an average salary of $7,500 a week, which in Las Vegas locations goes to $12,000.* She is paid $2,000 to $3,000 for a concert appearance or a one-nighter. For four days of appearances earlier this year in Australia, she received $17,500.'

When her contract with Mercury ended in the fall of 1959, she walked right into a contract with Roulette Records and began recording in April 1960 for record producer Teddy Reig, whom she had met in the 1940s. Roulette was owned by Morris Levy, a backer of Birdland, so for Sassy recording for the label was like going home again. Head-liners at Birdland – Count Basie with Joe Williams, Dinah Washington, and Lambert, Hendricks and Ross, to name a few – also recorded for Roulette. 'It was gangster-dominated,' recalled a well-known artists' manager. 'Artists claimed they didn't get royalties or statements. That has been said a lot. Everyone had problems or felt that they had been ripped off.' Sassy herself, as she was being interviewed years later by Marian McPartland on 'Piano Jazz', was reminded of her years at Roulette. 'Enough said,' Sassy said in a deadened voice. From a musical standpoint, however, her recordings for Roulette rank among her finest. 'Her vocal style seems to have come into full maturity at this stage,' wrote Hiraku Aoki, who would write the liner notes for Polyg-ram's 1980s reissue of Sassy's complete Mercury recordings. Sassy signed again with Mercury in 1963, but she was one of Roulette's biggest stars during her few years there.

Jimmy Jones arranged and conducted a Roulette album issued in 1960 as *The Divine One* that features effervescent, uptempo, swinging songs such as 'Have You Met Miss Jones?' Sassy substituted *old* for *Miss*. There was a difference in her sound, her taste and control, from the Mercury recordings of the 1950s. That year, too, her recording of 'Serenata' for Roulette rose on the *Billboard* pop charts, along with two recordings she had made during her Mercury days, 'Eternally' and 'You're My Baby'. In July 1961, she recorded *After Hours*, an intimate, relaxed album done with guitarist Mundell Lowe and bassist George Duvivier, both subtle, versatile musicians' musicians. 'I felt proud of that album,' Lowe recalled. 'We recorded it in about three and a half hours, from six to nine-thirty, in a single evening. Teddy Reig brought tables, food and drinks to the studio on West 106th Street in Manhattan. Every song was recorded in one or two takes. Sassy's work was devoid of vocal tricks.' She sang with exquisite control, stressing her jazz feeling and improvisational genius on such songs as the uptempo 'Great

---

*Another close personal friend gives $7,000 as a figure for a week's engagement for Sassy in Las Vegas in this period.

Day'; there was none of the flamboyant vocalising that characterised much of her other work. 'Teddy Reig later told me that it was the only album she ever made that made any money,' Lowe said.

In his newspaper column, 'Platter Chatter', George Albanese wrote of *After Hours*: 'The title itself indicates the intimate, totally relaxed mood of this album. In this low-glow atmosphere, Miss Vaughan sings a bouquet of her own special favourites, each delivered with exquisite voice and discriminate phrasing. The single criticism I would offer is her tendency to "bend" notes using the glissando. While the occasional use of the glissando might enhance the total, too frequent use will mar an otherwise excellent performance. It's much like using too much seasoning on a choice roast of meat. I must direct attention to the marvellous accompaniment of . . . Lowe and . . . Duvivier, who make up the whole orchestra. To be sure when Miss Vaughan sings like this, she doesn't need banks of lush strings to achieve the desired effect.'

She pared down her style for 'Just in Time', too, harnessed her voice and sang with exactly the right rhythmic impulses to create one of the hippest songs with the most jazz feeling she had ever done in her life, accompanied by guitarist Barney Kessel and bassist Joe Comfort for another critically praised jazz album, *Sarah Plus Two*, recorded in Los Angeles in 1962. Her tightly controlled, swinging jazz interpretations for Roulette stood out intriguingly against the background of the ballads, which make up the majority of her recordings.

Mundell Lowe loved working with her 'because she was such a good singer and musician that there was never any competition or skulduggery between us. No ill will ever cropped up. Some singers made work so difficult for me that afterwards we barely talked to each other. That never happened with Sarah.'

Lowe not only loved her singing; he was attracted to the perky-looking woman, who was always warm and friendly to him. In the early 1950s he had worked in the house quartet at Cafe Society Downtown, with Duvivier, drummer Bill Clark and pianist Dave Walters. Sassy had worked in the club for a couple of weeks at a time in those days. Mundell had met her even before then, in the late 1940s, when clarinettist Tony Scott, his roommate in an apartment above Cafe Society on Sheridan Square, introduced them; Lowe also recorded with her for Columbia. 'Sassy always seemed happy to see me whenever we bumped into each other in Birdland. I would see her at the bar. She was so shy that it was difficult for her to hold a conversation. But she always seemed bright and spirited, really appealing.' He had wanted to get to know her better, but there was no opportunity. 'There always seemed to be someone ahead of me, first George Treadwell, then the men directly behind him.' So Mundell and Sassy remained just friends.

Sassy was presenting herself to the world, through the press, as a happily married woman. She and CB had also adopted a daughter. The *Ebony* magazine article published in 1961 was a serious profile, one of the few attempts at an in-depth study of her personal life ever done, with photographs of her and CB and their new daughter, Debra Lois. Sassy and CB 'tried to have a baby', Modina remembered. 'Sarah said she could never have a baby. She went to the doctor and found that out when she first was with George. CB said they could adopt, but first they still tried to have one,' Modina recalled. They tried herbs and various techniques for lovemaking, Modina said, 'but it didn't work out'. From the Midwest, they brought home a pretty little girl, their adopted daughter, to Englewood Cliffs. The *Ebony* article was a celebration. Allan Morrison wrote that 'she had for years longed for a child' but 'had emerged childless from the marriage to [George] Treadwell'. 'My life was being wasted,' she said of that marriage. 'I knew it wasn't going to last.' Morrison said that she had become so resentful of Treadwell, she 'bristled' when his name was mentioned. 'This is what I always wanted,' she said softly while cuddling her baby. 'I never had a child before because I was either too busy to take time to have one or because I wasn't happy. This baby has brought a lot of happiness into our home. She has made a big difference already.'

Morrison wrote: 'Sarah describes herself as a seeker after peace and happiness, and within two years of her divorce from Treadwell she began another attempt to find that which had eluded her so long. Her second marriage to bulky, boyish Clyde B. Atkins is now three years old and appears to be a thriving arrangement. Sarah adores Atkins and credits him with successfully reorganising her business affairs, elevating her status professionally, and financially, and bringing into her life a kind of strength and love that she never knew before. Of his famous wife, Atkins says, "Sarah is one of the great stars of the world and should be recognised as such."'

The article presented Sassy as a purposeful woman who knew what she wanted and who would never let anyone hurt her in her career again. 'I've been hurt, hurt deeply, and I want to avoid being hurt again,' she told Morrison. She planned to make all the big decisions, never deplete her physical and mental energies again, and make sure her income kept growing bigger. Morrison also offered his own observations of Sassy, who was then thirty-seven years old.

'Sarah's personality puzzles some, annoys others. She seems indifferent to public approval, cold, aloof, and even unfriendly. This is not a fair impression, however. Those who know her intimately can attest to her warmth and generosity, good humour and intelligence. The external Sarah can be curt and defensive. Inside she is a woman alive with feeling and the joy of living, curious and passionate, eager to love and be loved and accepted not as a celebrity but as just another human being.

'As a little girl, she had a . . . deep, almost traumatic complex about her appearance. A feeling of inferiority developed, from the conviction that she was "homely"; her dark skin seemed to compound what she felt was a monstrous handicap. A sensitive, imaginative child, she dreamed freely and extravagantly. She says she used to dream that a gorgeous Prince Charming would stride into her narrow, little life and carry her away to a place where there was no poverty and where colour didn't matter. Most of all, she dreamed of changing her colour. "I often wished I was a medium brown colour," she once told a reporter. "I imagined people of that colour were regarded more highly than I. To most persons who knew me, I thought I was just another little black girl for whom the future was just as dark as it was for thousands of others like me . . ."'

Morrison offered no opinion of C. B. Atkins, and Sassy didn't give any hint of turmoil in the marriage; she told Morrison that she was actually a very nervous woman who didn't show her true nature on the surface. She usually saw no reason to tell a friend – and certainly not a reporter – about how she really felt or what was going on in her private life. And she had long ago discovered the way to dispel her problems was by singing.

But many friends spotted her trouble with CB quickly. One night at a dinner table in a restaurant, Annie Ross was disturbed when CB wouldn't let Sassy go to the ladies' room unless all the other women in the party remained at the table. That struck Annie Ross as chillingly odd. Carmen McRae, too, recalled: 'Sarah couldn't go to the ladies' room . . . unless we were all sitting at the table. It was strange.' Carmen also knew that 'CB used to hit her. He thought that was the way women should be treated.' Carmen supposed that 'he just wanted to show his authority . . .' Others recall CB as especially possessive and domineering.

Aretha Landrum, a woman with whom Sassy had gone to grammar school and attended the First Mount Zion Baptist Church, had long been accustomed to going with a group of friends to hear Sassy sing whenever she performed in Atlantic City or Asbury Park, New

Jersey. Sassy's hometown friends used to rent rooms for the duration of her engagement in those places. After she came offstage, she met them and took them out for drinks and meals, conversation and laughter. 'She made sure we had everything we wanted,' Aretha remembered. But during her marriage to CB, Sassy stopped calling her friends' rooms and never got together with them after the shows. She passed by their tables and said, 'Call me.' When they called her, CB told them that Sassy was busy on the telephone or giving interviews. 'CB tried to tie her up so that nobody saw her but him,' according to Aretha.

Carmen McRae thought that Sassy let the blockade of her friends go on because she was afraid of CB, scared to death that he would hit her. 'She was scared to say something because this m.f. was going to knock her under the bed,' Carmen said. Before her marriage to CB, Sassy had been a woman who 'hung up her stardom and was into jeans, a friendly woman', when she was offstage, said Aretha Landrum. 'She used to talk to anybody who stopped her on the street in Newark and have long conversations. Afterward, she'd turn to me and ask, "Who was that?" I said, "I don't know. I thought you knew." The women laughed together about Sassy's free and easy manner. But Sassy didn't socialise like that in front of CB.

Duke Niles, a Manhattan song plugger, thought that CB was 'a rough type'. Word circulated among Sassy's friends that CB went to collect her fees when she sang in Las Vegas, and then he headed to the gambling tables where he immediately lost the thousands of dollars Sassy should have been given. 'He was a gambler,' Carmen McRae said. That would become clear to everyone who knew the couple. Ronnell Bright, whose early connection to CB made him privy to more of the Atkinses' personal life than others were, travelled to California with Sassy and CB to see Nick Castle, the dancer, who was going to stage Sassy's upcoming show at the Waldorf-Astoria. They stopped in Vegas on the way. Ronnell Bright said: 'CB was a gambler. That was CB's real calling.' At the Flamingo in Las Vegas, Ronnell recalled that CB won $40,000 shooting craps during a period of a few days. But by Saturday night he had lost it plus some of Sassy's money.

In 1960 Modina left Sassy's group to stay home to take care of her children; by then she had a son and a daughter, and the daughter was starting school. So Modina, taking a leave of absence, unbearably homesick for the excitement and challenge of the road life, was living in Newark when the owner of the Copacabana called her to find out why Sassy hadn't shown up for work one night. Sassy was booked for several weeks and hadn't shown up or telephoned. Modina guessed that

Sassy missed every night of her engagement at the club because she had been fighting with C. B. Atkins.

When the baby was a year and a half old, in fall 1962, Sassy simply picked up Debby and left everything else behind in the Englewood house, Aretha Landrum remembered. Sassy moved in with her parents in Newark; by 1961 they had sold their Avon Avenue house and were living on Weequahic Avenue, in a house Sassy had provided for them. Eventually a fire damaged the two-family house on Avon Avenue where Modina had lived across the street from the Vaughans, and Asbury Vaughan would decide to sell that house, too; he didn't want to be encumbered with the responsibility for it anymore.

Sassy, accompanied by Aretha Landrum, started to go around the corner at night to a little club with music on Clinton Avenue. Sassy began singling out John 'Preacher' Wells, who worked in the club, as a special friend in the crowd of familiar faces. As a child, Newark-born John Wells had been nicknamed 'Little Preacher' by the neighbourhood people, because he had spent so much time with his uncle, Reverend Wells, the preacher at Wells Cathedral, his own church. Little Preacher, who was about three years younger than Sassy, had known her slightly when they were children. By the time they were in their thirties, the age difference meant nothing. He befriended her during the tense days at the end of her marriage to CB.

Soon she and Preacher were living together in an apartment she rented in the Weequahic Towers, a building near her parents' house. Sassy's problems with C. B. Atkins finally reached the newspapers; in October 1962 she filed for divorce in a Philadelphia court, charging that CB had threatened her life over the telephone. But she withdrew charges and left the courtroom arm in arm with him. Then on 3 November Toronto's *Telegram* carried a headline, 'Sarah Claims Life Threats, Asks Divorce'. The *New York Times* printed an item saying that Sassy had filed a suit in Trenton, charging Atkins with physical and mental cruelty. The Toronto paper reported in greater detail that Sassy charged Atkins had threatened her life while she was appearing at nightcubs and theatres in Atlantic City, Las Vegas, Washington, Philadelphia and Canada.

Preacher and a friend, Clyde B. Golden Jr, a small, wiry man whose nickname, 'Pumpkin', stuck to him for his whole life, decided to go to Sassy's house in Englewood Cliffs at her request and retrieve her furniture and possessions. The police stopped them; Preacher was arrested and actually spent a brief time in jail. Sassy had paid for everything in the house that CB had reconstructed, but the furniture was now community property, Preacher recalled. Preacher soon started to put Sassy's finances in order for her. By his own admission, he didn't know anything about show business, but as Aretha Landrum would say, he liked music and at least he was honest. He also had a knack for making money. Soon, he was Sassy's lover and manager – a familiar arrangement for her.

Actually there was no money to put in order at first, because CB left Sassy with virtually nothing. Pumpkin, who became close friends with Sassy, estimated that she was $150,000 in debt after that marriage. Newspapers published small items in March 1963 that the IRS seized her house in Englewood Cliffs for non-payment of the joint 1961 income taxes owed by Sassy and CB.

'It's very hard for a woman on her own on the road,' Annie Ross said. 'You're making a lot of money, and you're a woman with a certain kind of power. There are always guys [who want to use you]. That's their identity. And Sassy was always peculiarly trusting, when she first met someone. Her naïveté was part of her charm.'

Pumpkin knew that, by 1963, 'Preacher put her back on her feet financially.' She was solvent again. Aretha Landrum remembered, 'Preacher opened a cheque account for her. She had never had one before. Her red velvet chequebook holder said, in gold lettering, "Sassy Vaughan". The cheques were printed "Sarah Vaughan".' Sassy showed the chequebook to Aretha, saying, 'Can you believe this?'

Sassy and Atkins wrangled over who would have custody of Debby; the conflict was so tumultuous that those among Sassy's friends who knew the details preferred not to talk about them for publication. In the end, Sassy prevailed and kept Debby, who would always use the family name Vaughan. When singing engagements took Sassy away from home, which was most of the time, she often left the child with 'Nana', Ada Vaughan. Sassy also had a nurse named Inez Brown taking care of the baby. In a PBS documentary tribute to Sassy many years later, Debby recounted that she travelled with Sassy a great deal both inside and outside the United States before she started school. Then she had to stay in Newark. Aretha recalled, 'Whenever Sassy was home, she and I used to take our kids to the park and sit on benches together, talking and having fun.'

Sassy and Preacher set up a management office in Newark and usually travelled together. In Las Vegas, they maintained an apartment in a hotel across the street from the Riviera casino. For about seven years, the pair shuttled between Newark and Las Vegas, living and working together in a generally amicable way – punctuated by some quarrels, noticed one of the musicians in her group. The relationship between Sassy and Preacher was never a great love affair, Pumpkin knew, but it was a constructive relationship between good friends, an assessment with which Carmen McRae agreed.

C. B. Atkins was completely out of the picture for Sassy. He had the prestige of having been her manager, and he went on to marry Little Esther Phillips, a highly regarded rhythm-and-blues and jazz singer, who had a hit with 'What a Diff'rence a Day Makes' some fifteen years after Dinah Washington recorded it. Little Esther's personal and professional life had tumultuous ups and downs. She stayed with CB until she died in the late 1980s. 'I imagine he was just as domineering with her as he had been with Sassy,' Ronnell Bright said, adding, 'Little Esther had looked up to CB because he had been Sarah Vaughan's husband.' The last time any of Sassy's friends saw CB, he was living in Chicago, and he had suffered a stroke. Carmen McRae had stopped talking to him for a while because of Sassy. 'But CB turned out after Sarah to be not a bad man,' Carmen McRae came to believe. 'He was sorry for how he had treated Sarah.' Sassy stayed on the road with Preacher and her musicians. In 1963, after her Roulette contract ended, she headed back to Mercury.

EIGHT

Muddling through the 1960s

Ronnell had left Sassy's group in 1960 to work for Lena Horne and was replaced eventually by Kirk Stuart. In 1963 Richard Davis, the bassist, and drummer Ray Mosca went along with Ronnell to work for Lena Horne. Sassy hired Buster Williams, a twenty-year-old from Camden, New Jersey, for the bass chair in 1963 and began raving about Buster to everyone. He had been playing with singer Betty Carter in Birdland when Kirk Stuart had approached and asked if he would like to work in Sassy's group. Buster began working with Sassy at the Edgecombe Hotel in Chicago. From there he went with her to Juan-les-Pins in the south of France and on to Copenhagen, where Sassy recorded thirty-six songs, four with Quincy Jones's orchestra, the rest with a trio – Kirk, Buster and drummer Georges Hughes – for two albums, one called *Sassy Swings the Tivoli*.

It is such an exciting album. Sassy sings 'I Feel Pretty' with so much conviction shining in her gorgeous voice that she becomes the prettiest girl who ever sang that song. Beginning the song straight-forwardly as it was written, she soon 'takes it out', swinging and improvising until its original rhythm is unrecognisable. She swings 'Misty' with great femininity, and then Kirk Stuart joins her with a soft, velvety baritone. When he sings, 'Would I wander through this wonderland alone?' she calls out, 'Oh, never.' And when she comes back in to finish the song, she moans with a trace of self-mockery and sighs the last word, *love*. 'Lover Man' inspired the audience to clap with their own, special European cadence, a regular chanting style of clapping similar to the Dixieland two-beat rhythm. Sassy started the next song, 'Sometimes I'm Happy', in that same rhythm at a fast tempo and turned the song into a scatting aria. Nobody else has ever combined such natural jazz feeling with such a ripe, robust and gorgeous voice. Buster, who loved pretty music, was very happy to be working in the group. Sassy sang better than any singer he had ever heard before – or since, he reflected years later; she had the uncanny ability to make her voice shimmer. From her, he learned the enormously important lesson of playing in tune. If that seems like an elementary lesson, it's one that young musicians often have to work at for a long time. Sassy sang exactly in tune and could hear instantly if any musician was out of tune. 'I took special care to make sure I played up to the mark for her,' he recalled.

While in Copenhagen, she recorded 'Lover Man' twice, and in one of those recordings, she substituted the words *hot hot hot* for the lyrics a couple of times. She was perspiring a great deal on stage. 'I don't know why hot hot hot,' she sang. She was beginning to perspire during performances – to the point that it would soon become an unsightly and uncomfortable problem for her.

After the Tivoli engagement, the group joined Count Basie's band and toured England for a month. Buster had heard about a famous bass shop in London, where he went looking for the bass of his dreams and found it, an unusually shaped antique of fine shiny brown wood dating back to the last half of the nineteenth century. When he told Sassy the price, she bought the instrument for him. Eventually he paid her back most but not all of the money; the remainder she decided to make a gift. In 1990, when Sassy died, he was still using the same treasured bass.

When Kirk Stuart left her group later in 1963, Sassy called Ronnell Bright and asked him to return. Then Buster and Ronnell practised together every day, because it was such a pleasure for them to play together. Buster loved Sassy because she could sing so well – intense emotions welled up in him at the sound of her voice – and because she was 'rough' and never put on airs with him. He could go into her dressing room, throw his arms around her, and hug her; she would say, 'Oh, Buster . . .' and joke with him. He smoked marijuana for the first time with her. Later his religious beliefs precluded his smoking.

Once she became tipsy after a performance and acted in a seductive manner toward him, telling him, 'Oh, Buster, you play so pretty . . .' She teased him with the offer of a little pay bonus. Nothing came of the brief game. By the next morning, Sassy forgot about the flirtation and never alluded to it again.

In addition to recording a few of Ronnell's compositions, she sang his tune 'Sweet Pumpkin'. (Despite its title, it had nothing to do with Sassy's friend, Pumpkin Golden.) As Ronnell and Sassy drove or flew around the country, Ronnell sometimes advised her: do such and such a song. She forgot lyrics, and she used syllables as launching pads for adventurous improvisations. Ronnell called her attention to lyrics and thought that he may have illuminated them for her at times. Sometimes she thanked him by saying, 'That's good,' and deciding to do a song he suggested. They travelled more by land than plane after she broke up with C. B. Atkins because she was trying to conserve money, Ronnell thought. And she and Ronnell also whiled away the travel time by trying to identify notes they heard from car horns and train whistles. Many times she said, 'What note is that?' 'It's a C,' Ronnell might answer. 'No, it's a D,' she would say. As soon as they could, they would find a piano and settle the dispute.

For Ronnell, his tenure with Sassy was a great musical experience. Though he had arrived in Sassy's group with classical training, he learned more about harmonies and the construction of music from Sassy. 'It was like working with Bird. She never liked to do a thing the same way twice, and she encouraged us to do our own stuff.' In 'Poor Butterfly', she changed keys – a technique that builds excitement and heightens any mood, and which most singers couldn't master, because they didn't have Sassy's musicianship. Without warning them that she was going to change keys, she forced her accompanists 'to grope for a way to follow her in front of audiences', Ronnell remembered. He felt exhilarated by the paces she put him through, just as her other accompanists, including pianists Sir Roland Hanna and Bob James, would in the early to mid-1960s and other pianists would in years to come.

Bob James said, 'If you fed her something new and different, like a chord, she could take it – and [improvise] so far that none of us could keep up with it.' Sir Roland Hanna said, 'I didn't usually like to work with singers, but I worked with Sassy for love of her musicianship.' She gave the men plenty to talk about after the shows, when they sat around and discussed what she had done and how much creativity and ingenuity she had elicited from them. 'She was full of fun and laughter and always on the edge and had a surprise going all the time,' Ronnell said.

One night at the Chez Paree in Chicago, after a performance, she found her musicians sound asleep in the dressing room. They were exhausted from travelling and working – they had been country-hopping, alighting in such places as Antibes to open a jazz festival in July that year, then flying off again to the next date, and the next. But she felt fresh. So she decided to wake everybody up by bringing in the nightlub's camerawomen, who set off their flashbulbs.

She often sang Erroll Garner's 'Misty', which critics singled out as a wonderful vehicle for her. 'It encourages use of her tonal range and guttural slurring of some passages,' wrote Robert Dana of the *New York World-Telegram and Sun*, admiring her December 1963 engagement at the Waldorf-Astoria's Empire Room. Dana felt that Bright's working as the musical director made Emil Coleman's orchestra backing Sassy somehow sound like a reasonable facsimile of the Count Basie orchestra, with which, Dana could remember, she had enjoyed great success at the hotel's Starlight Roof in 1957. She started her Empire Room set with an uptempo 'Everything's Comin' Up Roses' and 'Cheek to Cheek', then composedly announced 'I'd like to open my show.' Dana thought the cool hue of her mint-green dress emphasised and enhanced the subtlety of her manner. She then sang several ballads – 'Gone with the Wind', 'Comes Love', and 'Just One of Those Things' – before embarking on 'Misty'. A fiery 'Lorelei' was tamed right afterward by a sensitive 'Poor Butterfly'. She was still being asked to sing 'Broken Hearted Melody' often enough that she included it, to the delight of the audience – 'This rock-a-dilly tune has all the elements to bridge the gap for all cults of music lovers,' Dana wrote, unaware of her own ineffable boredom with the song. She had never come up with an artistically worthwhile way to change or embellish it. (Modina Davis remarked how Sassy would come offstage after singing that song and always say she was mystified by the audience response. 'Don't I look funny, hollering and yelling up there?' she asked.) She sang 'Walk with Me' a cappella, to a silent, awestruck audience, and ended with 'Smooth Operator' and 'It Don't Mean a Thing'. The variety of her repertoire at that time, as well as the excitement of her style, aroused audiences.

Her partying offstage never prevented her from showing up to give a wonderful performance. When she and the trio were working at the Starfire Club (which had a bowling alley) in San Jose, California, they visited guitarist, pianist, singer and composer Slim Gaillard at his house. A character in his own right, Gaillard wrote 'Flat Foot Floogie' and 'Cement Mixer (Puttee Puttee)', and he could play the piano with his long-fingered hands upside down. In his own home, the novelty was his pet ocelot. Buster Williams noticed that the ocelot was chewing on Slim's furniture. Slim kept pouring drinks for Sassy and the men, but the audience never had any hint that she had been drinking before she stepped onstage.

Around that time, Nancy Wilson's manager asked Ronnell to become her accompanist, for about double the money he was then earning with Sassy. 'I had a wife and kids to support. It was a matter of economics,' Ronnell recalls was his reason for joining Nancy. Buster thought a tiff with Sassy might have prompted Ronnell's leaving, too, but no memory of it remained with Ronnell, who admired and loved Sassy so much as an artist and a person that he never wanted to dwell on any of the exasperations that came up from time to time. Buster soon joined Nancy's group, too. Before doing so, he played with Sassy a while longer, first with the gifted Patti Bown as the pianist. Patti recalled Sassy 'as a lady'. Then Buster contacted Bob James, who was a youngster building his career and little known to the public.

James never auditioned for her and before working for her had met her only once, when she had sat in at Birdland while he was working there. She had asked him if he knew 'The Sweetest Sounds I Ever Heard'. He knew the song and played it to her liking.

He appreciated that Sassy was a superb piano player with a good understanding of arranging. 'She could push me aside and show me how to [play for a singer] . . . The first thing she taught me was that a singer makes strong demands with tempo. Every singer has a favourite tempo for every song. I was used to playing with instrumentalists and doing a variety of tempos for the same song. She liked to do it one way for her breathing and comfort. It was hard for me to remember about the tempo, but it was an invaluable lesson . . . And she could improvise.' Years after his job with her ended, he wrote a song called 'Wings for Sarah', which explained how Sassy signalled to her group to slow down the tempo – she flapped her elbows back and forth. Audiences may have guessed she was being swept away with emotion, he related in the PBS documentary tribute that aired after her death, but she was actually signalling to James that she felt acute discomfort with the tempo. It didn't matter that Bob, to whom the rest of the rhythm section looked for direction, already felt as if an eternity were passing between the beats. She wanted him to slow down and make the accompaniment soft, supportive, and yet seem impromptu.

Sassy needed consistency in her musical accompaniment to show her off to best advantage. During the March following Ronnell's departure from her group, when she appeared at Basin Street East in Manhattan, critics noticed that her new accompanist, who wasn't credited, hadn't become quite used to working with her. On 2 June 1964 the audience in Toronto's Club Indigo and the Canadian critics had no reservations about Sassy's work. Frank Morriss of the *Globe and Mail* wrote that she sang 'Maria' from *West Side Story* as if Leonard Bernstein had written it for her. 'For Sarah Vaughan is a magnificent law unto herself and the large audience was quite ready to let her take hold of any piece of music, and any lyric, and fashion it to her own ends . . . She is an astonishing, ever fresh singer who has genius. She is a stylist in the very best sense in an era when the term is applied to anyone who decided to muck up a number with unnecessary frills.'

Morriss loved her storming 'All of Me' and her slow, long lines in 'Poor Butterfly'. 'She uses [her astonishing voice] in an astonishing way. On top it has the delicacy of a coloratura soprano with the flexibility that goes with this type of voice . . . At the bottom, it is a deep contralto and if sometimes she switches registers too suddenly, it is the only mistake she can make.' Gerry Barker of the *Toronto Daily Star* wrote that she was so unique, it was impossible for anyone to copy her flair and style. After the second show on opening night, the customers threw the flowers from their tables on to the stage. Sassy was stunned. (The legend was that Dizzy Gillespie was in the audience and started the flower-throwing. The same thing would happen to her soon in Rio de Janeiro, even without Dizzy there.)

Bob James noticed that despite adulation from audiences, she didn't like to talk to them between the tunes she sang. He heard anxiety in her voice when she talked and noticed that she forgot the names of her musicians when it came time to introduce the trio. He knew she thought of herself as an instrumentalist. 'She would forget lyrics sometimes, partially because she was thinking of the notes, the lines, the phrasings more like a horn player. The lyrics [were] not that important to her,' James reflected. She could relax during a long run in one place and remember the musicians' names. 'But when she [sang] she [was] home free.'

James recalled how exciting the experience was, for her and for him, when she performed at the White House for the first time. Lyndon Johnson was hosting a state dinner for the Prime Minister of Japan. 'And she was really nervous – extremely – in the afternoon before the performance which was to be in the East Room. For me, it was a chance to play the famous Steinway made with ornate legs shaped like eagles designed for the White House. But the East Room is not like being in a theatre or a club or a concert hall. It is fairly lit up, with all the famous political people and guests sitting only three or four feet away from the performers. It's like working in a living-room. Afterward we had our pictures taken with President and Mrs Johnson. Dean Rusk and his wife and all those people were there. We were invited to the dance after the show, too. Sarah, myself, Larry Rockwell, the bassist, and Omar Clay, the drummer. So we're standing around, not knowing what to do. President Johnson asked Sarah to dance. She was thrilled . . . She and Lyndon seemed to get along well.'

Her bouts of nerves before performances always riveted her friends' attention, too, if they were backstage and witnessed, as Robert Richards did many times, how she walked around saying, 'I can't do it, I just can't do it.' And then she would walk onstage.

All the while she kept convincing the small group of important jazz critics in the United States that she was one of the best singers the country had ever produced. For the *Saturday Review* of 26 August 1967, Martin Williams, a pioneering jazz critic and historian, offered a retrospective critique of Sassy's recording career in the 1950s and 1960s. The public was now more accustomed to her adventurous style.

'Sarah Vaughan has one of the most remarkable voices that any of our popular singers has ever possessed . . . to find comparable voices one needs to turn to the opera or concert stage . . . Her voice has range, body, volume. More important, her control of her voice is phenomenal . . . her pitch is just about impeccable, and she can jump the most difficult intervals and land true. No other singer has such an effortless command of dynamics. I know of no one who can move from a whisper to full volume in the course of a few notes and make the move sound less affected than Sarah Vaughan. When, as a young singer, she discovered her vibrato, she indulged it distressingly, but today her use of it – . . . say, to end a sustained tone – should be the envy of every singer alive.'

Williams went on to analyse some of the technique that made her different from any other kind of singer, especially a classically trained singer. 'She can take a note at the top of her range and . . . bend it or squeeze it; she growls and rattles notes down at the bottom of her range; she can glide her voice through several notes at mid-range while raising dynamics or lowering or simply squeezing.' In addition to harking back to eighteenth-century singers, for whom improvisation was a requisite, she encompassed all the musical expression of jazz in America. And in reviewing her career as a tug-of-war between her pop and jazz recordings, he singled out some of his favourite recordings by Sassy done for Columbia, Mercury and Roulette.

For Columbia, she had improvised a new melody for 'Mean to Me' and effected a 'discreet' reading with little embellishment of 'Come

Rain or Come Shine'. 'From that point on, as she discovered more and more of the phenomenal nature of her voice, it seemed that fewer and fewer popular songs could contain her. There is, for example, a gloriously dramatic version of 'Dancing in the Dark' in which every note seems to be bursting out of the confines of that song, and it is not exactly a simple one. The performance . . . should not be missed; it is part of a two-LP set with the . . . title *Great Songs from Hit Shows* . . . which is also not to be missed.' She had become a standard for the Establishment to measure everyone else against. Everyone had caught up with the adventurous children of the bebop era.

If he had to choose only three songs as his favourites by her, Williams wrote, he would choose 'Ain't No Use' on Roulette: 'She teases that song, she cajoles it – to miss her sly but guileless humour is to miss her art – and she uses or implies almost all her vocal powers in doing so.' He praised her versions, on the album *Sassy Swings Again* for Mercury, of 'Everyday I Have the Blues' and 'I Left My Heart in San Francisco' as 'wild vocal *tours de force*, and while they last they are marvellous'.

'The version of "All Alone", however, is apt to stay with us,' he continued, 'a humorous plea for company . . . until a kind of floor-show bravura possesses it . . . In any case, it is good to know that this superb voice can express itself through small popular ditties, because it's very unlikely that we have a composer who will write her what she deserves. Ah, but if we did, there would be an improvisational oratorio or opera for Sarah Vaughan.'

It was difficult for most people to choose favourites among Sassy's songs. Her version of 'I Cried for You' for Columbia was full of improvisation; she sang it as if she was gloating with joy about no longer being unhappy for any lost love. She was clear-voiced, swinging and imaginative on 'Mean to Me', with Budd Johnson's saxophone as a perfect foil. If there was any change in her voice from the late 1940s through the 1950s and into the 1960s, it may have been that it got better – richer. But it was still difficult to detect a real change or a deepening; she could give a lyrical reading to 'Serenata' for Roulette by the 1960s, save 'My Dear Little Sweetheart' from becoming a country-and-western tune by the elixir of her pretty voice, and then adopt a dramatic, rich, uplifting tone for 'Green Hills of Summer'. 'Them There Eyes' was a swinging jazz romp. When she sang 'A Taste of Honey' for Mercury, one could savour the hint of honey in her throat, until she seemed to clear it and swoop around the octaves fetchingly to end the song. She adjusted her voice and lyric reading to each song. The richness and maturity, however, had always intimated its presence, from the earlier Columbia recordings with Treadwell's groups, including Miles Davis with his eerie haunting trumpet tone, to the Roulette repertoire.

Photographs of her begin, in the mid-1960s, to show her fuller figure. She lent her name to the Women for Humphrey organisation in July 1968, though she was not ordinarily associated publicly with politics, except as a performer at many benefits. Her support for Humphrey may have been Preacher's idea. Mainly, during 1968, she was dreaming of a new musical adventure for herself. Writing in the *Toronto Telegram* of 4 June 968, Helen McNamara advocated what that new direction should be.

McNamara suggested that the planning board for the Toronto Symphony Jazz Series slated for 1968–9 pay a visit to the Hook and Ladder Club in town to hear the voice of Sarah Vaughan; it 'would be a dazzling asset to the Jazz at the Symphony series'. At the Hook and Ladder Club, Sassy shone even though her pianist was new, and she needed rehearsals with him; about five hundred people crowded into the club ostensibly to hear her but actually, it seemed, they preferred to talk to each other, annoying Sassy to distraction. A few times she asked them to be quiet. 'An adventurous rendition of "Misty" passed almost unnoticed,' Miss McNamara observed. 'By the time she . . . started on "The Nearness of You", softly and quietly, she was getting slightly and rightfully impatient. "It's noisy, noisy, noisy in here," she carolled, which must have been the most musical scolding any audience has received. But it served her purpose.' The audience quieted down for her uptempo 'All of Me', which she followed with 'It's a Most Unusual Day', 'Day In, Day Out', 'On a Clear Day', and 'Tenderly'. 'The rich qualities of her voice . . . [seem] to improve year by year,' McNamara wrote. 'If she has appeared under more favourable conditions, it was still apparent that she is a singer of extraordinary talent. A true jazz singer, possessing all the requisites (an exquisite sense of timing, a rare improvising ability and vocal range encompassing deep throaty notes and pure treble tones), she is exactly the kind of performer that would do justice to both jazz and classical music on a Jazz at the Symphony series.'

In September 1968, when she sang at the Rainbow Grill at the top of 30 Rockefeller Plaza in New York, she received similar attention from John S. Wilson, who wrote in the *New York Times* that she showed a new subtlety; she had eliminated the swoons from her style, and, most fascinating of all, she now had a wider range. (Actually it was the rare performance in which Sassy did not venture a good moony swoon or two, but perhaps not on the night Wilson heard her.) She was celebrating the twenty-fifth anniversary of her professional singing career, which made her conscious enough of the passage of time to joke with her audience, 'You know, I was only two when I started.'

Wilson wrote: 'The passage of all these years has finally brought to her something that she has seemed to have been searching for during most of her career. From her earliest years, she has had a remarkably flexible voice with a 2-octave range through which she could move seemingly without effort to pure, luminescent highs as well as strong, mellow, full-bodied lows.' (Actually she had a 2½-octave range at that time, normally from about C below middle C to D above middle C, 'though she could go up to A-flat or A or maybe even higher than that on a good night', reckoned pianist Bob James.) Wilson recounted that the audience stood up and cheered for her.

Offstage she told Wilson that she felt her voice had matured, that her range had been extended at both ends of the scale, and she admitted to a desire to do 'classical stuff'. She wanted Leonard Bernstein to write a modern opera for her. 'I'm dying to meet him. I'd like to hear what he'd have to say about the idea.' She lifted her chin, and her eyes twinkled when she said that if she met Bernstein, she would say, '"Write me something, please." If he's familiar with me, I don't think it would be difficult.'

Still living with Preacher Wells at the time, Sassy welcomed Tom Mackin, a staff writer for the *Newark Sunday News*, to interview her in her 'swank apartment', as he described it, sixteen floors up, with a big chair with soft cushions in the living-room for Sassy. Until she appeared at the Rainbow Grill, she hadn't performed in a New York nightclub for four years; her previous club date had been at Basin Street East. Though she loved the New York audience, she had increasing reservations about the sound systems and other facilities in nightclubs (actually she complained about the sound nearly everywhere). But keeping herself familiar with New York while staying out of its clubs – which had diminished in number and popularity in the rock era – she had performed two outdoor concerts with audiences of 5,500 people at the Wollman Rink in Central Park. She had done a concert with Louis Armstrong in Philadelphia. She was constantly on the road, moving from Los Angeles hotels to Caesar's Palace to Montreal clubs to Europe, where she gave concerts in eight countries in 1968; she was going back to Europe when she left New York in 1969.

The itinerary information, Tom Mackin reported, came from

Preacher, who was in charge of telling both the press and Sassy where she was headed, just as George Treadwell had been. She told Mackin she was tired. 'I sure would like to rest some,' she said, cuddling Debby, then a seven-year-old first grader at the Maple Avenue School in Newark. 'I used to take her with me, but now I can't take her out of school. She doesn't mind so much, as long as I bring her autographs of the stars I meet,' Sassy said. Debby later said she had started travelling when she was three months old and, before starting school, had gone around the world five times with Sassy. Ada Vaughan by that time had also adopted a daughter, named Donna, the child of a woman who had travelled on the road with Sassy and who was unable to take care of the child herself. So Sassy had a stepsister about thirty years younger than she, and Mrs Vaughan had a new family to raise.

During her Christmas-time respite in Newark that year, Sassy told Mackin, she would play some golf and paint a little. Golf, of course, was not in season, but painting, an indoor pastime, was possible. She showed Mackin a few of her paintings, a clown, a landscape, and a still life which she said she had begun to do in oils when she was playing in Caesar's Palace in Las Vegas. Her father had been painting portraits for a while, including several of Sassy that her friends admired; his painting had given her the idea to dabble. She didn't mention that she had also learned to sew and liked to travel with a sewing machine, making clothes for herself and her friends as a way of relaxing in her hotel rooms. (She also didn't tell Mackin that 'one of her favourite pastimes in Las Vegas was hanging out at night with Frank Sinatra and playing pranks on friends in the middle of the night. Her daytime life was not very interesting, but she liked to hang out and get into mischief with friends in show business all night,' Bob James recalled.) Mackin saw a half-packed fine leather trunk in the corner of her living-room; he asked her how many trips she had made, and of course she had no idea. She was earning about ten thousand dollars a week, the reporter wrote, though it isn't clear if he meant ten thousand dollars for a one-night concert in a theatre or a week-long club engagement; she was probably earning that amount for both gigs by then.

She had just been honoured at a Sarah Vaughan Day in Newark, when she was handed the keys to the city at a dinner. She had requested that the proceeds from the dinner go to the Mount Zion Baptist Church for a new Christian education building for children, she told Mackin. She also mentioned that she had added a Beatles' song, the pensive 'Yesterday', to her repertoire. It was one of the few songs from the era that she had liked and paid any attention to yet.

When she left Newark to go to work, she left Preacher, too. Their liaison ended. It would take a while before they became friendly again; later Sassy visited him in his house in Las Vegas. Exactly why their intimate relationship ended, neither Pumpkin Golden nor Aretha Landrum really knew. Aretha said, 'Nobody can say what really happens with other people when they shut their doors.' The friend with whom Sassy had hung out when she worked in Los Angeles agreed that Preacher was rather aloof; he didn't like to party all night with Sassy; so that crowd didn't know him very well. For one thing, few people had Sassy's endurance for nightclubbing and morning-aftering. Sassy's East Coast musician friends never got to know Preacher intimately, either. And he characterised himself as a 'loner'.

Preacher, who played a subsidiary role at first, may have become more proprietary, just as George Treadwell had done, Aretha thought. A struggle may have developed about who was the boss, she surmised. 'Everyone got very egotistical behind her, a star. She said, "Hey, listen, I am the star, I am paying the salary." But she had to be very angry to say that. But she did say it. A lot of times I would have said it more than she did, when someone was telling her where to go, what to do, what to play. She was like all women, looking for someone to love and to be in her corner, with a closeness, an understanding, and a sharing. It started out that way,' Aretha said, for Sassy and Preacher. Aretha never questioned Sassy about why she and Preacher parted. Nobody did; if Sassy confided in her friends, then they knew what was on her mind. But she cut off questions when there was something she didn't want to divulge.

Musicians and business people who worked with her knew that Sassy could be quite provocative, demanding, and even bratty, without any reluctance about asserting herself in all sorts of large and small matters. Pumpkin heard her tell people who made faulty and inconvenient arrangements for her hotels and travels to come on the road with her. 'Come and see for yourself what you're doing to me,' she'd say to them. Once Pumpkin also heard her tell Preacher, as she was going onstage, 'I need you when I come offstage, not when I'm going onstage.' She didn't like to be told what to do when she didn't need direction. 'She wasn't moody,' Pumpkin said, taking an opposing view to many of her road companions and business connections. 'She was either tired or rested,' Pumpkin commented. Debby Vaughan would eventually say that her mother had been exceptionally strong; that had always been the crux of her difficulty with men. And Annie Ross explained the reason for the difficulty: 'Where are you going to get a man who can stand up with equal force?'

After Sassy and Preacher separated, she rented a condominium near Malibu and then moved to a house near Benedict Canyon in Los Angeles. Carmen McRae lived nearby. So did Gail Fisher, the actress who played the secretary in Mike Connors's television show, 'Mannix'. Fisher's husband at the time was manager John Levy, a former professional bass player, who had played in Stuff Smith's group along with Jimmy Jones. So Levy had met Sassy in New York in the mid-1940s. Briefly he managed Sassy's career, but he had several other clients, and Sassy wanted virutally undivided attention from a manager. 'That was the problem there,' said James Harper, her accountant in Los Angeles, who took over the management of her career for a little while. Even though she had old friends around her on the West Coast, she confided to Aretha that she didn't really feel as attached to her rented place as she had to the house which the government had seized in Englewood Cliffs, New Jersey.

Sassy was not exactly at a loss for male companionship. She had two men friends between 1968 and 1970 who sometimes travelled with her, one from the Midwest, another from the West Coast. Both were regarded by musicians who worked in her groups as 'street people', 'hustlers'. 'They were slick men with a sharp way of talking and dressing that always fascinated Sassy,' the Newark-born singer Andy Bey recalled. 'One of [her slick companions] wore a diamond pin in the shape of a question mark on his tie,' said Jimmy Cobb, the drummer who would join Sassy's group in 1970.

Carmen McRae said, 'She met these [guys] and went crazy. But I understood her and her reasons for doing what she did.' About Sassy's love affairs, Annie Ross thought: 'Look what she gave out onstage! She needed to get that back. You can't sing like that and not feel sexy. As you get older, you get a little selective, but Sassy never felt less sexy.'

Sassy included prominent people, too, in her growing list of friends whom she could trust or rely upon. Al Davis, for one, the owner of the Los Angeles Raiders, made a natural friend for Sassy, who loved to watch sporting events.

Because of her career, Sassy lived in a state of nearly perpetual stimulation, always preparing to go back onstage the moment she stepped offstage. She never really calmed down. George Wein, who over the years battled with Sassy and came to regard her as 'a mixed blessing' but an indisputable 'angel' for the way she sang, thought her wild life-style, in which she mixed pleasure and business, hurt her career. She still hadn't sought out first-rate professional management by the 1960s; later, George would think she never did.

'I was sorry for her problems,' he said. 'She could have had such a more enjoyable life if she had come from a different background and had a different philosophy, and she was hurt by people who violated her trust. She suffered from coming out of the Newark ghetto. She rose above her background to a degree but it was always there. Prejudice and fears of prejudice were against her. She suffered more so than a lot of other black artists. I don't know why.' By some miracle, she overcame her naïve approach, because she could sing through any adversity. The glory of her voice, despite all the turmoil in her life, remained inexplicable to Wein – and to everyone else. 'She survived in spite of her husband,' he said.

At the time she broke up with Preacher, Sassy's career was in a crisis even though her voice was indomitable. Though she wanted Leonard Bernstein to compose an opera for her, she had not tried to contact Bernstein herself, and neither Preacher nor anyone else had done so on her behalf. Still hampered by shyness, she had no confidence about her chance of being welcomed by Bernstein. So she continued in her usual groove. It was more apparent than ever that focused, forward-looking management of her career had disappeared with George Treadwell. Occasional guest appearances on the Johnny Carson, Mike Douglas, Merv Griffin, and other television shows kept her before the public. One belated film opportunity arose when she sang Handel's *Messiah*, adapted by Quincy Jones for a 40-person chorus and 110-piece orchestra for the 1969 movie *Bob & Carol & Ted & Alice*. She sang the *Messiah* brilliantly, but it didn't lead her to more or larger projects of that nature. Instead she made the rounds of the casinos, cocktail lounges, clubs, jazz fetivals and jazz concerts. Her fans continued to flock to her concerts. But rock had swept the country, and its stars had accumulated all the glamour. Sassy's records were now played on the radio stations that played golden oldie and jazz records. Though she had recorded with studio orchestras with strings, as well as jazz groups, she had not yet had a booking to appear with a symphony orchestra, despite Helen McNamara's suggestion in the Toronto paper.

Furthermore, after her last recordings for Mercury in 1967, there was a hiatus in her recording career, primarily because of the overwhelming popularity of rock. Rhythm and blues, too, and soul had captured the attention of the public. Sassy had no clear idea of what to do for herself except to keep singing the same 'sophisticated' music she had become famous for. By then forty-four years old, Sassy was letting the proud prow of her voice lead her around in circles.

Robert Richards, an artist, was living in New York in the late 1960s; earlier he had become friends with Dinah Washington and Anita O'Day. One night he went to hear Sassy singing in a club, where he ventured backstage to meet her, and she welcomed him into her dressing room; later, he remembered affectionately that she was always pleased to see attractive young men come to her dressing-room door. From their first conversations, she sensed his respect for her as an artist. 'The only demand I made on her was for her to sing. I showed up at ringside tables, which I paid for myself, to hear her perform. I also made it clear that I was interested not only in her artistry but in the person who made this sound,' he reminisced. In those relatively lean years for her in the late 1960s, when he saw her playing in the few clubs featuring jazz, not rock, remaining in New York, he always went backstage after the shows and brought her presents. He knew that she was earning a good income for her work, but she was having a difficult time, because her kind of music had been eclipsed by rock.

A jazz lover, he remained fascinated by her singing, no matter what the trends were in pop culture, and listened to her records all the time. He told her about how he had heard her record 'Black Coffee' when he was a teenager in Sanford, Maine, and how he had fallen in love with it for its oddity; it had inspired him to think that he could leave his small hometown and find a more exciting, less restrictive life in the big city. 'Oh, don't tell me that,' Sassy said to him. 'It gives me such a responsibility.' He told her not to feel responsible. He had always been looking for inspiration to go out into the world. He had cut pictures of elevators, trains, even stairways out of magazines – anything that seemed even remotely like a means of transportation out of Sanford. She loved his sense of humour, she loved to laugh, and she was always very happy to see him at her performances and to know he was there. They began to telephone each other when she was on the road or back home in Los Angeles. She would call him often simply to tell him what kind of day she was having and to find out what he was doing.

In the late 1970s she would write him a letter about her memories of the early days of their friendship and her feeling toward him:

Dear Robert,
    I'm not one with words, but I want to try and say this to you. I remember when things were going a little less great than they are right

now. The late sixties and early seventies weren't always kind to me. But to you I was still the best and number one. And I could always look out into the audiences (and I could see them), and find your face encouraging and approving. You made me want to sing good, and it helped me more than you know.

And you always looking so fine and swanky and coming back and bringing me the kind of gifts other people brought to Lena [Horne] and Diana [Ross] or those other glamour queens because you knew that in my heart I was a glamour girl even if it couldn't be seen. And I love you for catching that. And so my friend, when I sing in New York, I sing to you. You are always in my songs. Thank you for loving me and don't stop.

Your (I hope), favourite vocalist,
Sarah

P.S. Don't be embarrassed. Just accept the compliment.

At the time, 'she didn't have a recording contract because she couldn't get one on her terms', Richard said. 'She wanted to choose the material, and the contracts offered were for her to sing songs that she didn't want to do.'

Reviews of her performances in New York City were now few and far between; she didn't sing there as often as she had once done. She concentrated on booking herself for 'events' – jazz concerts or big clubs. *Ebony* magazine ran no big feature stories about her in the 1960s after the major 1961 interview. *Down Beat* magazine paid attention, however. Leonard Feather invited her to take his series, the 'Blindfold Test', for which he played recordings by other vocalists and asked her to guess who was singing and to rate the performance with one to five stars. He was astounded to note that he hadn't given her a blindfold test since his salad days in 1952, when he had been living in a top-floor apartment at One Sheridan Square in Greenwich Village, and she had been singing at Cafe Society in the building's basement.

'Cafe Society . . . is of course long gone,' he wrote. 'Everything has changed: the Eastern scene for the worse, the great Miss Vaughan for the better, though even back in the 1940s it seemed impossible that anyone could advance beyond the standards she had already established. Somehow she has found a way to improve on perfection. Sarah . . . has never won a . . . Grammy, although these awards are supposedly based on artistic merit rather than sales. At the time of this interview, she had not made a record session since February, 1967; meanwhile, Big Mama Cass and Tiny Tim were racking up big record sales.

'Sass spoke very softly and carried no stick; in fact, she was as bashful as always and seemingly eager to find something affirmative to say about the odd mixture of vocal records played.'

She confessed that sometimes she mistook Arthur Prysock for B. She had a tiny criticism of the way Prysock ended a song Feather played: 'Seems like he could have sung more – stuck something in there – I would have!' Prysock got three stars. She had reservations about Barbara Streisand singing 'He Touched Me'. 'Whoee! That's a dirty song. The only thing I can say about that record is, she was *touched*. It's nice in spots, a little dramatic I think . . . but with the arrangement and all, it all goes together – the arrangement was pretty exciting.' She wanted to know the story of Miriam Makeba's song, sung in Xhosa, and she struggled to find words about a record by the blues singer Jimmy Rushing, whose name she forgot, though she knew he had sung with Basie. 'That's good music,' she managed, but it didn't really interest her. Helen Merrill, who liked to sing flatted fifths, intrigued Sassy with 'Day Dream', accompanied by Thad Jones on cornet, Dick Katz, the pianist and arranger, and Ron Carter, the bassist. 'I don't know who the singer was . . . I liked the sound.' (Helen had left the country after recording a few jazz albums – later acclaimed as classics – because she was having difficulty finding any work in the United States.) 'The musicians are excellent. I don't know who he is, but he's my kind of piano player . . . and the bass sounded good. Everything is excellent, the arrangement, everything. I'd give it five stars,' her highest rating of the test session. Nancy Wilson singing 'This Bitter Earth' got two stars: 'I like Nancy's singing, but on this one she really sounded like Dinah.' Aretha Franklin took four stars for singing 'Come Back Baby'. 'That's a good record,' Sassy said. 'It's that down home, good swingin', pat your foot record. I like Aretha, though not every-thing she does. There's only a few people, singers, that I like doing anything – Billy Eckstine is one, Tony Bennett . . . Carmen and Ella . . . Tony Bennett's been making some nice records, all of them are good, and pretty . . . that's what I want to do, songs like that. I would give five stars to Tony's "If I Ruled the World". I thought that was just beautiful . . .'

Her accountant, James Harper, and many other friends thought that in addition to the frustrations she faced in her career, she was unhappy without a special man in her life. She hung out with musician friends around the clock and around the world. In Los Angeles, she went to Donte's, a favourite hangout for musicians, and with Carmen McRae and Morgana King, Sassy sat in with a group featuring guitarist Joe Pass. The women scatted together. Sassy could sing anything the men played and, in Pass's opinion, she came out on top of the other women.★ Drummer Grady Tate, who had first heard Sassy sing in a San Antonio, Texas, arena in 1951, when he was stationed at Lackland Air Force Base, thought then that he had never heard anything more beautiful than Sassy's singing. They remet through musician friends and became close after Sassy broke up with Preacher. Grady noticed that Sassy had more energy for the sport of hanging out than anyone else he knew, but he acquitted himself well when he tried to match her.

'She always found something to do or laugh about,' Grady said, and her exuberance was obvious in her singing. She constantly improvised, rehearsing the format but never the exact improvisations in her performances. She was the most interesting of singers. Singers of all styles of music flocked to her bandstand to hear what she was going to do. Each time Grady Tate listened to the ways in which she treated songs, how lightly, playfully and coquettishly she sang certain things, and then how seriously and gravely she addressed other material, he recognised her genius; she could rivet his attention and control his moods. A singer as well as a drummer, he felt educated by her sound and her ability to communicate with an audience. As her gift overtook her onstage, her audiences succumbed to her. Offstage she never wanted to sleep, Grady knew. He believed that was why she could keep going long after others had collapsed. Sleep had to overpower her.

★It wasn't always that way. Although Sassy had the most beautiful voice of any woman who ever sang jazz, Carmen McRae was always praised as one of the greatest interpreters of lyrics. Reviewing a concert in Los Angeles, when Carmen sat in as a guest with Sassy, Leonard Feather in the *Los Angeles Times* remarked that Carmen, 'Ms Head Tones', as he called her, outshone 'Madame Chest Tones', Feather's amusing way of pigeonholing Sassy and differentiating her from Carmen.

The young Sarah Vaughan on tour during the early days of her success in the late 1940s (Courtesy Institute of Jazz Studies, Rutgers University)

Johnnie Garry took this photo of Sarah one day when they were relaxing on a golf course. She taught him how to play and even bought him his first set of golf clubs (Courtesy Johnnie Garry and Jazzmobile)

The fine Tennessee-born pianist Jimmy Jones, one of Sassy's favourite accompanists (Photo by Red Wolfe; courtesy Institute of Jazz Studies, Rutgers University)

Glamour, sass and spirit: publicity shot of Sarah (Photo by Maurice Seymour; courtesy Associated Booking Corp)

From left to right: Dizzy Gillespie, Earl 'Fatha' Hines and Billy Eckstine
(Courtesy Institute of Jazz Studies, Rutgers University)

The great Billy Eckstine, a very important influence in Sarah's life, late 1940s.
Drummer Kenny Clarke and bassist Tommy Potter are in the background
(Courtesy Institute of Jazz Studies, Rutgers University)

*Publicity shot of Sarah from the 1970s during her time at Mainstream Records
(Courtesy Institute of Jazz Studies, Rutgers University)*

*Marshall Fisher with Sarah at a Mainstream recording session in May 1972
(Courtesy Raymond Ross Photography)*

*Sassy knew how to party – even on stage. With fellow singer Betty Carter,
1980s (Courtesy Institute of Jazz Studies, Rutgers University)*

Part of The Trio (with Jimmy Jones and Richard Davis), drummer Roy Haynes worked with Sassy for five years (Photo by Archie Hamilton; courtesy Institute of Jazz Studies, Rutgers University)

Michael Tilson Thomas and Sarah, 1982. They worked together very successfully on the songs of George Gershwin

NINE

A New Man, a New Record Contract, a New Outlook

In 1968, accountant James Harper also became Sassy's personal manager, co-ordinating hotel and travel reservations for her bookings, taking care of contracts, sending cheques to her musicians, and acting as a central clearing house for any business or information between Sassy, the bookers, and the places where she was scheduled to play. The arrangement didn't work out very well, because she still wanted a personal manager to travel with her.

He preferred his work as an accountant and struggled to take care of her personal management. When she cancelled engagements, as she often did, he simply postponed them for a later date. He knew that other people involved in her bookings often weren't abe to reach her for days at a time. (Frank Rio, an Associated Booking Corporation vice-president who had become familiar with her life-style when he became her booker during her marriage to Treadwell, stopped working for her for a few years at this time.) When she had a man in her life, she wasn't so elusive and erratic, especially because the men in her life usually acted as her managers. Sassy played one concert in a theatre in Wilmington, Delaware, which James Harper arranged. He felt that he had done something with far-reaching good consequences for Sassy; the William Morris Agency was doing her bookings then and didn't perceive her as a concert artist. The theatre itself was leery of her drawing power as a solo artist, so Harper told the management he would take financial responsibility for the first show if it flopped. She sold out two shows in the theatre. Harper later saw the success as a harbinger of things to come.

Drummer Jimmy Cobb, who played for Sassy beginning in 1970, had first met and became friendly with her in Los Angeles in the early

1950s, when he had been working in Dinah Washington's group. He was twenty-one years old, only five years younger than she, but one night as they were having a drink together, she asked him flirtatiously, 'What's a young boy like you doing with Dinah?' It had amused him to be considered a kid. Sassy admired his drumming and eventually called him to play for her; he didn't think he wanted to work with a singer again and passed the gig to another drummer. But in 1970, when Sassy called Jimmy Cobb again, he changed his mind and said he would try working for her. Her pianist then was Czechoslovakian-born Jan Hammer; the bassist was Gene Perla.

One of Jimmy's first gigs with her alarmed him. Not only did he have difficulty in learning to play slowly enough with his brushes when she sang very slow ballads, but his brushes stuck together as the group was performing in an open field on a damp night. No sound was coming from his brushes. He felt panicky, but she remained calm and didn't complain.

Cobb would work with Sassy for the rest of the decade. They would appear at the Fairmount hotels in New Orleans, San Francisco and Dallas. They played in Harrah's with Sammy Davis and the Cal-Neva lodge in Lake Tahoe, Nevada, and the Sahara in Las Vegas. There was nothing more difficult later than keeping track of when they had played where. Most years seemed very much alike, with the regular stops in hotels and festivals, and new clubs opening one year and closing the next. Cobb loved playing with her because she gave him so much room in which to improvise; he learned to play slowly and lightly and still sound tender on the ballads, and he played the untempo numbers the way he would have for any virtuosic horn player who could move with Sassy's lighning speed.

Jimmy remembered one engagement at a casino in Las Vegas in 1970. After a show, he went to the bar where he met a white man with a black beard, dark hair, and bright blue eyes. The man, who appeared to be in his thirties, said, 'I've been listening to Sarah Vaughan all my life.' He had first heard her records on the Dave Garroway show in Chicago. 'I sure would like to meet her.' Jimmy Cobb said, 'C'mon with me.' He took the man to meet Sassy and introduced them. When they started talking, Jimmy wandered away; by the time he walked back, she was inviting the man, whose name was Marshall Fisher, to come to her condominium in California. Jimmy knew something was definitely brewing.

Marshall didn't simply visit; he began living with her in California first in the condominium, then in the house near Benedict Canyon, 'a cute little house', according to Jimmy, a comfortable place without ostentation, big enough for Sassy, Marshall and Debby, who visited Sassy when she was off the road; otherwise Debby still lived with Ada Vaughan and went to school in Newark. Sassy was living with Marshall near Bendict Canyon during the earthquake in January 1971. It was her first earthquake, and it terrified her; afterward she always lived in dread of another one.

Marshall began working as her road manager and soon as her personal manager, too, together with James Harper, who stayed in the home office and was delighted to have Marshall help with business affairs and act as a buffer between himself and Sassy. Jimmy Cobb noticed that Marshall also tutored her in all sorts of things; he improved her vocabulary, teaching her the meanings of words she didn't know. And 'he taught her about the world and how things worked', Jimmy said. She began calling Marshall her 'guru'. He helped her with the practicalities of life; with his guidance, she soon acquired a sprawling house in Hidden Hills, California, a private community of estates set in bright green rolling hills covered with palm trees. The residents of Hidden Hills owned horses and made a pretty tableau, riding their cantering horses over the hills. There was a gate, a checkpoint through which visitors had to pass. Sassy's house had many large rooms and a big, square swimming pool. Those who had known Preacher Wells fairly well kept in mind that he, too, had helped Sassy organise herself, especially financially. 'After [Preacher], there was no more trouble with money,' recalled Joe Williams.

One day she telephoned Pumpkin and said, 'Hi, I've got someone I really want you to meet.' Aretha Landrum received the same kind of call. In 1970 Sassy decided to make a family-style Thanksgiving holiday with Aretha and her children at Aretha's house. Sassy told Aretha: 'Put on the pots, I'm bringing someone to meet you. You're going to love him.'

From the moment Aretha met Marshall, she liked him. There was just something nice about his manner with Sassy and everyone else. 'He fit right in. The racial difference didn't mean a thing to Sassy or any of us,' Aretha said. Even though Aretha had always liked Preacher, 'Marshall, Marshall, Marshall is my favourite,' she decided. Carmen McRae, who would soon meet Marshall, too, felt the same way about him. 'Marshall Fisher was a doll, a sweet man,' she said.

Although George Wein couldn't think of anything important Marshall might have given up to become part of Sassy's entourage – he was described in *Ebony* magazine as having had a food-and-drink concession in the Tropicana in Las Vegas, and others called him a restaurateur – to Sassy it didn't seem to matter what Marshall had done before he became her manager. He threw himself heart and soul into the new job. Sassy's career became the focal point of their friendship, which was after all her *raison d'être* and the reason Marshall had wanted to meet her. None of Sassy's intimates doubted for a moment that Marshall loved her, and they knew she cared for Marshall. Though reporters usually referred to him in print as her husband, he and Sassy never legally married. But he was treated as if he were her husband because he became 'a hustler for her *music*, not her *money*', as bassist Walter Booker, who would begin working for Sassy in 1976, summed it up. That was the consensus of all her friends and acquaintances. 'Marshall was a Midwesterner, and he was Protestant,' said Larry Clothier, who worked in Sassy's road company on and off between 1966 and 1985. Marshall was slimmer and about ten years younger than Sassy, but the age difference didn't seem obvious to Larry or anyone else because of Sassy's vitality.

As they travelled together, the word spread in the music world that Sassy had found a man who had her best interests at heart. Clothier, who would eventually start his own firm and manage Carmen McRae, grew to love Marshall as a brother. 'He [was] one of the nicest people in the world,' Larry said. 'Marshall would do anything for Sassy. Sassy wasn't used to that kind of treatment. Marshall would never have hit her in a million yers. He took care of her. Anything she wanted, he tried to do it or to get it for her.' In Larry's opinion, Marshall was the one responsible for encouraging Sassy to concentrate on performing with symphony orchestras, so that everyone would realise that she was the great singer that she and Marshall knew she was.

But neither of them could think of a way to interest symphony orchestras in performing with her. So she continued her usual routine. In 1971 pianist Jimmy Rowles, a friend of Sassy's who had recorded with her, referred pianist Bill Mays to her. She auditioned Mays for about eight bars on the piano at her house, then said, 'That's enough, you have the job, let's have lunch.' They set off for a year with her in the United States, Canada and England, together with Jimmy Cobb and bassist Bob Magnusson. Magnusson's lyrical playing particularly charmed Sassy, who cooed about him, 'Oh, he puts in those little flowers.' They played a series of concerts with the Duke Ellington band; those musicians learned Sassy's charts by ear speedily, then split up into sections to study their parts with Mercer Ellington. They ended up 'really cooking', Bill said; he was thrilled to have the chance to play with Duke's band, which travelled to England with Sassy's group to do another concert.

There was also an extraordinarily funny job at a racetrack in Chicago, where the group played between the fourth and fifth races. Everybody in the grandstand was much more interested in watching the races. Nobody in Sassy's group could figure out why the booker at the William Morris Agency had arranged that job for her.

Bill Mays thought that Sassy and Marshall Fisher seemed happy, and she was great fun to be with. After performances, her group usually congregated in her hotel suite, drank gin and tonic, and played a game called Spill and Spell, which resembled Scrabble. She had a sewing machine and passed the time by making clothes. She didn't always know what she was going to make when she started a garment. Sometimes she ended up with dresses and suits for friends – a caftan for Pumpkin, a red suit for Annie Ross, gowns for herself. Bill enjoyed the casual, intimate atmosphere she created for her group offstage. Onstage he revered her musical strength – her range, her pitch, her scatting and singing, and her stage presence. Bill took Jimmy Rowles's advice – learn the lyrics of the songs and, when he got a brilliant idea for the piano accompaniment, play only half of it; as Sassy's accompanist, Bill was never to show off everything he knew nor to try to play as a virtuoso. His role was to enhance Sassy and never to let his playing intrude upon what she was singing. Some musicians couldn't and didn't want to learn to make themselves subsidiary to a singer, but Bill enjoyed the challenge, because Sassy used difficult music, and she required her accompanists to play with excellence and to improvise. 'She didn't want to hear the same thing all the time,' Bill said. She made it clear that the more creative he was, the more he could inspire her.

But he was disappointed that Sassy's show was so 'set', he later said. 'She had hundreds of tunes in her book, some arranged by Bob James, Chick Corea, Jan Hammer, Jimmy Jones and Jimmy Rowles, but she kept using the same thirty or forty songs, including "Broken Hearted Melody" by public demand, all the time. She would always end her sets with "Tenderly".' The variety of her shows resided in her treatment of songs. Occasionally she began 'Stairway to the Stars' a cappella; when the group came in, the men had to guess which key she was in. But Bill was puzzled about why she limited herself to singing relatively few songs. As time went by, other musicians who worked with her or went to hear her sing would develop some theories – that she was tired, or bored; because she travelled constantly, she didn't have time to experiment with new material. None of the musicians who worked with her ever asked her why she rarely varied her repertoire. Pianist Carl Schroeder, who would work for her later, said that Sassy's show had to be planned so she could perform at a high pitch of artistry no matter what was going on behind the scenes. He remembered a time when the group flew from Los Angeles over the North Pole to Nice; then they only had time to eat, do a sound check, dress, and hit the stage. Sassy just didn't have the leeway to experiment with her repertoire. She had to be ready with a polished show for the kind of audiences who came out to see her perform.

As Bill was playing one of his last gigs for her at the Fairmount Hotel in Dallas in late 1971 or early 1972, he decided to shave off his beard and cut his long hair. He also took off his glasses for the performance. When Sassy walked onstage, singing as she usually did during an entrance, she didn't recognise him; she was so nonplussed that she stopped singing. Later they laughed about it.

He recorded one album with her – *A Time in My Life* – her first album for Mainstream, in November 1971. Ernie Wilkins, who had emerged from the Count Basie band, arranged and conducted the album. Bill very much wanted to record another album which Sassy was planning, but he wasn't invited to. He went to her hotel suite and asked her why. 'She told me she didn't have artistic control and couldn't choose her own personnel. I thought that couldn't be true. From my experience working in the recording studios in Los Angeles, I knew that artists had control. She insisted that she couldn't choose the personnel this time. And she didn't like me questioning her word on the matter,' he recalled. He decided to leave her group and go back to play in the California studios.

Bill recommended Carl Schroeder, a New York born pianist, to take his place in Sassy's group. Carl went to the Fairmount Hotel in Dallas to observe Sassy at work. Jerry Gray's orchestra, the house band at the hotel, had a drummer known as JZ. One evening, Sassy, Jimmy Cobb, Larry Clothier, who was passing through town, and Schroeder were sitting in the cocktail lounge, listening to Bill Mays play some classical music informally with the room's gypsy violinist. Then JZ took Bill's place at the piano and played a tune from *West Side Story*, supplying his own lyrics: 'There's a hope for us, Somewhere some dope for us, Lots of hashish and reefer, too, sweet cocaine, ooo ooo . . .' He went on with many choruses. Sassy's group howled with laughter. It was the sort of incident that often made people who worked or travelled with Sassy think that she had a special knack for finding things to laugh about. She was always out on the scene, where anything could happen.

For several reasons, Sassy's outlook was particularly upbeat at the time Bill Mays left her. Her new recording contract with Mainstream was very important to her. It was owned by Bobby Shad, the artists and repertoire man with whom she had worked so well at Mercury nearly twenty years before. Shad was highly regarded by people in the industry for his great skill in the recording studios – his ability to hear music, the *sine qua non* for a record producer. Shad had telephoned Sassy and invited her to record for his new company. After she did *A Time in My Life*, Bobby Shad arranged for her to record with four very gifted arrangers and conductors – Peter Matz, Michel Legrand, and the team of Jack Elliott and Allyn Ferguson. Bobby's wife, Molly, who had loved to go to Sassy's recording sessions at Mercury's studio, felt Bobby had pulled Sassy's career out of the doldrums; she hadn't had a recording contract for five years. 'My husband was one of the most important people in Sassy's career,' Molly later said. 'He knew what was good for her to sing.'

For her recording session with Michel Legrand, Bobby Shad presented her with 'Send in the Clowns', a Stephen Sondheim song from the show *A Little Night Music* on Broadway. She wasn't sure if she liked the song, but Shad insisted that she record it. Robert Richards talked with her by telephone on the day she recorded it. She said that she hadn't liked the other songs done that day very well but thought that 'Send in the Clowns' had possibilities; she wanted to get a copy of the sheet music to study on her own. 'She began exploring the song, originally recorded as an uptempo number, and decided that it was perfect for her; she could blend her jazz, pop, and operatic instincts for her interpretation, which she started to treat as her characteristic aria,' Robert said. It eventually replaced 'Tenderly' as her signature song.

Sassy, then forty-seven years old, made an indelible impression on a twenty-three-year-old recording engineer, Jimmy Gilroy, at the Record Plant studio between Eighth and Ninth avenues on West Forty-fourth Street in New York. She used to arrive with Bobby Shad to record voice-over sections for the music already recorded separately by the instrumentalists. The first day, arriving at about noon soon after she woke up, Sassy said to Jimmy, 'How are you doing, kid?' He said, 'All right.' Her voice was husky, 'a whisky voice,' he called it. She said, 'Kid, go out and get me some lemons and sugar.' When Jimmy came back, he cut the lemons in half for her; she dipped them in the sugar, bit into them, and sucked them. 'They cleared her throat instantly,' Jimmy noticed. He also was struck by the gentle way the producer talked to Sassy. 'He was always very careful and polite with her – "Sarah, will you please . . .?" "How about . . .?" She was into her "Sailor" mode for her replies.' For three days, she, the producer, and Jimmy went through the same routine, except that after the first day, Sassy shocked Jimmy by grabbing him playfully by his pants when she arrived for her wake-up lemons. 'It didn't make me nervous. In fact, it relaxed me,' he said. 'She was in command, and she obviously had no doubts about herself. Her physical appearance had nothing to do with my awe of her. It was her earthiness. The most amazing thing of all was her singing. She did every song in two or three takes. Within three days she finished the album. The job was over – too soon. I could have listened to her forever.' Jimmy had been accustomed to groups doing so many takes that albums stretched out to become three- to six-month projects.

Her Mainstream albums received praise throughout the early 1970s. Of her album *Feelin' Good*, John S. Wilson of the *New York Times* wrote that she had refined her style. Peter Matz, Michel Legrand and Allyn Ferguson, the arrangers, he wrote, had 'kept the strings lean and spare, allowing Miss Vaughan to kindle her own vitalising glow. There are no tricks this time, no affectations – just some of the most glorious pop singing you might ever expect to hear.' He picked out three songs, dissected them, and praised her feeling for the lyrics, too; those songs – 'Easy Evil', 'When You Think of It', and 'Alone Again (Naturally)' – exemplified what he called 'Miss Vaughan at her very best'.

Wherever she sang, she inspired awe. Laurie Johnston of the *New York Times* went to Sassy's concert with Dizzy Gillespie in an auditorium in the prison on Riker's Island – her first performance there – in May 1972. She glimpsed Sassy having her curly red wig adjusted by a blond valet in a chilly bathroom. She was complaining, 'My throat is killing me.' Then she went onstage, wearing a black choir robe-style gown with long slits in the skirt, Johnston wrote, and 'had most of the audience of five hundred on their feet with her first notes of "I'll Remember April".' Johnston herself loved the concert and asked some prisoners for their views. One said, 'I'm supposed to leave here Friday, and I'm going to be in the Rainbow Room every night.' Sassy was appearing there.

That summer George Wein moved the Newport Jazz Festival into New York City. The festival left Newport because it had started to attract hoodlums who started a mêlée at the resort, throwing bottles and disturbing the peace. Don Heckman reported in the *New York Times* that the star of the first Newport Jazz Festival in New York City at Philharmonic Hall in July 1972 was Sarah Vaughan. 'Beautifully gowned, vivaciously responsive to her audience, the divine Sarah sounded better than ever. Her instrument has gained in range and interpretive powers, she can scat sing with the best, and she is a good enough performer to balance her programme with old and new material.'

When Bob Magnusson, one of her favourite bassists, decided to leave the road and retire to San Diego for a while, Carl Schroeder called Ron McClure, then living in San Francisco, to join the group. McClure, committed to jazz experimentation, stayed for only six months. 'She was probably the greatest singer of all time,' he said. But she was a hard person to work with. 'I got off to a bad start in one of my first gigs with her, in the Troubadour Club in Los Angeles. One arrangement was difficult. I went to the wrong ending – the second ending instead of the first ending. Sassy said, "What's the matter, m.f.? Can't you read?"' The audience enjoyed it. 'She slaughtered me on stage,' Ron recalled. 'That was pretty cold. I thought she could have showed more patience on one of my first nights with her.'

Ron was also upset because 'she repeated the same twenty-two songs every night. I thought that the work came so easily to her that she didn't have to push herself anymore, and so she didn't. She did her hits. She was real lazy.'

He noticed that Sassy made mistakes, forgot lyrics, and covered up artfully for herself. Of course, she almost always put across the sense of the lyrics even if she forgot the exact words at times in performances. His embarrassment at having been corrected on the bandstand rankled in his memory.

Sassy's young blond valet took the brunt of her nervousness before she went onstage, McClure observed. 'She gorged herself on drugs, alcohol, cigarettes – and she sang like a bird. Just before showtime, she ate an amazing amount of food' – something most singers never dared to do – and then she would conduct a frantic search for her Alka-Seltzer, berating her valet all the while. '"I told you, dammit!" She treated him like a . . . prisoner,' Ron said. Annie Ross had always been astounded that Sassy never needed to warm up or rehearse before a show, and that she could eat a big meal. Those were little miracles, Annie thought. But Sassy's bouts of nerves and her appetite appalled Ron. 'We never hung out. She was nice when I was in the room. Once she said I sounded good,' he recalled. But they never were close. He didn't become friendly with Marshall Fisher, either. 'I talked with him about the business. He paid the bills. He gave me wake-up calls. I never saw her relationship with Marshall Fisher as being very warm. Marshall loved her singing more than anything else, I think. I don't know if it was a romantic, sexual love . . . She might have just been complacent.'

Hugh Wyatt of the *Daily News* in New York noticed that Sassy placed extraordinary demands on her accompanists, Schroeder, McClure and Cobb, when she performed at the Copacabana in March 1973, her first engagement there since she had sung at the club with the John Kirby sextet in 1947. McClure played his bass with the bow – a technique called arcoing – for the introduction to the romantic 'Rainy Days and Mondays', and Sassy's interpretation was so intensely moving that 'women in the audiences screamed in appreciation', Wyatt wrote. John S. Wilson of the *New York Times* liked it when she told the audience she was going to sing 'a little bit of jazz' and performed only with her trio, not the Copa's musicians. The simpler the setting, Wilson said, the easier it was to hear her undiluted virtuosity. He loved 'Rainy Days and Mondays' and another slow ballad, 'My Funny Valentine'. For 'Street of Dreams', she sat down to play her own piano accompaniment. And she sang 'Everything I Have is Yours' a cappella to satisfy a request from the audience, though she had no arrangement for the tune and scatted the lyrics, which she didn't know. 'Miss Vaughan seems to be bringing to this engagement a summation of the experience she has gained during the twenty-six years since she last was there, a very varied and rounded display of a talent that has grown steadily over those years,' Wilson wrote.

John Rockwell, reviewing Sassy and her trio in concert with Michel Legrand's orchestra at Carnegie Hall in July 1973 (on the same bill with tenor saxophonist Stan Getz), remarked in the *New York Times* on the striking similarity of Sassy's and Getz's sounds; Getz was known above all as a beautifully melodic, romantic player. Jimmy Cobb, too, thought that Sassy reminded him of a saxophone, because she had so much power and control of her voice.

Despite all the glamour of the engagements, Ron McClure gave his notice and was replaced by John Gianelli, who prepared to go with Sassy's group to Tokyo.

Sassy moved on without worrying about Ron's fate. Bob Shad arranged for her to record a beautiful album, *Live in Japan*, in perform-ance with her trio, Schroeder, Gianelli and Cobb, at the Sun Plaza Hotel in Tokyo on 24 September 1973. She sang several of her favourite songs, 'A Foggy Day', 'Misty', 'Wave', 'Round Midnight', 'Summer-time', which Carl Schroeder would one day advise her to sing a cappella to the delight of audiences, and 'Poor Butterfly', among the more than two dozen tunes recorded that day. As she was singing 'Poor Butterfly', a young Japanese woman ran on to the stage, hugged Sassy around the waist, and hung on throughout the entire song. Sassy kept singing right through the incident. Jimmy Cobb watched her stunning sangfroid with fascination.

He also marvelled at her self-confidence soon afterwards onstage in Lake Tahoe, Nevada. The group was playing with the house band, which used such a fast tempo that Sassy could barely get the words out. Afterward, she lay down flat on her back on the floor and pretended to have fainted. She was playful that way, playful all the way; she wasn't shy onstage at all. Now she often sang her old favourite, 'If You Could See Me Now'; as she grew older, the song seemed to become especially apt, for she had metamorphosed in every way into a daring leader.

After the great success of the Tokyo concert, Sassy returned to the United States by way of London, where a promoter arranged a concert for her at the Victoria Palace Theatre. It was followed by a reception at Ronnie Scott's jazz club in Soho. Stan Britt, a Briton who was compiling interviews with American jazz musicians, taped a forty-five-minute interview with her. 'She was very shy and diffident to begin with but halfway through she opened up, and she gave one of her funny little laughs at the end,' he said. He was happy to capture her characteristic, high-pitched giggle on tape. She didn't introduce Marshall Fisher, but Stan Britt noticed 'a white man. He kept in the background and seemed cheery. He asked was she all right and did she want a drink.' Britt had no idea that Marshall was her lover.

In 1973, Asbury Vaughan died. Sassy went back to Newark to the First Mount Zion Baptist Church, and she sang 'The Lord's Prayer' at his funeral. Then Sassy convinced her mother to move to her house in Hidden Hills, promising that her friends could fly to California to visit often. Sassy was going to buy their plane tickets. Ada agreed, packed everything, and took Debby and Sassy's stepsister, Donna. There the four women tried to get along. 'She respected her mother. That was the respect of that time, and Sarah never lost it,' Pumpkin said. 'Sarah's roots were her survival.'

Sassy was very protective of her family, taking a deep interest in the friends Debby found in Hidden Hills, her social life, the hours she would come home, and her activities in school.

Settling her family in her house, Sassy soon went on the road again, taking Pumpkin to Nice, France, for an engagement. She was still girlish and impressionable, he recalled. When Omar Sharif walked through the Sporting Club restaurant they were in, Sassy said, 'Ooooh, that's Omar Sharif!' She seemed very flustered, like a teenager hoping to get a celebrity's autograph. Duke Ellington's former singer, the handsome romantic baritone Herb Jeffries, had a similar effect on her when she saw him in that restaurant.

In 1974, Sassy had a chance to record with Jimmy Rowles and his quintet; Jimmy arranged all the songs, including 'Morning Star', his own tune with lyrics written by Johnny Mercer. 'I had a gig at Playa del Rey,' Jimmy recalled. 'And all of a sudden, here [Sassy] comes, all the time, hanging out with Carmen. Every place I went with my trio, the two of them would come.' They sang with Jimmy's group. 'My wife and I became close friends with Sassy and Marshall. And it was all music,' Jimmy recalled about the times when they had dinner together, and she sat down and played the piano. Frequently she called him to play for her. Once during a performance in Houston, Texas, she whispered to him, 'Do you know "East of the Sun"?' He said, 'Yes.' She said, 'Find a key quick while they're still clapping.' One of his favourite songs was 'Icy Stone', which Sassy sang on a Mainstream album. 'The goose pimples [went] all over the room' when she sang that song, Jimmy always felt.

Then Sassy stopped recording for Mainstream. According to Molly Shad, the end came because of an argument over a photograph; 'Sassy sued us for some kind of [album] cover that Bobby didn't really have control over. She just tried to find problems all the time.' According to an Associated Press story in March 1975, Sassy sued Mainstream Records for $216,000: 'Miss Vaughan's suit alleges that under her contract, the New York record company and its president, Robert Shad, owe her more than $15,000. She seeks $200,000 in general and punitive damages.' Molly held Marshall responsible for tensions between Sassy and Bob Shad. 'Marshall wanted total control,' Molly said. 'He even wanted to produce a record. Bobby told him to do it, but he didn't know how. Sassy never needed anyone telling her what to do. She just needed someone to keep her from falling through the cracks. But she wasn't strong enough,' Molly said, and was 'too influenced by the men in her life'. Bobby Shad always tried to keep Sassy happy, Molly reminisced after her husband's death, 'because you got the most out of her when you kept her happy. He never blamed the artists. He took the blame himself and accepted the bad part of it. He always did that for all artists,' she said.

Sassy would go without a record contract for another three years.

TEN

The Divine One Becomes a Concert Artist

Michael Tilson Thomas, then the conductor of the Buffalo Symphony Orchestra in New York, was thinking about Sassy. Only twenty-nine years old in 1974, he had heard many of her great recordings over the years. From their early years in Brooklyn, Michael's father and uncles had personal connections to the Gershwins – Michael's grandfather, Boris Tomashefsy, was a star in the Yiddish theatre – so Michael was particularly sensitive to Gershwin's music. Michael, who grew up listening to all sorts of music – Bach, Stravinsky, Sarah Vaughan and George Gershwin – had always thought that Sarah had the greatest voice of all the jazz singers. It had suppleness and flexibility, and she kept her voice in astounding shape. It had become a bit lower over the years, that was true, but he noticed 'the gorgeousness of her voice had stayed very much the same; that was remarkable, considering all the smoking and everything else she did', he later said.

He was planning a Gershwin show with the Los Angeles Philharmonic for the Hollywood Bowl in 1974. If it was to be a real Gershwin show, it should have a vocalist along with the orchestra music and piano pieces he planned to include. Who could sing this music? If anyone could perform the music with brilliance and style, it was Sarah Vaughan, 'obviously', he told himself. Very often when people performed Gershwin's music, they made it less interesting than the original music. He knew that Sassy would understand Gershwin's harmonies and remain true to their essence while embellishing them with her unique style and taste.

So Michael, then living in Los Angeles, his hometown, contacted

Sassy in Hidden Hills; even her location was convenient for rehearsals with him. She gave him the business card that said 'The Devine One' – a charming touch, Michael thought, though he didn't notice the purposeful misspelling which she affected to sass the language. The card had the number for her office, called The Devine One Corporation, which she had set up in the early 1970s in a townhouse that she bought on Canon Drive parallel to Rodeo Drive in a luxurious area of Beverly Hills. 'She liked to go and hang out there and have another place to be private,' recalled Robert Richards about the office.

Marty Paich became the arranger for the Gershwin project. He, Michael and Sassy met for sessions at Sassy's house. 'We sketched out what the tunes would be, how the medleys would work, and what could happen,' Michael said. 'Right away I was happy because the arrangements were rich, and Sassy's ideas were terrific.' Experienced jazz musicians were hired – pianist Dave Grusin, bassist Ray Brown, drummer Shelly Manne, saxophonist Bill Perkins, and Pete Cristlieb on tenor saxophone. They made the orchestra swing.

'She was very, very nervous, she could get so nervous,' Michael said. 'We were going to do a medley that began with "Summertime". I was supposed to go onstage and start the orchestra, and from offstage Sassy was supposed to sing and then walk onstage singing "Summertime". The first time we did it, from offstage came this strangled squeak, which was Sassy trying to get some notes out. Standing offstage, she was paralysed with fright. We realised that she had to overcome that moment of walking onstage. She was really amazed [to be] doing this with a big orchestra.

'When we worked together at her Hidden Hills house, I loved to look at her scrapbooks. She had collected many photographs of her early years with the Hines band and of herself with friends in Harlem clubs, especially in after-hours party scenes. Everyone looked so elegant to me. The style and details of the dresses and suits, the hats, the clubs, everything in the pictures fascinated me. I never got tired of looking at them. In one photo, she was seated at a table in a club with Dizzy Gillespie and some very good-looking people. She was very thin and wore a hat that amazed me. It was really just the top half of a picture frame, a stiff piece of material that looked like something you could put plants on. It went up one side of her head, then across her head in a stiff line, and then down the other side of her head. The hat had no substance other than as a frame for her face, and all around the material, she had curls in an elaborately done hairstyle. When I looked at those pictures, I thought she must have had very happy memories of that time in her life.'

During preparation time for the concert, she autographed a photograph of herself and Michael at the piano in a rehearsal, 'Oh, Michael, do you think it's going to work? Let us pray.'

In the end, they enjoyed working together for the show and the critical acclaim very much. Sassy did not perform the whole concert. She opened with the 'Summertime' medley, which included 'It Ain't Necessarily So' and 'I Loves You, Porgy'. Later in the concert she did a medley of 'But Not for Me', 'Our Love Is Here to Stay', 'Embraceable You', and 'Someone to Watch Over Me'; then, as a separate piece, she sang 'The Man I Love', ending with a 'huge, high note', recalled Robert Richards, who travelled from New York to California especially for the concert. She closed with 'A Foggy Day'and 'I've Got a Crush On You'. All these songs she used as part of her regular repertoire in many shows for the rest of her life.

The thrill of making music together whetted Michael's and Sassy's appetites to work together more. Right after the Hollywood Bowl concert, her group went to Buffalo to perform with Michael and the Buffalo Symphony Orchestra. Then Sassy, her trio – Ray Brown on bass, with Jimmy Cobb and Carl Schroeder in 1974 – and Michael moved on to the road, playing with symphony orchestras in several cities. Michael and Sassy added more Gershwin songs, some of which they performed as duos with Michael playing the piano and Sassy singing. They changed 'The Man I Love' radically and would eventually record a highly embellished version for Columbia. They worked ou 'Sweet and Low Down' and 'Do It Again'. Over the years, they developed an all-Gershwin show for Sassy, with new songs and new variations added to keep themselves interested. Michael thought her trio was one of the hippest he had ever heard; it was paradise for him to hear those people make music together.

Michael met Marshall Fisher and many of the business people who worked for Sassy. Sassy also brought some close friends along with her on the road from time to time. But Michael didn't involve himself particularly in their personal lives; he was never interested in anyone but Sassy. He was also impressed by the people who attended her shows and visited with her backstage. Joni Mitchell, then at the height of her fame, arrived one night. After Joni left, Sassy said to Michael and Carl Schroeder, 'This blonde girl was here and said all these nice things.' Carl and Michael had to explain to her who Joni Mitchell was and that she was actually quite good.

After the performances that he, Sassy, and her trios played, they got together backstage for a little musical fun. 'I'd play Berg, Schoenberg and Stravinsky. I remember playing the last two or three minutes of Berg's Violin Concerto with its wonderfully evolved chords that are as complicated, as beautiful, and as painful as any chords that exist in classical repertory. It's actually harmonisation of a very simple little Bach melody, and the harmonies are way out there. And each time I played it, they'd say, "*Oh no!* Say it isn't so, Michael. Have mercy!" The chords sounded bizarre to the musicians, even though they had grown up loving bebop.

'We laughed, cried, and played another chord. We played music back and forth for one another,' Michael recalled. She teased him about being her friend from outer space, because he did so much work in contemporary and avant-garde music. Often she said to him, 'Michael, when you play those chords, I just go out so far, and when you stop playing, I come back to the room, and I think: I don't know where I've been for the last five minutes.' He knew she was half putting him on and having a good time doing it. Learning that Sassy loved to hang out, tell old stories, and hear new music, any kind of music, he played all sorts of curiosities for her, from the classical repertoire to vaudeville. Sassy, for one, was very familiar with European classical music from her earliest piano lessons. But Berg was a long way from Chopin, Debussy – and Bird; Bird didn't play atonal, cacophonous music. And neither did Sassy or any of the musicians in her groups when they played with her.

Carl Schroeder played Sassy's repertoire exceptionally well, Michael thought; Carl was an 'extraordinary musical intelligence, very special', because he had a sophisticated perspective on classical and all music, 'an extremely evolved view', Michael thought. Carl himself stated his forte bluntly: 'I could swing. Michael couldn't swing.' Carl had actually studied music formally for only a year and a half at the Berklee School of Music in Boston and then had begun working professionally, first with blues groups, then with rhythm-and-blues groups, and then with jazz. Carl had accompanied many singers. He knew exactly how to space out the chords he used for Sassy; his timing for the chords was 'incomparable', Michael thought. 'Carl knew her voice was rich, so he played few notes and spaced his few chords over a wide range; he gave her the maximum amount of play area' – space in which she could sing her own embellishments without any intrusion from the accompaniment. 'A typical arranger would just lay down a big, rich chord and say to himself, well, this is rich, and her voice sounds rich, so therefore it will all work together. Carl knew exactly what she was thinking when she was straight and when she sang far out.'

Michael discovered that she alternated between moments of tremendous ambition, when she said something like, 'I want to be an opera star, and this should happen, and that', and moments when she sloughed off the work. 'She wasn't that compulsive as a worker,' Michael observed. 'I don't want to say that she was lazy, but it was so easy for her to be spontaneous and leap into the great unknown, and she had enough material to work with for what she wanted to do with her voice. That was why she limited her repertoire, I believe. And she didn't have to practise rigorously.' Michael would work with her several times throughout the 1970s. 'More and more, as the years went by, she used to say to me, "I don't really want to leave my pink bedroom. I'm very happy here with my spinet, my poodles, and my life. I deserve to be here."

'When she travelled, she could be so elated by her show,' Michael observed. 'But the circumstances of her life on the road were punishing. And, because for many years in the business, people hadn't treated her or any jazz artist with the respect and reverence that they should have had, she felt some bitterness,' Michael learned, referring especially to the racial prejudice she encountered. 'She had also endured years of record companies and promoters taking advantage of her,' he remembered her telling him. And so, he said, 'she was often looking to see if there would be a problem, "Oh, here's a problem, the limo is late, and this means these people aren't taking me seriously" '. That was her attitude. She became very agitated at such times. So there was the joy of working with great groups weighed against the hassles of travelling. It was a chancy, annoying thing for anyone in music to do, travel,' he said – and he agreed with her. 'Furthermore, she was trying to [make] her own business arrangements, and the people she hired to help her – well, maybe her people were nice folks, but she didn't pick the most official or detail-obsessed staffers. So problems did arise about the way things ran . . . I could understand her point of view. On the one hand, musicians want to feel good with the people they have around them on the road and have the company [be] friendly, but maybe friends aren't so efficient and organised. That conflict exists for everyone.'

Tilson Thomas discovered that Sassy had an unusual way of working out a song. He would play a minimal amount of accompaniment, just enough to support her. She would sing a song a few times in an absolutely straight, square way, exactly as it was written on the sheet music. Then she would suddenly take one little phrase out, inventing her own embellishments; then she would go back to the straight version, take out another phrase, and do that again and again, exploring. It was as if she was saying to herself, 'If I take that out here, that happens, and I have these options. And if I go there, I have these options. But if I just stay straight here, I could move here instead.' Also, in various performances, with her trio and with orchestras to come in her future, she would find a riff or an idea that she liked and, after the performance, she would go back to that and develop it for future performances. Other times she went back to the beginning with a song and sang it straight and explored it again to find another way to sing it. Michael thought that was the way she kept her music fresh for herself.

Sassy had played no concerts with symphony orchestras at all when Schroeder first joined her. Throughout the 1970s, while Schroeder was in her group, and through the 1980s, too, the trio worked, sometimes with Michael Tilson Thomas, other times on their own, integrated into orchestras, including the Los Angeles Symphony Orhcestra at the Music Center with Michel Legrand conducting in 1975, the Philadelphia Symphony, the Chicago Symphony, the Washington National Symphony at the John F. Kennedy Center in 1975 and 1976, the San Francisco Symphony, the Hollywood Symphony at the Hollywood Bowl, the San Diego, Denver, and Kansas City symphonies, and many regional orchestras.

On the night of a performance in Kansas City, a terrific snowstorm halted transportation; only a dozen musicians and fifty people in the audience showed up. Still Sassy sang as if there were a full symphony behind her and a packed house. In other settings, she also sang magnificently despite musical mishaps, including conductors who, unlike Michael Tilson Thomas, couldn't appreciate what Sassy was doing. One European-trained Frenchman working with a Midwestern symphony orchestra announced to Sassy that he had taken her charts and corrected all the 'bad' notes. 'He had actually taken out all the "blue" notes and made them into major triads, so that the music ended up sounding like Schubert,' Carl Schroeder recalled with wry amusement. 'In fact, there were no "bad" notes. So we're rehearsing it, and we come to this real sexy chord, and all of a sudden there's this nice plain-vanilla major triad, and [the conductor] says, "Oh, yes, there's a wrong note there. I had to feex it." ' 'Put back the funk,' Schroeder told him. The symphony organisations would often put assistant conductors in charge of Sassy's dates, and the assistants, who had strict European training and were largely unfamiliar with jazz, constantly tried to take out 'wrong' notes – 'the *beautiful blues* sound', Schroeder said.

Schroeder wrote some 'uptempo stuff' for her to sing with the symphonies. 'She wanted me to challenge her. The question was: how much? "Excite me," she said. "If I like it, I'll use it."' Her razor-sharp intonation inspired awe in symphony players. 'She could nail it dead-on every time,' Schroeder said. 'For the symphony guys, that's their whole concern, to play in tune. They struggled to do it, while she did it so easily,' he observed. 'Then they would tell me how astoundingly well Sarah Vaughan was singing. To us it was just another good night with Sass. The symphony guys couldn't swing, and they couldn't improvise off a blues chord to save their lives, and they couldn't scat. Some of them tried to scat with meaningless results for Sassy's benefit. We just looked at them politely.'

In October 1974, Shaun Considine, reviewing records in the *New York Times*, praised several of Sassy's old albums, calling *After Hours*, *Linger Awhile*, *Sassy*, *The Mancini Songbook* and *Misty* 'among the most innovative and the most exhilarating ever recorded'. All this was a prelude to praising the album *Sarah Vaughan and the Jimmy Rowles Quintet*, released that fall by Mainstream. 'If possible her voice is richer than before. She still uses it like an instrument, weaving in and out of the melody of "A House Is Not a Home", bending the low notes of "Morning Star", and extending the highs of "That Face", purring, scatting and soaring, seemingly effortless but always in control, backed by five of the finest musicians on the jazz scene today. First and foremost, Miss Vaughan is an interpreter of melody; the lyrics come second (and do not suffer for it).' Considine ended by saying that 'some legends are indestructible, thank God'.

ELEVEN

Contemplating Posterity

Concentrating on personal appearances, Sassy stayed very busy. In 1974 she took her trio nearly round the world, first working in a Holiday Inn in Maseru, Lesotho, in South Africa, then playing in Japan, Hong Kong and Europe, and flying back to South Africa to a Holiday Inn in Swaziland. The itinerary was astounding enough; on top of it, Jimmy Cobb recalled wild incidents that befell the group. In an Italian city, they were booked to play a free concert outdoors in a field. Although tuxedos constituted uniforms for the musicians, they were told not to wear them that night because the audience comprised socialists or some group of people who embraced a political philosophy that eschewed tuxedos. Someone helped Jimmy carry his drums to the stadium in the field. When they reached the gate, the helper said he wasn't going any further; he was afraid of the unruly people in the audience. Jimmy said, 'Man, what am I doing here? If you Italians are afraid, why am I going in here?' He had to carry his drum set alone. While the concert was in progress, one man in the audience jumped up in front of the stage, 'buck naked and screaming', Jimmy said. Sassy asked him, 'Did you see that?' Yes, that guy's crazy,' Jimmy answered in his usual soft-voiced, low-key way. He kept playing. The group made it through the concert and quickly left the field.

In December 1974, she went on a jazz cruise on the SS *Rotterdam* – a cruise to the Bahamas for which a group of jazz artists was entertainment. Julian 'Cannonball' Adderley's group was also working on the ship, with his bassist, Walter Booker, whom everyone called 'Bookie'; a one-time medical student, he had quit school to concentrate on playing the bass. Tall and powerful, with 'a ferocious rhythmic drive', as Carl Schroeder said, he became one of Sassy's hanging-out buddies. 'She had many parties in her cabin,' recalled Larry Clothier, who went along on the cruise as part of Sassy's road staff. On the way back to the United States, the ship picked up the Basie band in Bermuda. Nobody was getting any sleep because everyone wanted to party together.

One night when Larry, Booker, Marshall and Sassy, among others, were having drinks and telling jokes in her room, the phone rang. Someone said it was the White House calling for Marshall Fisher. thinking it was a prank, Marshall took the phone. But it really was the White House. Sassy was invited to go to Fort-de-France, Martinique, to entertain President Gerald Ford and France's President Giscard d'Estaing, who were meeting on the island.

At first Sassy was told she would fly on a presidential jet, but when she arrived in New York, she found out that the government had chartered a Pan Am 707 for her and her entourage, Larry, Marshall, Jimmy Cobb, Carl Schroeder and bassist Frank De La Rosa. Without any rest period, they boarded the plane, landed in Martinique at midnight, and were driven to the Hotel Meridien, across the bay from Fort-de-France. Sassy and her group had the feeling they were isolated in the countryside; at first they didn't know that the hotel had been cleared of all guests, and that was why it was eerily quiet. They woke up to find that only the two presidents and their staffs were staying there. For the most part, they spent their time around the hotel pool, relaxing with President Ford and President d'Estaing.

The *New York Times*'s John Herbers painted a picture of the idyllic setting: 'Previous meetings . . . between American and French heads of state have been held in more austere places such as Iceland . . . President Ford, who has been without his own pool since he moved to the White House four months ago, went swimming in the evening and morning and at noon . . . "This is beautiful," said Mr Ford. "I love to swim." . . . At the dinner tonight, Sarah Vaughan, the American singer, who was brought here by President Ford, provided the entertainment. After two days of French and Caribbean food, the menu for the dinner sponsored by the United States was California cucumber soup, New York sirloin steak, Florida corn on the cob, Idaho baked potatoes, Boston lettuce, Iowa blue cheese, ice-cream and coffee. Mr Ford is to return to Washington tomorrow, after another brief conference . . . and, undoubtedly, further swims.'

'We flew back to New York in David Rockefeller's jet,' Larry recalled; it was a trip that he and Sassy savoured.

That year, a congressman from California, Thomas M. Rees, praised her voice in a speech in the House, saying, 'Sarah Vaughan has consistently provided the world with the very best in entertainment. For many years she has been an ambassador of good will for the United States, sharing her joyful gift of talent with people in the Orient, in Europe, in South America, in Australia – indeed just about wherever people walk on this earth . . . If music is, indeed, the universal language, "the Divine Sarah" is indeed a linguist without peer . . .'

Whenever she visited New York, she liked to hang out with Booker, with whom she had become friendly on the SS *Rotterdam* cruise. He was living in an apartment with an acoustic recording studio, which he had built with his own hands. They hung out together for days at a time, not for romance but for eating, drinking, smoking and talking about music and life. Sassy dabbled at playing the piano in Walter's studio – very impressively, he thought. She also sang some songs, some her original compositions, which he taped; nothing was finished or polished. Discussing her past husbands and lovers, 'she said she felt lucky to have gotten away from them', Booker recalled. She talked about her friendship with Billy Eckstine. (When Booker later played in a gig with Sassy and B on New York's PBS station, Booker observed: 'The way she treated him and looked at him made me realise that she had more respect for him as a singer and a person than for anyone else she knew.') Booker had the constitution and inclination to keep up with Sassy for a long night; from his medical school days, he had learned how to revive himself in the light of dawn.

Jimmy Cobb, who liked a quiet, regular life-style, remembered how she and one of Booker's predecessors had decided to hang out together one night after a gig at Lake Tahoe. 'The next afternoon, I went to her suite. She was gone, still having a party someplace, but the bassist was stretched out asleep on a couch in the living-room. He was still wearing his tuxedo from the night before.' A man had to be physically strong to try to keep up with Sassy, even though she was fifty years old.

Sassy appeared at the St Regis Maisonette Room in New York in January 1975. John S. Wilson, reviewing her, quibbled with a few of her stylings only because he was comparing them to others which he thought were superb. 'On some of her songs – "My Funny Valentine", "Fly Me to the Moon", "Rainy Days and Mondays" – the richness and colour of her voice and her exquisite control of dynamics are used to produce brilliant interpretations. Yet on other songs – "Tonight", "On a Clear Day", "A Foggy Day" – the results are disappointingly superficial. But the disappointment occurs of course only because of the startling evidence of her capabilities on other songs.'

Right after her appearance at the St Regis, she flew to Los Angeles, where she heard Leontyne Price in recital at the Chandler Pavilion. Accompanying Sassy were Marshall Fisher, Larry Clothier, and pianist Nat Pierce's ex-wife Sylvia, a friend of Sassy's. Sitting in the fourth row centre, Sassy's friends were struck by the similarities in stage bearing between Sassy and Leontyne – the way they stood, held their heads, moved their mouths. Leontyne Price had studied for years, Sassy never at all. Though Sassy's friends realised they couldn't compare the very different singers, Larry and Marshall knew that Sassy was as great in her improvisatory art as Leontyne was in the field of classical music. When they went backstage after the recital, Sassy lingered for fifteen minutes, chatting alone with Leontyne, while Marshall and Larry waited outside the dressing room. The men became enthusiastic about the idea of arranging a recital for Sassy with Leontyne. Then Sassy raved about the beauty and strength of Price's voice to Carl Schroeder; from her he learned that she envisioned herself performing a recital with Leontyne. Several times Sassy's offices tried to arrange it, but nothing ever came of the efforts. Leontyne Price didn't have time, her business people said.

In 1975 *Ebony* magazine published a story by Louis Robinson, who visited Sassy's Hidden Hills house to interview her and found it full of friends and family. He recapitulated her career and put her current musical situation in perspective. 'The problem with Sarah Vaughan is that she is a queen without a country, so she must reign over a kingdom populated merely by those with the sensitivity, taste and musical knowledge to appreciate the vocal miracles she performs night after night, year after year. Overshadowed by such comparatively *nouvelles* sovereignties as Nancy Wilson and Diana Ross – themselves completely gifted singers – and dethroned by the thoroughly confusing electronics coup of the 1960s that thrust much mediocrity into the power echelons of the top 40, the Divine Sarah nevertheless endures at age fifty, sounding, some say, the best she ever has. The delicious jazz elegance of Sarah Vaughan has always been a little too rich for the masses to digest . . . Now it's almost as if she exists in the wrong era . . . her style is not one to go with electrified guitars, eight thousand watts of amplification, and a lyric which can only be understood if you're reading along on the record jacket. Thus an entire generation, weaned at a decibel level which threatens to make us all as deaf as Beethoven, has never even *heard* Sarah.'

He then recounted some of the highlights of her life, from the Earl Hines band to the praise from Congressman Rees. She had 'a voice which citizens of the African country of Lesotho travelled a thousand miles to hear. Nevertheless it was a voice which came into the declining era of jazz, clashing head-on with Elvis Presley, Bill Haley and the Comets, the Beatles, and all – both good and bad – who were to follow. But there are no sad songs to be sung for Sarah.' Robinson explained that even though she was fifty, she was serene in her career and happy in her personal life with Marshall Fisher, whom Robinson called 'her third husband'.

'I'm happier than ever and it shows while I'm on the stage,' Sassy told Robinson. 'That's because my personal life is wonderful . . . a great husband, a loving mother . . . and daughter . . . and many close friends. All of this has helped me to be more at ease with the public than ever. Today I talk to people and they talk to me. I love them and I feel their love for me.' Robinson mentioned that the worst conditions of segregation had changed for Sassy, too, when she travelled on the road. The bookings were now chosen with care and discernment. 'She spends two-thirds to three-quarters of the year on the road, playing prestigious dates . . . She is basically into concerts now because they offer more money for less work (her income runs into six figures annually). "You can make more for three concerts than you can in a week in nightclubs," Sarah commented. "I try to avoid them." ' Robinson also mentioned her concert at the Monterey Jazz Festival in California the previous summer, when he saw her in performance singing 'I'll Remember April', 'I've Got It Bad and That Ain't Good' – 'bringing "wows" from the crowd' – then 'A Foggy Day (in London Town)' and an almost operatic 'My Funny Valentine'. 'Now the crowd was totally hers. But backstage her husband was perturbed over the mikes. 'The biggest single problem in this business is sound,' he grumbled.

'Fisher appears to be almost totally concerned with Sarah's career. "It's a travesty to take an instrument like that and just let her do those dumb sounds," he says of such lyrics as "Broken Hearted Melody", and explains further that "hit" is "a dirty word around us". As a result of what Fisher and Miss Vaughan consider to be bad handling on the part of record companies, she did not have a record contract for five years (before Mainstream), and Marshall says, "We may be out of it five years again." And he doesn't like that entertainer's pot-of-gold called Las Vegas, with its astronomical salaries. "The only reason to play Vegas is for the money. There's no soul in Vegas." He also thought that most nightclubs were soulless. "It's a case of take the money and run," explains Fisher. "But we don't like to do that because it's a ripoff on the customers. It's a ripoff on Sarah because she is not presented

properly.'" Robinson finished by saying, 'Her husband is determined
to protect [her place in musical history] through her golden years by
seeing that she is properly represented.' The exorbitantly nurturing
Fisher told Robinson, 'It's time for Sarah to leave Sarah to posterity.
There's only one of her. There's nobody coming up like her. There
possibly never will be.'

Ebony published photos of Sassy singing at an annual jazz party
thrown in Colorado Springs, Colorado, and also at home with ten
friends, among them bassist Red Callender, Carl Schroeder, trumpeter
Al Aarons, and with her mother in the kitchen, cooking a huge panful
of food for all her friends to eat at the commodious dining table. Also
in the picture is Debby, a slender, very pretty teenager with chiselled
features and a sweet, pensive expression. Sassy herself looked relaxed
and natural, wearing a sleeveless, flowing dress that hid her ripening
contours.

Louis Robinson wrote that Marshall had 'married' his idol. Robert
Richards later said, 'I think that Marshall Fisher was probably the best
friend she ever had, because he cared about her and her career. So many
of her friends came to the parties and had no interest in her performances, and they never evinced any interest in anything except that she
was a star. Some of them never even went to see her perform. She and
Marshall had a pure love for each other.' Molly Shad thought that Sassy
didn't have an easy time of it, travelling around the country in the
1970s with 'a white man'.

Sassy toured in Europe that year and made a recording called *Jazz
Jamboree*, with Carl Schroeder, Bob Magnusson back from his leave of
absence in San Diego, and Jimmy Cobb, on the Polish Pronit label –
certainly an obscure label guaranteed to have little or no circulation in
the United States. She sang ten of her usual standards – 'Tenderly',
'Round Midnight', and 'A Foggy Day' among them. That year, too,
she toured in the Caribbean, including Haiti, taking Pumpkin along.
By now he was beginning to fill up a second passport.

At the Newport Jazz Festival in 1977, John S. Wilson wrote, she
sounded even better than the previous year, citing 'the electrifying
beauty of her voice on "Poor Butterfly", a seemingly unlikely song for
Miss Vaughan that she turned into a definitive vehicle for her talents'.
If Wilson had any reservations about Sassy's performances, they were
usually that she didn't settle down to do her best work until she had
warmed up with a few songs.

About Sassy's outdoor concert on 4 July 1976 with the American
Symphony Orchestra at Battery Park City in New York, Peter G.

Davis wrote in the *New York Times*, 'The most rapturous applause was reserved for Sarah Vaughan's inimitable, slow-motion delivery of "The Lord's Prayer" and "America (the Beautiful)" – unlikely material for Miss Vaughan, perhaps, but still an extraordinary display of vocal control and jazz embellishment.' The previous night she had received an ovation for 'America' with the same orchestra at Carnegie Hall.

She headlined with Harry James at the three-thousand-seat Valley Forge Music Fair in the summer of 1976, winning praise for her a cappella interpretation of 'Summertime', a song with which she often moved people to tears, even if the critics didn't mention that proof of her power, and she performed with Woody Herman and His Thundering Herd in September 1976 at the Westbury Music Fair on Long Island. Woody and Sassy had already performed together in California. She sang to benefit the Reverend John Garcia Gensel's Duke Ellington Center at St Peter's Lutheran Church in New York, and for Rahsaan Roland Kirk, a remarkable saxophonist who had then recently suffered a stroke. He later died young. Sassy sang with Count Basie, Dizzy Gillespie, pianist Bill Evans, drummer Elvin Jones, bassist Eddie Gomez, saxophonists Lee Konitz and Warne Marsh, trumpeters Freddie Hubbard and Jon Faddis, Dizzy's protégé, saxophonist Sonny Stitt, Eddie 'Lockjaw' Davis, with an unusual baritone sound to his tenor sax, reeds player Anthony Braxton, bassist and composer Charles Mingus, the bassist George Duvivier, and drummers Tony Williams and Art Blakey. Though paralysed on one side and able to work with only one hand, the heroic Kirk played saxophone for his own benefit.

TWELVE

The Divine One Goes to Harvard

In 1976, Sassy was scheduled to play at a tribute to Cannonball Adderley in Los Angeles. Marshall asked bassist Walter Booker to play 'East of the Sun' as a duet with her. Soon she hired the friendly, gregarious Booker, who danced around his bass as he played with an extraordinary rhythmic drive and with lyrical abilty, and who felt, as most of her musicians would from then on, that she regarded him as a younger brother. At the same time, she seemed like a kid sometimes herself, the usual opinion endemic in her trios.

Booker came into Sassy's life when it was uncomplicated; her relationship with Marshall Fisher was free of obvious emotional turmoil and any physical violence. 'She enjoyed driving around in her little Mercedes-Benz; she made enough money, had a lovely home, her mother and daughter with her, and everyone around her as well as her audiences loved her,' Jimmy Cobb observed. A dog fancier, she owned four at a time; Lady, a stray and a mutt, was the smartest of the bunch. 'The others had pedigrees, small pedigrees,' Bookie reminisced years later with a smile. She could afford her tastes and habits, and she could indulge her penchant for hanging out with musicians, 'the guys', said Jimmy Cobb.

Booker felt that he and Sassy communicated mystically onstage. She never gave him any instructions about how he should play for her, but she advised him, 'I like to pick good notes. The right note is not always the best note for me. I like to hear the good notes.' So Bookie learned the difference between the right note and the good, harmonically interesting note. When he picked a special note, a good, inspiring or complementary note for her, she would turn around and wink or smile at him, especially when they performed ballads. He thought that she listened first to the chords that the bass played and had spent years developing her great ability to hear chords. With her peerless voice and knowledge of the structure of the chords, she wasn't afraid of trying anything. He loved her complete self-confidence onstage. She admired him very much, too. Carl Schroeder recalled the day that the group travelled to perform a live concert with the BBC orchestra in London under the gifted conductor and arranger Robert Farnon. 'The orchestra made up of eighty-five men absolutely could not swing, but Booker made them swing,' Carl Schroeder recalled with admiration. 'He and Cobb were doing it together. They had them hovering over the ground.'

On the road, she and Bookie became such close friends that he felt free to telephone her suite simply to ask her what she was doing. If she said 'meditating', he knew she was sewing in the living-room – for some reason she never sewed in the bedroom – and he was welcome to visit her when she was meditating.

Booker, too, noticed that Marshall Fisher gave her fealty; he would do anything she wanted him to. Booker also knew that she hadn't been accustomed to that type of treatment from men. Joining the inner circle of her friends and family, Booker sometimes stayed at Sassy's house in Hidden Hills and enjoyed the mighty preparations for meals that she made in her own elegant kitchen; both she and her mother were excellent cooks. And along with everyone else, Booker saw Sassy put on more and more weight. She had developed into a round, mature woman and still kept gaining in girth.

Larry Clothier, also a frequent guest, remembers that Ada, whom he loved and admired, didn't stand for disrespect from anybody. Once when he was wearing shorts, she slapped him so hard on the thigh that she left an imprint of her hand. 'You're a grand rascal,' she said to him, because she knew he was dating one young woman on the sly while he was more seriously involved with a friend of the Vaughan family.

Despite Ada's principles, Sassy lived her own free-form life as she wanted to. If she felt like drinking, smoking or even taking cocaine, she did so in her private quarters in the house, out of her mother's sight. Jimmy Cobb remembers that when Sassy had taken some cocaine, she seemed frozen, with her teeth clenched. In fact, she probably was frozen, he reasoned. He never saw her in that condition when she went onstage, however. According to Walter Booker, Sassy 'smoked two packs of cigarettes a day, she and Marshall. When I stayed at her house, and I saw her smoking all the time, all the time, I didn't like to see that, because she was a great singer. It didn't seem to hurt her voice, though . . . She could still get up to those high notes. In the years that I played for her, her voice cracked only once,' Booker recalled. 'But she had great control,and she fixed it right away so no one could hear it. Other singers' voices cracked all the time. That confidence which she had onstage probably kept it from cracking. She forgot words of songs, but her voice never cracked.'

Someone once asked her how she managed to sing so prettily, and Joe Williams had heard her answer: 'I drink booze, I smoke cigarettes, I stay high, I stay up all night, I hang out.' By now, she was developing a rich, commodious baritone register. John S. Wilson wrote: 'Sarah Vaughan had one of the finest voices with which a singer of popular songs has ever been blessed. Not content with this, however, she became a determined stylist with a fondness for tonsil-rattling vibrato and for sudden swoops from her normal soprano to low-register contralto, which gave the impression that she had jumped down a well.' But the sound was dramatic and effective, while her soprano retained its shimmering beauty.

After the shows, when her fans milled around to lavish praise on her, she found the perfect line to replace the stock 'thank you', saying instead, 'God is good'. Bookie loved to overhear her say that in her little high voice so filled with shyness, so strikingly different from the commanding tones she used onstage. It was in this period of her career that she confided to Patricia O'Haire of the *New York Daily News*: 'I try to look relaxed onstage, but believe me, honey, it's only an act.' The dichotomy in her personality charmed Booker.

Carl Schroeder remembered, 'I liked her. I loved her. As a singer, she was once in a lifetime. In my life, there will never be another singer at the level of Sarah Vaughan. Many singers know little about music and think they knew everything. I decided long ago that arrogance and stupidity are a deadly combination. But Sass knew about music, and she was a pro as soon as she hit the stage and stunned you with the power of her voice. As a person, once you got past her shyness, it was like talking to the person next door. She liked people who treated her that way. She was uncomfortable with people fawning over her.

'She sometimes called for requests from the audience, then rarely did them unless somebody asked for a song that she'd like to do. If she didn't know the lyrics, she toyed with them. If we didn't know the songs, she helped us through by actually singing the chords and incorporating them into the delivery of the song. She helped me through a lot of times. I defy any other singer to do that. By arpeggiating –

singing those chords – she bailed me out many times when *I* didn't know the songs,' Schroeder said.

'She also had a gift that most singers didn't have. She knew when to improvise and when not to. She could walk the line between the melody and improvisation exactly the way a great saxophone player could,' returning to the melody for a little while, leaving it, returning, diverging, creating new passages, and always enhancing the original composition.

One night in a club in Texas – 'a Mafia club', Carl Schroeder recalled – she was supposed to be paid before the last show of the night. 'It was in the contract. But she wasn't paid. One of the owners told her he didn't have the money. She came to the bandstand and said to us: "Pack up the drums. *Pack – up – the – drums.* We're leaving." The house was packed. Then she goes downstairs . . . with these big three-hundred-pound Mafia guys with funny-looking noses. "Oh, my God, Sarah, what are you doing? These guys are carrying guns. These guys are Mafia guys. They'll kill you," I said. She walked out of there with the money. I don't know what she said to these people. But we walked out of there with the money. That's when I knew how strong she was. I had said to myself, Oh, my God, she's not coming out of there. I feared for her life. I'll bet she called them a whole lot of things . . . because she could. She was strong. She didn't like to be that way but she could, when she had to, she was very strong.'

Another night, arriving to play in a hotel in Chicago, she heard that the piano was out of tune. 'It was tuned, but it kept going out of tune,' Schroeder said. She hated the idea of singing with it. Schroeder said to her, 'I can manage with it, and tomorrow we can rent another piano.' He saw there was 'a packed house, opening night, the press', everyone waiting for her. But she didn't want to work with that piano. 'She locked herself in the bathroom of her suite. The manager came knocking on the door, but she stayed in the bathroom. We left the next day. The hotel evicted her.' Schroeder thought that her toughness 'was born out of her experience in the bebop era. This is a positive type of strength. I never met a musician of any gender stronger than Sarah.'

In 1977 she and Michael Tilson Thomas planned to do two more Gershwin concerts, one at the Hollywood Bowl in California, and another in New York, a Sunday afternoon that was part of a classical series at Carnegie Hall. Michael, who wanted to rehearse for the Carnegie Hall concert, knew the haphazard way that she usually got her shows together; he had been backstage when she played Avery Fisher Hall with her trio that year. She had a little ceremony, as he viewed it, of making up her face while she talked to Carl Schroeder about what they were going to do that night. 'Okay, we'll do "A Train" up,' she said. 'We'll do "Valentine" down, down, real down.' Michael wanted to make himself clear about the preparation he required even though he had already worked with her at length. He told her by telephone, 'I'm a classical musician. I have appreciation of jazz, but this is a whole other world for me. I know you don't need any rehearsal at all, but, honey, I need rehearsal, so please come over, and let's rehearse.' She said, 'Okay, we'll get together. Call me.' On the day she had designated, he called her at noon. A very sleepy voice answered, 'Wawawa . . .'

'Sass!'

'Michael . . . oh . . . so late . . . sushi.' She had been up all night and had eaten sushi.

'Listen, what's going on?' Michael said.

'I don't know. I haven't gotten up.'

'Sass, we must rehearse today. *When* are you coming? *When* are you going to show up?'

'*When* it gets dark. Look for me *when* it gets dark.'

She showed up at his apartment at about eight o'clock that night – a great night for him, because it was the first time that he and Sassy had ever been together for an extended period with nobody else there. She played the piano for him. 'Her playing was wonderful,' he says, even though she kept her fingernails very long, and long fingernails always made clicking noises on piano keys. 'She had to keep her fingers curved up in the air the wrong way,' he noticed, and he told her, 'If you'd only cut your fingernails, imagine what kind of a pianist you would be.' She played some music she had composed – she was always toying with composing. And she talked in her soft, sometimes high, rushed voice, about getting a lyricist to write for her. He thought that she should do so. She never did much about her own music. Carl Schroeder would have been ideal for helping with her music, Michael thought, but Sassy never approached Carl about working with her on her own music.

Sassy told Michael that recently she had been invited to address an audience of hopeful young singers and musicians at Harvard University. The school asked her to discuss the question: What does jazz mean? Sassy took her trio with her. Carl Schroeder answered a question about how Sassy adjusted her 'book' – her repertoire book with the music she carried around – for trio, big-band and orchestra performances. A flute solo with a symphony orchestra was adapted for the bass in a trio gig. Sassy said that she sang essentially the same way with trios, bands and orchestras; she demonstrated how she changed her interpretations in general by singing 'Body and Soul' straight, then singing a few bars in a different way, and then again in a different way, and perhaps even a fourth way. She was very proud of her appearance at Harvard and talked about it a lot to Michael Tilson Thomas. It wasn't something that she bragged about to most people, but she confided in Michael. 'She was very proud of it,' he recalled.

THIRTEEN

Tom Guy Films
Listen to the Sun

By 1977, her friend Pumpkin had bought a house in South Orange, New Jersey, to which he welcomed Sassy, Marshall and their entourage every time she came to the East Coast. He decorated a room in blue for her and installed a telephone which only she used. Often she preferred to stay with friends instead of in hotels in many cities. She put a Yamaha piano in Pumpkin's house for her use. 'She would go downstairs to the sauna and come up and play the piano,' he recalled. She liked the pampering and informality that her friends' houses afforded her.

Tom Guy, a friend of Pumpkin's, in his twenties in 1977, was producing a jazz series called 'Express Yourself' for the public TV station in New Jersey. A native of Newark, he had become a film producer and director while in college at Texas Southern University. He told Pumpkin that he wanted to make a film about Sassy. Pumpkin, in the process of opening a men's clothing store on the Upper East Side of Manhattan, invited Tom Guy to the opening party. Guy saw Sassy walking down the street toward the store with Marshall Fisher; she was wearing a blue jeans suit and a cap cocked to the side. Guy talked to Marshall for about two hours, explaining what the film would consist of. Tom wanted to film Sassy on the road, offstage, and in performance, including a performance abroad. Marshall was intrigued and enthusiastic. Sassy wanted to do the film, but she resisted the idea of having to do an interview in which she discussed her life with Guy. 'She didn't like to talk about herself,' Tom Guy would learn. Still, he proceeded; Marshall in particular wanted to see Sassy capured on film both onstage, as she sang and aroused audiences to cheer and scream, and backstage as she greeted fans.

Tom talked to an executive of the New Jersey Symphony Orchestra, who said, 'Let me tell you a story.' The New Jersey Symphony Orchestra had planned a performance with Sassy, but then the symphony went on strike. Sassy was owed money. Instead of asking for it, she said, 'No problem. Give me the date when you have it together.' The New Jersey Symphony Orchestra's man was willing to do anything to cooperate with Tom Guy for a film. As it turned out, he didn't film her performance with the symphony. Guy approached Count Basie and Dizzy Gillespie to see if they would share with him on film their memories of Sassy, and they said essentially the same thing that the orchestra's man had said: 'If it's for Sassy, we'll do anything you like.' Guy began by filming her in performance at the Levin Theatre at Rutgers University/Douglas College campus. She was very pleased with everything – the invited audience, the sound system.

Then they went to Newport, Rhode Island, where she played a concert produced by George Wein at Fort Adams. Tom Guy travelled with her in the car, which she drove to Newport, and filmed her as she was driving. She talked, laughed and sang during the trip. Though she flew when she had to, she preferred the freedom and relaxation of driving her own car.

From Newport she drove to Washington DC, did a Fourth of July concert in Rock Creek Park, and then backtracked to Philadelphia to perform at the Robin Hood Dell amphitheatre. Years earlier, she had done a concert there; the overflow audience had sat on tombstones in a nearby graveyard so that it could hear her. And from Philadelphia, the entourage moved to Houston, Texas, where Sassy performed a concert with the Houston Symphony Orchestra under the direction of Marty Paich; then she went to the Hotel International at Tijuca, a beach just outside Rio de Janeiro, Brazil, where she sang in a hotel auditorium.

All the while, Tom kept trying to get her to sit down and let him interview her about her past. She kept postponing the interview; he felt she wanted to concentrate on the present and the future. She hated interviews anyway, and she thought it would be a great effort for her to put her mind on the past. But Tom kept pressing her because he didn't have a narrator for the film; his idea was to have Sassy speak for herself. After a few abortive attempts at interviewing her, she said to him, 'You're going to bug me to death for that interview, so I'll just write it myself.' Then she took him with her to Petrópolis, a suburb of Rio, where she was staying at a lovely hillside house with a pool owned by some Brazilian friends. She found a spiral notebook, wrote her own history, and went to the sleeping quarters reserved for the servants, where she and Tom Guy sat on bunk beds. She read her story, focusing on Billy Eckstine and Dizzy, the early days, and all her inspirations. 'My goal, believe it or not, is rather hard to find,' she wrote, 'because everything today must be rather commercial to be in the top 50. I just refuse to throw my talent out of the window just so I can have a number 1 hit. If I have lasted this long, I shall continue.' Tom thought that her melodious recounting sounded like her singing, and he used her recorded voice for the film's beginning.

She seemed alert all the time, and she never hid what was on her mind. When she saw that he was gaining a little weight later in their friendship, she said so. He felt a bit embarrassed, but she laughed and said, 'I'm just telling the truth.' She could be that way about anything. And if Billy Eckstine had enjoyed his unique view of Sassy as his 'baby' and 'Little Sister', Guy regarded her as a 'Big Sister', just as her younger musicians did. Guy admired her for the way she shouldered the responsibility of her work.

He helped to produce a week of inaugural activities for the opening of the Paul Robeson Campus Center at Rutgers. Sassy agreed to do the last night's concert, a benefit for sickle-cell anaemia. She would be getting far less money than she usually received for her concerts. A reporter asked her, after she walked offstage, 'Do you think that your appearance here raising money for sickle cell will be a more universal approach in terms of attracting a black audience?' The question was confusing, but Sassy unravelled it for herself and answered, 'I don't think black and white. I have to tell you that. I think of human beings, people . . . My mother raised me that way.'

Guy never saw her fight with Marshall, and he never sensed that she might be having a romance with another man. But Sassy did have another man on her mind while she was in Brazil in 1977. She missed that man. Almost immediately after the tour, Sassy and Marshall split up. Tom, who had become friends with the two of them separately and as a couple, was surprised and dismayed.

FOURTEEN

A Letter to Marshall Fisher

Life might have gone on in a routine way for Sassy and Marshall, if she had let it. But anyone taking clues from her voluptuous singing alone would have guessed that she had no taste for controlling her exuberance or her appetites for excess. And she wanted change at times more than she needed security, or so it seemed to her in her fifties, when she was still full of energy and zest. Aretha Landrum speculated that Marshall might have tried to assume too much authority for Sassy's taste.

Pumpkin thought that Sassy was 'fishing', just flirting with the new man, and he guessed that Sassy had begun her flirtation after Marshall started travelling on the road with the equipment; he would drive ahead to engagements, while she flew. 'She'd be in my house, and he was on the road,' Pumpkin recalled. 'I never understood that, but I never interfered.' Pumpkin knew for sure that 'she didn't like it' when Marshall drove with the equipment. Once, when Marshall called her from the road, Pumpkin asked her what was going on, and Sassy answered, with a combination of perplexity and exasperation in her manner, 'Don't ask me. I don't want to know about it.' The new arrangement puzzled Pumpkin and Aretha, because they remembered how Marshall had always tried to adjust to anything Sassy wanted. Neither Pumpkin nor Aretha would ever really understand why she made the decision to end her relationship with Marshall.

Carmen McRae explained Sassy's attraction to Waymon Reed, a trumpeter with the Basie band. 'Waymon could [make love].' Walter Booker thought: 'She wanted to be in love.' Robert Richards, who knew that Sassy and Marshall had loved each other as the best of friends, thought Sassy decided to break up that relationship because 'she wasn't sophisticated enough to know that friendship is love'. Marshall, he thought, had 'become an authority figure rather than the Prince Charming she thought she had to have at that stage in her life'.

And Carl Schroeder added his own insight into Sassy: 'She needed to sweep everything clean. She was very shy with strangers and nervous about performing, and that may be why she kept the same musicians with her for long periods of time. She was also always looking for a man with whom she could be happy – or happier.' Waymon's trumpet-playing excited her.

Jack Kleinsinger, a young New York State assistant attorney general moonlighting as a jazz concert producer, had been working as a stage manager during the summer of 1976 for George Wein at the Nice Jazz Festival. He remembered clearly that Marshall, with his son along, 'was driving everyone crazy, complaining about the sound. He even had a quarrel with Carl Schroeder – something about rushing the tempo – something that Marshall had no expertise in. Sarah was having a tough time then. I think [Marshall] was making her crazy. She was a little frantic.' Kleinsinger was under the impression that Sassy was physically sick from her various excesses and that she and Marshall might even be breaking up at that time. Sassy let Kleinsinger know that she appreciated his introduction of her and her trio in French onstage. 'She was amused that I was a state prosecutor by day and a fledgling jazz producer on my own time,' Kleinsinger recalled.

'She and Marshall became like roommates,' said Walter Booker. 'That was how it happened that she fell in love with Waymon Reed.' Yet she appeared to break off with Marshall with difficulty, hesitating perhaps with the instinctive knowledge that she was about to pursue another dream of romance that could turn out to be another frustrating trap.

She had an ironic sense of humour that led her to joke about many things and poke fun at herself. She told jazz critic George Kanzler Jr of the *Newark Star Ledger* that she came from Newark in Excess County, New Jersey, instead of Essex County. To Patricia O'Haire of the *New York Daily News*, Sassy said, 'I was born in . . . good old Excess County. No, that's not right. Access? That's not right, either. E-s-s-e-x,' she spelled it out and laughed. 'I never could pronounce it! I remember I used to be punished in school because . . . the teacher thought I was making fun, and she used to make me stand up against the wall. I even used to go home and practise it, and here it is, all those years later, I still can't pronounce it.' When the young, robust Waymon Reed came into her life, she welcomed him too readily. And she joked to Walter Booker about the 'thing' she had for trumpet players. She thought that the pressure of playing trumpet cut off the supply of oxygen and damaged a trumpeter's brain. (Musicians and medical experts have theories about the physical side-effects that many instruments have on players.) Sassy knew that her own quick mind, so immersed in improvisation and inured to an itinerant existence, could fail her when it came to making decisions about everything but her music. But her insights didn't curb her impulsiveness.

Once the love affair between Sassy and Marshall had ended, Walter Booker observed, she began travelling on the bus with the Basie band, having fun with Waymon and his bandmates. Sassy admired Waymon's playing, which other players found fascinating, too. If the Basie band was playing anywhere within a hundred miles of where Sassy was performing, she made the trip between her shows without batting an eyelid. She loved a long drive. But most of all, she was infatuated with Waymon Reed.

Waymon's playing had already caught the attention of Jack Kleinsinger in 1975. When Waymon sat in at Eddie Condon's club one Sunday night, Kleinsinger was very impressed and invited him to play in a Highlights in Jazz concert, a series that Kleinsinger was beginning to produce at New York University's Loeb Student Center. When Waymon, playing with Frank Foster's Loud Minority orchestra, took a solo, Chet Baker perked up backstage and asked, 'Who's that playing?' The next year, on St Patrick's Day, Waymon and Jon Faddis sat in at a Kleinsinger concert at Loeb, playing with Lew Soloff – 'three of the best trumpet players in the business', wrote Ed Watkins, reviewing for the *Black American*. 'When all three were going at once, you had the kind of noise that can only be described as golden.' Kleinsinger was very happy with the trumpeters – and especially excited by Waymon, whom he came to like personally, because he was the least known. 'He liked to play. He was always very happy to get out his horn and jam. Everyone liked him at that time.'

In 1977 Sassy went to Newark without Marshall. She stayed with Aretha and, as she was leaving, asked Aretha to do her a favour. 'You have a mailbox right outside your house,' Sassy said. 'Would you please mail that for me?' It turned out to be a thick letter to Marshall, which told him that Sassy was ending their relationship. Sassy said things in the letter which she couldn't bring herself to tell him in person. 'I wouldn't have mailed it, if I had known what that letter said,' Aretha later told Sassy.

Pumpkin and Aretha wanted to continue their friendship with

Marshall, but he shied away from keeping up his friendships with his and Sassy's old friends. He told pianist Roger 'Ram' Ramirez, who had written 'Lover Man', that he was no longer with Sassy and felt relieved after seven years of stress. He also showed up at a gig where pianist Jimmy Rowles was playing in New York in the late 1970s. Jimmy didn't think that Marshall looked well; he had a beard, his hair was long. Jimmy said, 'Where's Sass?' Marshall told him, 'That's all over,' and he refused to discuss their relationship.

To what degree Marshall influenced Sassy's artistic choices during their relationship isn't exactly known. Larry Clothier thought that Marshall lifted Sassy's sights in general and forever, but the people directly involved with her bookings, money management, recordings, and musical choices had their obvious impact, too. Michael Tilson Thomas had engaged her for milestone performances. Bobby Shad had found 'Send in the Clowns' on Broadway and presented Sassy with that ideal vehicle during her Mainstream years. Earlier, at Mercury, he had paired Sassy with 'Poor Butterfly' during an exciting recording session. Even Frank Sinatra had exerted influence on Sassy's career. Just before her relationship with Marshall ended, Sinatra invited her to sing as the opening act in a two-week series of concerts at Universal Studios where he was performing. She was set up with a dressing room in a trailer. Legend has it that Sinatra once said Sassy sang so beautifully he wanted to cut his wrists and bleed to death while she sang to him. He kept stopping at her trailer and asking, 'Is everything okay?' 'It's okay,' she said. 'Okay, baby,' he said. Sinatra had even made sure she had a fully stocked bar. She sang so magnificently that pianist Larry Willis, who had been the keyboardist for the group Blood, Sweat and Tears, sitting in her audience at Universal one night, was astounded to find himself crying as she sang. Sinatra also invited Sassy to join him when he performed at the Palladium in London around the time of her success at Universal Studios. She was invited to sing for President Jimmy Carter at the White House – her third presidential invitation. All of these events probably would have taken place without Marshall's management. His strong influence on Sassy's career stemmed most of all from his supportive love during a period when so many new opportunities came her way.

In 1978 Pablo released Sassy's 1977 recording of *I Love Brazil!* Across the country, critics praised it. Leonard Feather wrote: 'She was surrounded by some of Brazil's most distinguished and distinctive instrumentalists (strings, flutes, guitars, percussion) and composers doubling as players. Even Antonio Carlos Jobim joins in, playing a keyboard on his own "Triste"; Milton Nascimento on "Courage" is on hand with guitar and vocal assistance.' Feather loved hearing Sassy singing songs she had not been heard to do before; incorporating songs by Marcos Valle, Dori Caymmi and Oscar Neves, the album was 'a five-star collection', Feather said.

Pablo was owned by Norman Granz, Ella Fitzgerald's manager. He wanted to sign Sassy because of the prestige of having her on his label; he would then have the two greatest female jazz singers in the world recording for him. One of his goals was to have Sassy record Duke Ellington's songs. But first she made the album done in Brazil. (Sassy's previous album of Beatles songs in 1977, eventually released on the Atlantic label, was done as her relationship with Marshall was ending; the album had a few songs that turned out well, though the rock beat and the simplicity of the music worked against the luxurious fluidity and richness of her approach. On the album cover, she gave thanks to Marshall Fisher for his help and called him her 'guru'.)

She was nominated for a Grammy for the Brazilian album, but she didn't win. Carl Schroeder was very disappointed for her about her loss. She herself said nothing about it; she just shrugged. But he played for her when she sang a song at the Grammy ceremonies; he waited with her for the name of the winner in her category to be called. 'Sassy sang her heart out, and then she lost.'

Tom Guy's documentary, *Listen to the Sun*, was aired on 21 September 1978 on New Jersey public television. He had pared sixteen hours of film down to forty-five minutes of performances and forty-five minutes of scenes from her personal life offstage. Guy had thought of the title for his film as he was driving his car one day. He regarded Sarah Vaughan as the greatest female vocalist, and he chose the sun, a symbol of the life force, as a symbol for Sassy.

For Pablo, she recorded an album called *How Long Has This Been Going On?* with pianist Oscar Peterson, guitarist Joe Pass, bassist Ray Brown, and drummer Louis Bellson. George Kanzler Jr, writing in the *Newark Star Ledger* on 19 November 1978, said: 'In most other countries, her voice would have already been declared a national treasure.' He remarked that she was singing better than ever on her new album of 'warm masterpieces'. Gary Giddins of the *Village Voice* said the new album was 'cause for breaking out the champagne for two reasons'. He thought it was one of the best albums she had ever made, and it reminded him of the way she had sung when she had first became known. 'Those who have come to admire La Vaughan as an opera singer without an opera may be disappointed, but those lonely for the kind of singer she was when Charlie Parker, Freddy Webster and Miles Davis were numbered among her accompanists will be elated – she swings just as hard, her tones are richer, and her concepts free of little girl coyness. And this collection represents more than a return to a casual jazz ambience. I can't think of another Vaughan album with such an abundance of blues locutions, variations and riffs.' (*Crazy and Mixed Up*, her last Pablo album, with many of the same musicians, had much the same quality, and freshness, and dashing spirit.)

Sassy concentrated on concerts, but sometimes she still played clubs. Once in the late 1970s, she appeared at the Grand Finale on West Seventieth Street in New York. Bertha Hope was the intermission pianist. Between her sets, Sassy disguised herself with sunglasses, a floppy hat, and a frumpy smock, and went to the bar to listen. After a while Bertha said, 'It sure is nice to see you listening to us.' Sassy said, 'Oh, I learned something. I can hear something that teaches me. It often happens.' That was the Divine One's attitude.

The earthy Sassy was about to marry Waymon Reed. And the tumultuous relationship with Waymon would shade her attitude for the rest of her life.

FIFTEEN

A Mistake Made
Late in Life

Michael Tilson Thomas asked her where she was getting married, so he could send flowers. She told Michael, 'Somewhere where there's no community property.'

Waymon was nearly sixteen years younger than Sassy. On their wedding day in 1978 at the home of friends in Chicago, the solidly built, short man with a bright smile seemed the picture of robust health and happiness. Pumpkin gave the bride away in front of a small group of Sassy's friends. At the age of fifty-four, when she married Waymon Reed, who had been born on 10 January 1940 and was then thirty-eight years old, Sassy looked regal in her wedding dress, but she was far from the demure, perky-looking slip of a woman who people had thought was adorable in the 1940s and 1950s.

Before his involvement with Sassy, Waymon had been separated for a few years from his pretty young wife, Greta, with whom he had a son, Waymon Jr, and a stepson, Keith. Waymon had explored the possibilities of pursuing relationships with two other famous singers – Carmen McRae and Ella Fitzgerald, Carmen recalled. Sassy knew the gossip; even so, she was willing to go along with whatever he wanted, and she accorded him some of the nurturing encouragement and attention that Marshall Fisher had once given her. She appointed Waymon her musical director, leader of her group, and road manager. In retrospect, Jimmy Cobb thought that the marriage to Sassy, with her house in Hidden Hills, made it convenient for Waymon to play in gigs on the West Coast. He wanted to write music and have Sassy sing it. He wanted to lead a group and become better known on his own. James Harper thought that Waymon dreamed of becoming a star as a recording artist.

She was becoming a very large diva who wore tent-shaped dresses; long gone were the gowns with the nipped-in waists and padded bodices that George Treadwell's mother had sewn for her. At some point during her professional and physical growth, Sassy had begun to perspire profusely on stage during performances. By the 1970s, she perspired so much during a jazz festival performance in the broiling-hot, basement-level theatre of the casino in Montreux, Switzerland, that she changed the lyrics of the songs and sang about the heat. Slathered with perspiration after about half an hour, she went offstage for a moment and came back somewhat dried off. Anyone with less stamina would have undoubtedly fainted.

On the road with Sassy and her trio – Jimmy Cobb, Walter Booker and Carl Schroeder – Waymon Reed tried to assert his new status. Booker thought that Waymon had a hard row to hoe when he saw what a close, warm friendship Sassy had with the men in her trio: 'I really think Waymon was jealous of Jimmy Cobb and me being so close to her. We had such a pact, and he was the outsider all the time.' Her musicians thought that Waymon convinced Sassy to fire Cobb and Booker. Waymon would tell his ex-wife, Greta, that it was Sassy's idea to fire the men, and that he felt bad because he was held responsible for the change. She didn't fire them herself. Frank Rio in Los Angeles called drummer Roy McCurdy to replace Jimmy Cobb.

McCurdy, who had worked along with Bookie for Cannonball Adderley, was playing with singer Kenny Rankin's group when he was asked to join Sassy's group for about $1,100 a week, he said. The excellent salaries for the sidemen had reached their levels during the Marshall Fisher years. (Union scale minimum in 1979 was ninety dollars per show for sidemen.) McCurdy wanted to be sure that his friend, Jimmy Cobb, approved of the new arrangement. So McCurdy called Jimmy and asked if he thought McCurdy should take the job. Jimmy Cobb said, 'Take it.' But McCurdy had the impression that Cobb hadn't even known until that moment that a decision had been made to replace him. Booker was let go, too.

Carl Schroeder quit in sympathy with them, although he never had a confrontation with Waymon Reed. But the departure of Jimmy and Walter, 'my rhythm section', as he felt about them fondly, made Carl decide that it was time for him to go. Playing for Sassy had been his 'finishing school', he said. The word was out in the music world that once you had worked for a considerable time in her rhythm section, you were a very polished musician. Carl felt spoiled by her musicianship; he never wanted to work with a lesser singer and, in future years, when he accompanied a singer, it would only be someone like Mel Tormé or Carol Sloane. Carl felt bad about telling Sassy why he was leaving, so he said he had to leave her group because of his bad back; he had undergone surgery for a ruptured disc, then had another operation for spinal fusion. He began to teach and play in Los Angeles.

Once in the group, McCurdy became aware that there were hard feelings about the move which most people believed had been engineered by Waymon Reed. Years later, Sassy would apologise to Jimmy Cobb, who had gone to New York and remarried. When Sassy and Cobb discussed what had happened, she told him she thought there was a bright side; he might never have had a family if she hadn't forced him to get off the road, she said. Jimmy thought that was a peculiar idea, but he didn't argue with her. Bookie heard that for a long time after she fired her trio she sometimes introduced McCurdy to audiences as 'Jimmy Cobb'.

Pianist Mike Wofford, who didn't know about the way the previous trio had broken up, later reflected that, if he had known, he might not have agreed to replace Schroeder. Bassist Andy Simpkins, who was recommended to Waymon by his old friend, baritone saxophonist John Williams of the Basie band, a good friend of Waymon's, replaced Booker. McCurdy was impressed by the arrangements in her book, some of them by Alan Copeland, an arranger in Los Angeles, who was at the new group's first rehearsal at her house.

McCurdy, then forty years old, had expected it to be a pleasure to see Waymon again. Waymon had been born in Fayetteville, North Carolina, raised in Tennessee, and moved to New York State, where he had attended the famed Eastman School of Music in Rochester, New York. McCurdy had met Waymon in 1960 and played with him in gigs and sessions in Rochester, McCurdy's hometown. Waymon worked in those days with tenor saxophonist Pee Wee Ellis; Pee Wee and Waymon joined the Paul A. Miller circus, then the Royal American Circus, actually a fair based in Florida. Pee Wee introduced Waymon to his first wife, Greta. Waymon proposed quickly, and they married after knowing each other for two weeks. Waymon got a job playing in the musical group backing James Brown, the reigning soul singer, before climbing on to the Count Basie band bus. 'It was his dream to play with Basie,' Greta recalls. As a youngster, he had played trumpet along with the band while listening to it on records. When they had known each other in upstate New York, Roy McCurdy had thought that Waymon was a quiet, friendly guy who made the sessions and played his trumpet seriously. Pee Wee and Greta had a similar opinion of

Waymon, whose penchant for flashy clothes was the only hint of extroversion in his personality. 'He was shy,' Pee Wee would recall about the friend whose musicianship he respected so much. Greta thought Waymon was 'a musician's musician' who 'was difficult to get to know', but he had some close friends among musicians he worked with, especially in the Basie band. He had 'tunnel vision' about music, she said, and studied and practised constantly. But in Sassy's group, 'Waymon seemed like a different man', McCurdy said.

One morning, while on the road with Sassy, Roy went downstairs in a hotel to have breakfast. Waymon was sitting at a table, waiting for Sassy. When Roy approached and started to sit down, Waymon said, 'This table is for Sass and me. Musicians don't talk with us. They have to sit someplace else.' Roy wasn't used to that kind of behaviour. Ordinarily when you travelled with someone and saw that person at breakfast time, you sat down to eat together. Another day, Waymon asked Roy, 'What do you think you do to deserve the kind of money you're earning? I never made that before.' Roy said, 'I deserve it. I worked with great people. I was with Cannonball and others for years.' But Waymon was upset by Roy's salary.

'Waymon and I couldn't get along,' Roy said. 'We clashed all the time, not about music, just about living. He wanted the musicians to be degraded.' Lean and strong, fastidious and habituated to exercising and eating healthy foods, never smoking or drinking, Roy McCurdy didn't feel kindly disposed to anybody who tried to demean him.

Mike Wofford, too, found it difficult to understand or tolerate Waymon's behaviour. Waymon was acting as the musical director, leading Sassy's group onstage. Like Roy, Mike Wofford thought there was nothing wrong with the music being played onstage. Sassy wanted Waymon, an excellent player, to lead the quartet through several opening songs, then play muted and creative lines behind her when she came onstage to sing. Mike knew she liked singing 'I Remember Clifford', Benny Golson's tribute to Clifford Brown, the trumpeter who had died so young. Sassy enjoyed that song with Jon Hendricks's lyrics and with Waymon's solos; Waymon even sounded rather like his own hero, Clifford Brown. But offstage, Waymon tried to assert his authority over the musicians and make them feel like second-class citizens at best. None of them was used to that type of leadership. It was an abnormality in the jazz world, a society of individualists who maintained high standards for their playing and worked extremely hard to earn and keep the best, most pressured jobs in their field. The musicians usually appreciated reasoned discipline and tolerated a degree of eccen-

tricity and even competition as a way of life. But Waymon took everything to an extreme. The consensus was that, as Roy McCurdy
expressed it, Waymon was 'an envious type of guy with a big, swelled
head'. By some miracle of professionalism, the rhythm section's offstage problems with Waymon didn't affect the performances. 'Waymon
never seemed jealous or resentful of Sassy's friendship with Billy Eckstine, who came to hang out with her whenever they played in the
same city,' McCurdy recalled. Except for his deference to Eckstine –
'Waymon wouldn't have dared to be rude to Billy Eckstine,' Robert
Richards knew – Waymon was often, though not always, unpleasant
to musicians. Greta Reed heard stories about the tension between
Waymon and Sassy's other musicians, and Greta concluded that the
offstage combination of Sassy and Waymon was deadly. 'He was used
to being his own man, and then he was a little puppet. He wasn't used
to that. He became Mr Sarah Vaughan more than she was Mrs Waymon
Reed.'

Roy McCurdy noticed that Sassy called for rehearsals often while
he travelled in her group, even though he knew she didn't need the
rehearsals. 'I think she just liked to sing, and she liked to hang out with
the guys,' McCurdy said. Mike Wofford thought Sassy tried to bend
over backward to focus some attention on Waymon, so that he
wouldn't feel as if he was playing a subsidiary role – though actually
he was. Once, on Johnny Carson's 'Tonight Show', she waved in the
direction of the side of the stage where Waymon and the rhythm section
were placed with their instruments. She told Johnny, 'And that's my
husband, Waymon, over there.' The camera focused on Waymon for
a second, but the audience didn't evince any excitement. Nobody was
interested; she was the centrepiece. 'Let's talk about you,' Carson said
to her right away.

'Waymon became Mr Sarah Vaughan', said Jack Kleinsinger, echo-
ing many of Sassy's friends. During a meal with Waymon, Roy
McCurdy, enjoying one of Waymon's pleasant spells, listened to
Waymon confide that he had everything he had ever wanted – 'enough
money, a great job, a fine home'. But McCurdy thought to himself,
'Yes, but it's all really Sassy's.' Mike Wofford found Waymon unbear-
able.

Norman Granz had guessed correctly, when he signed Sassy to a
contract, that her recordings for Pablo could benefit her career as well
as enhance his prestige as a jazz producer even further. In 1979 she
undertook an eighteen-city US tour with Mel Tormé and Gerry Mulligan and his orchestra. If anything can be said to have capped the decade

for her, it might have been three sold-out concerts which she performed at Carnegie Hall in the spring of 1979. One was done with Tormé and Mulligan, the second with experimental post-bebop singer Betty Carter and the great bebop lyricist Eddie Jefferson, who wrote the words for 'Moody's Mood for Love', and the third with Count Basie's orchestra together with Sassy's own rhythm section, Wofford, Simpkins and McCurdy.

Gary Giddins of the *Village Voice* missed the Schroeder, Booker and Cobb trio, which was actually listed on the concert programme; John S. Wilson had wanted to hear Basie, his bassist, and especially his drummer, Butch Miles, playing behind Sassy. But critics seemed to agree that the second concert with Betty Carter and Eddie Jefferson, both of whom preceded Sassy on stage, was the best of the series, with standing ovations for each of the three singers. Sassy herself had picked Betty Carter, whose adventurous harmonies pleased Sassy so much. Each critic referred to Waymon Reed in passing as Miss Vaughan's husband and director of the group behind her; that was all the attention he received. The concerts were part of the Kool Super Nights series, a reference to Kool Super Lights cigarettes. The Super Nights series was a precursor to the Brown and Williamson-sponsored Kool Jazz Festival in the 1980s, for which Sassy would sing every year.

After the 1979 concerts Sassy went on to appear with the Oakland Symphony, the Tulsa Philharmonic, the Boston Pops, and, for two performances in the Hollywood Bowl, with the Los Angeles Philharmonic and Count Basie's orchestra. A public broadcasting affiliate followed her to a concert in Iowa. She starred with Billy Eckstine and Tony Bennett in a PBS special called 'American Pop – The Great American Singers', taped at the Plaza Hotel before an invited audience in 1979. Joe Williams and Chet Atkins performed for it, too. She also appeared at 'Salute to the Apollo Theatre' for CBS with Natalie Cole and Lou Rawls. And at 'A Tribute to Pearl Bailey', Sassy sang with Ella Fitzgerald – one of the very rare times they sang together. Then Sassy taped a segment of the Dinah Shore TV show.

Whether by design or default, or some of both, Sassy had decided on the right course for herself when it came to her singing. The inimitable beauty of her ornate jazz arias had kept the changing styles in popular music from eclipsing her career. Her fans and admirers kept turning out to hear her artistry in live performances. When the renaissance of jazz and earlier styles of jazz-influenced pop singing began to re-emerge as trendy entertainment in the 1980s, nobody had to call Sassy back from storage. She had reigned above the trends as a concert artist in the classiest halls, far from the din of rock concerts. The elaborateness of her music had worked in her favour to enrapture the most sophisticated listeners.

At the turn of the decade, with Marshall and her other companions throughout most of the 1970s gone, Sassy's maturing, earthy, supple and superbly conditioned voice remained as a pillar for herself and the jazz world to lean on and point to with pride.

While Sassy led Roy McCurdy into illustrious circles, he was dismayed and embarrassed in public for Sassy by things that happened offstage. He watched Waymon argue in an airport with a clerk in charge of seat selection. The clerk tried to accommodate Waymon, but Waymon kept yelling at the man. Finally the man came out from behind the desk and put up his fists, ready to punch Waymon. Waymon backed away about twenty-five feet, dodging the fight, and still 'woofing' – barking at the clerk. The clerk kept saying, 'C'mon, c'mon.' Another time with the group, Waymon showed up at the airport looking elegant and successful in a beautiful suit, carrying his horn and a briefcase. Sassy had spent a great deal of money on Waymon, buying him gold jewellery among many other luxurious gifts. Suddenly, he started running along a corridor in the airport, until he fell down on the floor, sweating, with his horn and bags scattered around him. McCurdy couldn't fathom what had possessed Waymon to have done such a bizarre thing.

His ex-wife, Greta, had known him to have mood swings, bouts of depression, and a few temper tantrums. 'And he had a very low tolerance for alcohol. A little bit of alcohol could trigger him. He did strange things. That happened seldom. He was otherwise a very sweet, caring soul. I think he and Sarah were high a lot, and that had a lot to do with altering his personality.'

Most people didn't know that he became sick with cancer about a year after he married Sassy. Sassy knew; some of her friends – Grady Tate, for one – knew. But they didn't necessarily think Waymon's physical illnesses could have anything to do with his behaviour. During his bouts of wildness, Waymon was manifesting symptoms of what doctors call, in the vernacular, 'running fits', according to Dr Edward Holtzman, a psychiatrist in New York. If that is what Waymon was suffering from, he began running automatically, not intending to, and passed out during a convulsion due either to a tumour or a blood clot in the temporal area of the brain. The behaviour indicated that he had some kind of lesion in his head. The episodes of nastiness that people witnessed were also part of a type of seizure pattern in temporal lobe epilepsy that can cause personality changes. If Waymon had some form of that illness, as his symptoms suggested, there was probably organic brain damage. He also would have great sensitivity to alcohol – Grady Tate as well as Greta recalled that – and would have suffered from terrible headaches, a symptom no one recalls in Waymon. People trying to live and work with Waymon during his marriage to Sassy didn't know what they were looking at – and didn't care because of how difficult he was.

By the time Sassy played at the Hollywood Bowl in 1979, she had hired a road manager, a Bostonian named Charlie Lake, a well-liked fellow whom everyone called 'the Whale'; his company was called Whale Productions, a name he decided upon after Count Basie, impressed by how active Charlie always stayed as a bandboy with the Basie band, had said: 'Look at Charlie wailing.' (When a jazz musician wails, he's playing superbly; that's the expression.) Charlie, who had known and liked Waymon Reed from their days together in the Basie band, had been working part-time for Dizzy Gillespie when Sassy called and asked him to work as a road manager for her. It had been too much work for Waymon to take care of all the details of being on the road and to play the music, too, especially with all his handicaps. Charlie accepted the job.

Joining Sassy's group on Saturday night of the Labour Day weekend at the Hollywood Bowl, he went to her dressing room, where Waymon introduced Sassy to Charlie. Charlie found out that his own salary was going to be six hundred dollars a week plus expenses, about double what he had expected. The first thing Sassy told Charlie to do was to fire the drummer. The idea bothered Charlie, because he knew what a good drummer McCurdy was; he had played with many other fine musicians.

Charlie approached Roy in his dressing room and told him that Sassy was letting him go. McCurdy started laughing and kept saying, 'It was coming, it was coming.' Charlie said he was glad McCurdy felt that way about it, because Charlie was unhappy about his task. At the time he was dismissed, McCurdy told Charlie that Sassy couldn't summarily fire him without paying him for two more weeks; that was a union requirement. Sassy told Charlie that she could fire McCurdy without two weeks' notice because she was paying far more than union minimum. But McCurdy was correct; when he appealed to the union in January 1980, the union directed Sassy to pay Roy two thousand dollars. Sassy appealed the decision, but the union upheld it. Waymon went to the union's office in Los Angeles and paid the money.

After McCurdy left, Sassy asked Grady Tate to work with her for a while. Grady was working with her in San Diego, California, where they were supposed to meet for a rehearsal. Waymon came downstairs from his hotel room before Sassy and went to the bar, where Grady approached him. Waymon gave him a bizarre look, then bit a 'chunk' out of his own lip, Grady saw, so that blood ran down Waymon's chin. Waymon said, 'She's driving me insane.' Grady decided to get away and went back to his room. A few minutes later, he received a call from Sassy. She said, 'Come and get Waymon.' He was throwing things against her door, trying to break it down. Grady called the police and asked them to take Waymon away for a while. 'Treat him very carefully,' Grady requested, because Waymon hadn't been arrested, merely entrusted by Grady for safekeeping until after the musicians had done their work for the day.

They took him away, calmed him down, and a few hours later, when Grady went to pick him up at the station, Waymon seemed at ease. They went to Grady's hotel room, where Grady told him, 'You'd better stay here and relax awhile.' Grady fell asleep for a few minutes and woke up to the sound of the phone ringing. Sassy was summoning him again. Waymon was behaving violently. Sassy was fearful. By the time Grady got to Sassy's room, Waymon had run away. Grady followed Waymon out of the hotel and saw him standing in the middle of the street. Several cars were backed up on both sides of Waymon. He was yelling, 'Kill me, kill me!' Grady forced himself into the street to lead Waymon to safety. (After Waymon had been married to Greta for ten years, he once had drunk some bleach because of marital tensions, Greta recalls. 'He was a strange bird,' she says.) As far as Grady could see, Waymon was mentally and physically ill, 'suffering from everything a person could possibly have – diabetes, cancer, mental illness, everything'. Grady knew about Waymon's illnesses from Sassy. Waymon was hospitalised several times during the marriage.

Soon after the San Diego incident, he called Greta from a Los Angeles hospital, told her he had cancer, and asked her to visit him. The cancer began in a kidney, spread to his colon and then his liver. Although he and Greta hadn't been in touch during the first year of his marriage to Sassy, Greta flew to Los Angeles and visited him on weekends in the hospital a few times. 'He knew he was dying, and he wanted to apologise for a few things,' Greta says. Sassy didn't like it that Waymon asked Greta to visit. Nevertheless, Greta and Waymon stayed in touch after that. Their sons had been visiting Sassy and Waymon in

Hidden Hills right along; Waymon Jr liked Sassy and especially Debby, who were very nice to him.

When Norman Granz didn't want to use him as the trumpet player for the Duke Ellington songbooks being recorded for Pablo in a California studio, Waymon sulked so much on the first day of recording that Sassy was unusually quiet and uncomfortable in the studio. She talked alone with Waymon when she had a moment. The next day, just before the session was about to begin, the word circulated among the musicians hired for the date that Sassy was cancelling the job. According to union regulations, the musicians had to be paid, even if the date was cancelled, because of the short notice. Sassy didn't show up for the second day of recording. Later she persuaded Norman Granz to let Waymon play. The sessions for the Ellington songbooks were finished in New York, not California.

For nearly a year, Charlie Lake stayed with Sassy, moving from Massachusetts to California, where Sassy placed him in a hotel in North Hollywood and provided him with a car. Then she decided that she didn't feel like working for a while. Although she kept paying him, he felt odd, away from home with nothing to do. And when he did begin working with the group, he couldn't help but notice how she and Waymon fought. 'She thrives on chaos,' Charlie thought. 'If things don't go wrong, she can't stand it. She doesn't like things to run smoothly.' He thought she was quite bossy. At other times, she could be 'double good', but to work for, she was 'tough'. He thought she was tough to live with, too. Yet Sassy was very protective of her mother and daughter. Overall, Charlie Lake thought that if you weren't on Sassy's payroll, you could sometimes be great friends with her. Once he left her employ and worked for Dizzy again, Charlie's friendship with Sassy resumed.

She called her mother's old friends in Newark and invited them to Hidden Hills for holidays. To Mrs Maude Crews, who directed the choir at the First Mount Zion Baptist Church, Sassy said, 'Come on out for Thanksgiving. I'm tired of seeing the same faces.' Sassy didn't want her mother to be homesick for her crowd in Newark. Mrs Crews couldn't go, because her husband didn't like to fly. Sassy also supervised where Debby, now in her late teens, went, and with whom, and what time she would be home, still trying to shelter the girl. When Sassy was at home, she entertained friends with Debby and Ada together. Sometimes, Pumpkin recalled, Sassy telephoned him and exclaimed jokingly about Debby, 'Your child! . . .' But the mother and daughter got along well, Mike Wofford thought. Sassy had the consideration to make Waymon the beneficiary of her union life insurance, with Debby as his alternate.

'When it came to people she loved, she'd do anything for them,' George Wein said. But by the time Charlie Lake met Sassy, embroiled as she was in her exceptionally difficult marriage to Waymon Reed, she was 'an angry lady', according to Charlie.

Sassy wasn't always logical in her approach to the business side of her career. And she had spent so little effort on taking care of her health or protecting her peace of mind that she was becoming rather excitable and difficult. The years of stress and indulgence had begun to take their toll. 'Maybe her problems caught up with her,' George Wein theorised. Grady Tate, James Harper, Frank Rio, Larry Clothier, and others of her friends knew that Waymon was giving her constant problems, while Waymon's friends thought that the marriage exacerbated his troubles. 'He had the money, but he was not happy,' Greta says.

There were, of course, people who never had any experience with Sassy's sassiness or temperament. She once sent Robert Richards a blank cheque because she suspected he might need money. She also encouraged others, Tom Guy for one, to ask her for money if they needed it. Robert Richards knew she gave B money as a gift, whether B, then earning a great deal of money by anyone's standards in the early 1980s, needed the gift or not. Michael Tilson Thomas enjoyed only good times with her.

Without ascribing responsibility for her moodiness to Waymon or anyone else, Sassy's booking agent, Frank Rio, thought that Waymon didn't help her frame of mind at all. Rio, who spent all but a few years between 1953 to 1990 as Sassy's booking agent and knew all her husbands, beginning with Treadwell, had the longest business relationship with her. 'When she listened to me, she made the right choices, and when she didn't listen, she made mistakes,' he said, laughing as he recollected their long, complex relationship. He shrank from discussing her with the press, but he, too, did say she was sometimes difficult.

There were numerous incidents, some stemming from Waymon's physical ailments, that upset Sassy and the people around her. Sassy, Waymon and Freddie Hubbard went into Bradley's, a club in New York, where an old friend of Sassy's was playing. Bradley Cunningham, the sociable, rugged-looking owner, told the pianist, 'Hey, there's Sassy.' The pianist left the piano and went to hug her. 'I rubbed my face against hers, looking for a drop of her perspiration to share with her. Then I saw Waymon's expression; Waymon didn't seem to want anyone even to put a hand on Sassy's shoulder,' the pianist recalled.

He backed away and looked to Freddie Hubbard for help, but Freddie hadn't noticed what was going on with Waymon.

When Sassy and Waymon travelled to the south of France, Annie Ross visited them in their suite. Annie overheard Waymon asking Sassy to cut his hair. While she was doing that, he said, 'Gee, wouldn't it be nice to travel on the Concorde.' Sassy gave Annie a funny look and said, 'Well, *yes*, that sounds nice. But do you know how expensive the Concorde is?' Waymon said, 'Yes, but it sure would be nice.' Annie thought Waymon sounded like a beseeching child. Mike Wofford wondered if Sassy might have encouraged that sort of childish behaviour; she was the boss, and Waymon was the employee. But he was also her husband and a fine trumpet player; he had a right to share with her in everything. She had given him that right by marrying him, and she could afford the Concorde. Mike Wofford quit his job with Sassy after a year because of the strained atmosphere. Andy Simpkins, a well-liked and easygoing fellow, Mike Wofford thought, weathered the storm with seeming ease, letting it roll off his back. 'I focused only on the music,' Andy explained.

When they had married, in 1978, Sassy and Waymon had rented an apartment on West Fifty-fifth Street in New York. Robert Richards was invited to dine with them several times in the succeeding years. He saw Sassy and Waymon padding around the apartment in their slippers, having a good time cooking; they seemed friendly and affectionate with each other and with him. Grady Tate, too, knew how sweet and charming Waymon could be. But the last time Robert had dinner in that apartment in 1980, Waymon wasn't there. Sassy had a girlfriend with her. Though a stranger to Robert, the woman was clearly a confidante of Sassy's. The girlfriend advised her, 'You've done all that you can, and it just isn't working out.' Sassy seemed quiet and glum.

Sassy hid her private life from the public very well. Robert Palmer, reviewing her concert on 5 February 1980 at Avery Fisher Hall, remarked that her husband, Waymon Reed, with his usual sensitive contribution to her accompaniment, was missed. Waymon was hospitalised in California at the time. Gary Giddins, writing in the *Village Voice*, loved everything about her March engagement at the Grand Finale, one of the few clubs in New York that could afford Sassy's price. (She was earning an annual income in the high six figures; by the time of her death in 1990, she would earn at least a million dollars a year, Robert Richards estimated.) Giddins preferred the intimacy of her performance and her treatment of her songs in the Grand Finale to her Ellington songbook, some of which she had performed at Avery Fisher Hall, and he even liked her playfulness, when she lip-synched 'Misty' as drummer Grady Tate sang it, startling the audience at first. 'The intimacy' of the club 'loosened her up', Giddins wrote. 'She . . . scatted Waymon Reed's "46th and 8th" [including his trumpet solo from his record of that name on the Artists Home label] and burned through "Cherokee". There were several show-stopping ballads, of course. . . .'

It didn't bother Giddins that she introduced herself as June Carter. She had developed a comic bit in her shows of introducing her trio to audiences, then telling them, 'In case you've wandered in off the highway [or from someplace] and don't know where you are, I'm Della Reese.' Usually she used that singer's name, but she occasionally called herself someone else. Carmen McRae was very pleased when she heard that Sassy had once announced herself on stage in Japan as Carmen McRae. Giddins remarked that she took requests only when the audience requested 'Send in the Clowns'. That had become her signature piece. It was 'a remarkable performance', Giddins wrote, 'and though I always respond to it with "no, not again" . . . I always get goose bumps when she hones in on the big a cappella climax, "Losing my timing this late in myyyyyyyyyy career".'

Giddins hadn't liked Sassy's versions of some of his favourite Ellington songs on her Pablo recording because 'Vaughan occasionally threatens their integrity with her mannerisms. . . . The outstanding ballad selection, "In a Sentimental Mood", is the exception – brilliant Vaughan that dwarfs everything else on the record. She works the arpeggios with scrupulous care . . . with utter control, her low notes booming sonorously . . .' He was right; the songbook was, at times, disappointingly stiff, and if the stiffness in her voice reflected her emotional life for once, it was no wonder.

Charlie Lake, the road manager whose first duty was to fire Roy McCurdy, was fired himself in the wake of a fight that Sassy had with Waymon in a motel room. Lake had been staying next door to the couple. The fight had followed a successful gig that Waymon had played, leading his own quintet at Donte's in North Hollywood. Sassy had flown Tommy Flanagan in from Texas to play piano for the date. She tried to stay out of Waymon's way, hoping, Lake saw, to avoid controversy; she also sang beautifully for Waymon's group and filled the club for him. But afterward, Charlie Lake heard objects moving around and other sounds of a fight in the couple's room. In the throes of the struggle, she telephoned Charlie and said, 'And you're fired, too.' Charlie left right away. Soon afterward he heard the news that Waymon and Sassy separated.

Sassy hired a youngster as a road manager after Charlie Lake left the group in 1980; then she hired Bob Redcross, a well-known jazz figure, who had also worked for Dizzy and would do so again. And she had several managers in the 1980s; Harry Addesso, for one, who didn't have the background necessary to manage a singer of Sassy's stature, followed by the experienced, well-respected Milt Ebbins, who was then in his seventies, George Wein believed. Ebbins and Sassy parted company once, then started to work together again for a little while in the mid-1980s.

Divorced from Sassy, Waymon Reed played at the Kool Jazz Festival gig with the Count Basie band alumni in Saratoga, New York, in June 1981. By chance, Jimmy Cobb, Walter Booker, Roy McCurdy, and several other musicians whom Waymon had treated rudely were playing in the area at the same time. Apparently Waymon was afraid of what the men might do to him, Roy McCurdy said, because of their memories. 'That's right,' said Larry Clothier, who was at the festival, too. The men simply gave him the silent treatment and ignored him. McCurdy and Larry saw Waymon sitting alone, quiet and looking around suspiciously. That was the last time McCurdy saw Waymon,

Saxophonist Ralph Lalama, who had played with Waymon during the 1970s in the Thad Jones-Mel Lewis band every Monday night at the Village Vanguard, was working for drummer Buddy Rich's group in 1981 when Waymon joined Rich. Ralph asked Waymon, 'What are you doing here?' Waymon said, 'I came here to cool out.' Ralph said, 'You must be crazy.' It was well known that the mercurial Rich often screamed at people. 'He could holler at anybody,' Ralph recalled. 'But later I understood what Waymon meant. He had been hanging out and drinking every night in New York. He was taking chemotherapy for liver cancer, and on the bus with Rich, he was eating nuts and berries and trying to take care of himself. He wasn't drinking. Buddy Rich treated him well. So Waymon really did cool out. He was nice to hang out with. He was kind of mellow and happy to be there. And he didn't complain about Sarah. He may have said some little thing once in a while – but he didn't discuss her with me for the six months we spent together on that bus. In six months you talk about a lot of things. Waymon was playing very well; he sounded good. We had a lot in common, playing jazz.' When Ralph left Rich during 1981, Waymon was still playing with the group.

At some time during the last years of Waymon's life, he played trumpet in a long run of the road-show company of *Sophisticated Ladies* produced at the Shubert Theater in Los Angeles. During 1982 Waymon joined the musicians' union in Los Angeles. Trumpeter Snooky Young and saxophonist Marshall Royal, both alumni of the illustrious Count Basie band of the 1950s, were playing in the show with Waymon. Carl Schroeder, who went to see Waymon at the theatre, had the impression that the Basie alumni and several other musicians at the Shubert were helping Waymon through the job. He was having chemotherapy treatments and couldn't always play for the show. Someone was looking out for him, Schroeder understood.

Saxophonist Hank Crawford, who had known Waymon from their early career days in Tennessee, where Waymon had been raised, occasionally saw Waymon in a grocery store on Eighth Avenue in Manhattan. They lived in the same neighbourhood, Waymon living in the apartment he had shared with Sassy until the lease ran out. Sassy paid the rent. Hank, who usually saw Waymon alone and always found him pleasant and quiet, never noticed any disturbance in his personality. Although they weren't intimate friends, Hank admired Waymon's playing and asked the trumpeter to play on Hank's first album for the Concord label in 1983. At that time, Hank noticed that Waymon was sick. 'He was losing his chops,' Hank recalls.

The last time Grady Tate saw Waymon, in New York City in 1983, he was so sick from cancer, weak and thin, that he couldn't work. He also looked very sick when he went backstage at Carnegie Hall one night to see Dizzy Gillespie that year. Greta thought Waymon had lost so much weight, he looked pathetic. He stayed in her house for a few weeks, barely able to manage anything. She admired the way he faced up to his disease: 'He didn't bellyache or cry. He was very brave,' she says. Waymon Jr, took a leave of absence from Carnegie-Mellon University so he could take care of his father. Though Sassy had stood by him during his early battle with cancer, she wasn't in touch with Waymon by 1983. Annie Ross said that when Sassy wanted to sever the strings of memories to relationships, 'she went snip' – Annie made scissorlike motions with her hand.

A bartender named Henry Lafarque, who worked at the Possible Twenty, a jazz bar in Manhattan, saw Waymon occasionally after his divorce and thought the trumpeter was 'a very quiet, easygoing guy' who 'was hurt about Sarah. He always felt "done in". At least that's what he told me.' Ralph Lalama heard about a benefit being held at a jazz club, Sonny's Place, in Seaford, Long Island. 'I don't usually go to those things,' Ralph recalled, but because he liked Waymon so much, becoming friends with him after the marriage to Sassy ended, Ralph decided to go. He was surprised and upset to see how thin and ill Waymon looked. 'His face looked sunken in,' Ralph remembered. In late August or early September 1983, Larry Clothier saw Waymon at Grant's Tomb during a Jazzmobile concert played by Dizzy Gillespie. 'I thought that Waymon weighed about one hundred pounds; he looked terrible,' Larry remembered. A doctor told Waymon that he had three months to live; he went to Greta's apartment and told her, then headed to his father's house in Nashville. His mother, who had been an educator, had already died, and his father, William, had been the religious editor of the *Nashville Tennessean* newspaper, Greta recalled. She was about to take the children from New York to visit Waymon, when she got the call from her former father-in-law. Waymon died of cancer on Thanksgiving Day 1983, when he was forty-three years old.

★ ★ ★

Sassy was so disheartened by the failure of the marriage that she never started another romance. She told Pumpkin, 'If I ever say I'm thinking about getting married again, stop me.' Pumpkin thought she must have said to herself, 'I've tried and I've tried and I've tried, and it didn't work out, and I'm tired of trying.' Grady Tate said, 'Sassy blamed herself – not for Waymon's illnesses but for making the mistake of marrying the man.' She had known it would be a difficult marriage. She had known that she was impulsive when it came to men and that she kept making the same mistakes. But she knew that with hindsight. 'She became more reclusive after that marriage,' Grady observed. 'But when she hung out, she did so more than ever.'

In her flowing caftans onstage, she looked fatter than in her street clothes. It was possible to mistake her for an unassuming, neat, and chubby middle-aged housewife when she slipped away from her entourage for a moment and sat alone in a restaurant to have a meal. It was also possible to assess her as a happy, carefree woman when she found herself in the company of old friends, musicians she had known for a long time and with whom she could laugh and joke about the old days. When Thad Jones began to lead the Count Basie band after Basie died in April 1984, Sassy travelled to play with Thad in a Brooklyn park in a black neighbourhood remote from Manhattan. After the concert, she and Thad and a few others got into a car to go back to Manhattan, laughing and talking, friendly and easeful. Many of their old friends in jazz were dying, and the survivors who loved each other and remembered their early struggles together loved to see and hug each other.

Some people had the impression that Sarah Vaughan in those days was a temperamental, prickly, overly assertive woman. Though she was certain of her gift and love for singing and performing, she remained curiously insecure. In conversations, she rushed her words and talked hesitantly. She tried to compensate for her shyness by nerve, bravado and gritty determination – survival instincts that had guided her from her adolescent days into and out of Newark's clubs.

In her business office, The Devine One, set up in her townhouse in Beverly Hills, Harry Addesso, her manager in the early 1980s, a tall, well-built fellow, who dressed with panache and spoke in a rough but good-natured way, tried hard to make things run smoothly. But it was a taxing job for him. 'She's moody,' he explained to people who asked him to get her to do things – interviews, for example. He set up a date for Sassy to have an interview for a magazine article; he told her about it, and she agreed to it, but when the reporter arrived, she said brusquely, 'I don't know nothing about it.' She strutted away.

She was difficult because that was what her profession and her art required her to be, Grady Tate thought. Women instrumentalists had a hard path to follow; he knew their lot was unfair in the great, good jazz world, he offered, and women singers, too, had to deal with prejudice and sexual discrimination. Opportunists of all types popped up around every corner with their own ends in mind. But Sassy had weathered rough years; anyone who had been around for a while had to become somewhat jaded and embittered. And the failure of her last marriage compounded her entire life's experience.

Some people would ascribe her testiness – her refusal to sing without monitors, which allowed her to hear how she sounded during a performance, and her cancellation of jobs, and her squabbles with producers in the recording industry – to her failed relationships with men. Others thought it came from overindulgence in food, cigarettes, Cognac and cocaine. Still others who had known her for decades thought the rigours of her career and personal life had surely tired her out. All those opinions contained some of the truth. Her daughter Debby would say: 'Sarah Vaughan was such a complicated person. I'm not sure anyone can say, if they're being truthful, that they knew this woman.'

In the 1980s, Sassy was a very different woman and singer than she had been in her twenties, when the musicians in Earl Hine's band had doted on her bright, sweet, compliant expression. By the 1980s she came to view the world and her position in it very differently than she had on the night in 1951 when Grady Tate had watched her come onstage, a young woman wearing a white gown and singing her heart out with Les Brown and His Band of Renown in a Texas arena. She had sung with the most awesome sound of any singer he had ever heard. During her middle age, her voice became enriched, but her last dream of romance was dashed.

SIXTEEN

Winning an Emmy, a Grammy, and Other Honours

In July 1980, Sassy appeared again at the Grand Finale in Manhattan. *Village Voice* writer Arthur Bell discovered that she 'had thrown a couple of temper tantrums' during her run there, and the staff seemed to enjoy them as much as it did her singing. He didn't elaborate about her temperament, but he liked her version of 'Send in the Clowns' best of all her songs the night he saw her – 'a touching paean to those who have put career before love', he wrote. 'And I'm sure she really means it when she tells the audience "I love you" seven times.' The audience fed the line back to her seven times, too. Bell interpreted the response as reassurance that Sassy needed. But it might just as easily have been called *ease*. Sassy had felt more at ease with audiences beginning in the 1970s, she had told writer Louis Robinson in 1975, and her onstage gracefulness with people that had developed increasingly during her relationship with Marshall Fisher lingered on even after Fisher was out of her life.

Critics would sometimes complain that Sassy sang 'Send in the Clowns' too often, or that her voice broke with a sob they called inappropriate at the end of the song, and that she pronounced the word *my* as *moy*. But her change in the vowel sound made it resound with pathos; she simulated a moment's sorrow in exactly the right place for her interpretation. The song actually refers to the traditional call for the clowns to come running out to divert an audience's attention from a disaster during a circus performance. After so many years of relying upon her own judgment about how to sing and what she wanted to express, Sassy showed no signs of wanting to listen to advice from non-musicians. About her ability to sing a song repeatedly with exuberance, she had told a reporter early in her career, 'There are no tired songs, there are only tired singers.'

Her impatience in public had also grown commensurate with the time she had spent accommodating audiences and feinting with the music industry. Bertha Hope witnessed a quintessential Vaughanism during the 1980s. Bertha was sitting in the Village Vanguard audience one night when Sassy arrived to hear some music at that venerated jazz club. During the set, a man stood in front of her table to tell her how much he loved her singing. Sassy said, 'Thanks,' and added, 'Now will you please get out of my way?' Bertha knew that jazz musicians didn't always tolerate interruptions when they were listening to good music any more than they liked people having loud conversations in their own audiences, so Bertha excused Sassy's abruptness. She was sure Sassy's fan felt upset.

In the summer of 1980, Sassy's name was put on a plaque installed in the sidewalk in front of 'Black Rock', the austere, Saarinen-designed CBS building, the network's corporate headquarters, on the block where some Fifty-second Street clubs had stood beginning in the 1930s. The block was part of 'Swing Street' named in honour of those clubs. Sassy was invited to the ceremonies, called the Prez Awards (for Lester 'Prez' Young, 'president' of the tenor saxophone) because she was one of the musicians who had helped make Fifty-second Street between Fifth and Seventh avenues the world's centre of progressive jazz.

On 2 September 1980 Sassy's concert on a bill with Henry Mancini at the Garden State Arts Center again inspired one of her greatest admirers, George Kanzler Jr, to write a review for the *Newark Star Ledger* that evoked the spirit of all her performances. 'Not only is Sarah Vaughan at the height of her artistic powers . . . but on Tuesday she also was obviously in a good mood, perhaps happy to be playing to a home-state audience. For the Newark native was simply dazzling, and more than a bit playful . . . The playfulness came out exuberantly in her prancing, skipping scat singing over the . . . horns on "I've Got the World on a String", a song on which she also bent notes with the grace of a swooping falcon.' Vaughan's voice with its 'incredibly rich, honeyed lower register . . . on "Dindi" . . . the Brazilian song with lyrics that evoke the sea and sky' did a 'deep sea dive during the coda . . . It is a feat she performs even more dramatically on her second rendering of the bridge of "Send in the Clowns", a shopworn song only she can keep finding new vocal appeal in with each performance.'

For Duke Ellington's 'In a Mellotone', she maintained 'that swing-era feeling, romping with a graceful power through the lyrics and riding the riffing band horns in a scat solo full of joyous virtuosity'. And she approached Ellington's 'I Got It Bad and That Ain't Good': 'with utmost tenderness, caressing each word as she essayed it in a slower than usual tempo, practically stopping the beat to concentrate on drawing out the notes languorously . . . Vaughan uses songs to draw out and enhance their meaning through her artistry.' At the end of September 1980, the *New York Times*'s Richard F. Shepard was enthusiastic about her Gershwin programme called 'Rhapsody and Song – A Tribute to George Gershwin' performed with the New Jersey Symphony Orchestra and broadcast on PBS. 'What is there here you could possibly not like?' he said simply.

In one of the more ironic twists of her career, in May 1981 the National Academy of Television Arts and Sciences awarded her an Emmy for the Gershwin performance; the category was 'Individual Achievement – Special Class'. It came before she ever received a Grammy Award for any of her recordings! Repeatedly throughout the 1980s, she dazzled audiences at Carnegie Hall, during concerts in all seasons, sometimes with her trios, other times with Count Basie or Joe Williams or Tony Bennett or George Benson, just to name a few of the people who shared her stages and from whom she took over, dressed in her billowing gowns. She sang to standing-room-only audiences at the Village Gate; she joined a tribute to Duke Ellington on a sixty-minute programme, 'Kennedy Center Tonight', produced by EWQED-TV in Pittsburgh; she performed at Radio City Music Hall on a bill with Frank Sinatra, Count Basie, and comedian Rich Little to benefit the Memorial Sloan-Kettering Cancer Center. And she sang outdoors at Wolf Trap Farm in Virginia with only a feather fans as a weapon against the summer heat. During the performance, she said that because of the way she was sweating, she should come to Wolf Trap in February. 'It was her metabolism that made her perspire so much. I knew how much it upset her,' Mike Wofford said. Andy Simpkins, who travelled with her in the 1980s, always put on a jacket when he went to her hotel suites or rode in her limousines, because she turned up the air-conditioning so high.

In January 1982 Sassy was waiting at home in her hilltop house in Hidden Valley for Michael Tilson Thomas to arrive for a rehearsal for a February benefit for the pension fund of the Los Angeles Philharmonic. Writer A. James Liska, assigned to do a piece for *Down Beat* magazine, was admitted to Sassy's house, even to her private quarters, for an interview. CBS was going to record the concert. In a good mood, Sassy explained to Liska that she used one room, which opened out on to a large swimming pool, to sleep and work in; she liked that arrangement. She had decorated the wall over her bed with black-and-white photographs of jazz figures in simple black frames. An upright piano and an electric piano stood in her room along with a portable electronic keyboard which she liked to take with her on the road. No longer did she need to wait to get a piano to see what note a train whistle was blowing. At the time of the interview, she had three dogs living in her house. On top of her television, which was positioned for her to watch while she rested in bed, she had set her Emmy award. She had not as yet won a Grammy. 'I won that for a TV show I did, but nobody ever knew about it. People are always surprised I won that,' she said, and she laughed. 'It's unbelievable, that's what it is, that everybody likes me as well as they do. I still can't believe it,' she told Liska.

Michael Tilson Thomas arrived for the rehearsal, sat down at the piano, and told her, 'Take the time at the bottom, then get it back.' Sassy sat down on the edge of her bed to study the introduction he had written for 'The Man I Love'. Tilson Thomas said, 'You know all about that stuff.' She said firmly, 'I'll be glad when people find out that I do not know everything.' He said, 'You know everything there is to know.' Liska heard the sound of gentle reassurance in Tilson Thomas's voice. She said, 'I know everything I know.' She paused and laughed, Liska reported. Liking her own joke, she said, 'That's a good line.' Tilson Thomas had added some new material to the all-Gershwin programmes he and Sassy had performed previously. Sassy said, 'These new tunes have me a nervous wreck. I like new tunes. But they make me nervous. I can't help it.' Liska reported: 'Her voice changes to a raspy whisper, drawing attention to and perfectly befitting the story which is to follow. "I got ossified, you know. One night I got drunk just thinking about it. In my own house. I just went into the living-room and drank me some Cognac. Went to take a sip. Took sips . . ." She laughs.'

'Before Sarah goes on, she's real nervous,' Tilson Thomas explained to Liska. 'But the minute she's on . . .' The words of confidence have little effect on Vaughan, who interrupts with a reminder about her nervousness: 'I'm so nervous right now, and I'm always nervous before a show. Barbara McNair made a statement in *Jet* magazine that people who were nervous before they went on must be insecure. I don't know why she said that. Carmen says the same thing. Before I go on, I'm real nervous, and it lasts until I get the reaction from the audience.' Sassy added that sometimes things got worse instead of better; when people just stared at her, she could be so unnerved that she shortened her shows. Then the audiences went looking for her to sign autographs and told her that she had never sounded better. She would ask them why they had sat like slabs of stone; she had thought they couldn't stand her singing. Tilson Thomas tried to soothe her. 'Oh, come on now, just sixteen lousy bars,' he said, alluding to the introduction. Sassy said, 'They could be sixteen messed-up bars. I'm gonna have all this music on stage with me, you know.' He told her, 'Anything you like on stage is fine' and promised to follow her lead. 'You see? No sacrifice is too great for my art,' he said.

Sassy confided some memories of her career to Liska, saying that she had once gone through five years without making a record because, she said, 'the record companies wanted me to do something I didn't want to do', to make her sound commercial. She was too subtle a singer, people complained. She didn't like 'Broken Hearted Melody', she said – 'the corniest thing I ever did', as she described it. She reminisced about her work for Mercury, proudly recounting that one side of each 78 rpm release was commercial, and the other side was her choice. 'Usually the side I picked was the one that sold the record, though.' As she said that, she smiled in such a way to make Liska think she had 'self-assuredness'. And she mused that she wasn't a jazz singer or a blues singer, she was just a singer. 'I don't know why people call me a jazz singer, though I guess people associate me with jazz because I was raised in it, from way back. I'm not putting jazz down, but I'm not a jazz singer. Betty Bebop [Carter] is a jazz singer, because that's all she does. I've even been called a blues singer. I've recorded all kinds of music, but [to them] I'm either a jazz singer or a blues singer. I can't sing a blues – just a right-out blues – but I can put the blues in whatever I sing. I might sing "Send in the Clowns" and I might stick a little bluesy part in it, or any song. What I want to do, music-wise, is all kinds of music that I like, and I like all kinds of music. I want to do a country-and-western record, but I want to do it with my kind of background. I hate country-and-western the way it's done; it all sounds the same to me, so I want to do my own version.'

She let Liska know that she controlled her own recording projects to a great extent by that time, that she was toying with doing an album with some spirituals included, and that she had planned a new album called *Crazy and Mixed Up* for Pablo – a title which amused her very much. She said that she never felt jealous of singers who had a greater commercial success than she – the people who sang 'punk rock, soul-punk rock, rock jazz, jazz that rocks, jazz that doesn't rock, jazz jazz, jazz minus punk' – because she didn't have to sing the kinds of songs that she didn't like. She had reached a position in life where she could do as she pleased; even onstage, she let her feelings lead her in the songs and sometimes even let her mind wander to faraway matters – had the fence been fixed? had her dog gotten well? 'That's why I forget lyrics sometimes,' she told Liska. She thought she would like to do a tour with the Basie band, and she reminisced about some long past adventures.

She and the Basie band had done a seventy-one-day tour that ended in Detroit. Everyone, including Sassy, had gotten so drunk to celebrate that people had to go looking for them. 'They even found some of them in the curb. We must have drank up all of the whisky in Detroit. I was just one of the boys in the band,' she said. Another Basie story came to her mind. She had been on a bus with Basie, with Billy Eckstine and a friend of Eckstine's along, who tied Basie up with big link chains as he slept on the bus. When Basie woke up and found himself in chains, she recalled, he said, 'Damn.' 'Boy, what fun we had on that bus,' Sassy said. She went to the window and looked out at the lights of a nearby community. 'I've been singing all my life, and I've never really thought about anything else since that amateur hour [at the Apollo]. But I'm the same way now that I was when I was eighteen. I don't go for that star stuff. All the stars are in heaven.'

She had a rehearsal scheduled for the next day, after which she flew to Delaware for an engagement, then went to New York City, where she performed two concerts at the Beacon Theatre, relying on many of her usual standards, 'My Funny Valentine', 'Misty', 'I Hadn't Anyone Till You', 'Lush Life', and 'Send in the Clowns'. From there she went to the Ritz Theater in Elizabeth, New Jersey, for a weekend of concerts, and on Sunday morning she flew back to California to work with Count Basie at a library that day. On Sunday night, Monday afternoon and Monday night, she rehearsed. Her nervousness hadn't dissipated though she had worked on and off for a decade with Michael, and she could lean on him. Once she learned the music he had written for her, an aria for 'The Man I Love', he told her that it was really a countermelody for the bass line. She said, 'Oh, you clever little . . .'

She taped the rehearsal so she could listen to it alone and learn from it and make decisions about what she would do in the concert. (Eventually she made a present of that fascinating tape to Robert Richards.) As she and Michael rehearsed 'Do It Again', she sang the title repeatedly, ethereally, toying with the melody, the emphasis. Her voice is so soft and rushed when she speaks that one strains to hear her. But she and Michael understand each other clearly when they speak in half-sentences or play and sing together. 'Let me play the end of the piano solo just going into the . . . ,' Michael says.

'Yes, that's a good idea,' she says, experimenting to work out the ending she will eventually use for the concert.

He says, 'You'll do something interesting there.'

She says, 'Sure,' and sings it again and giggles.

He says, 'You'll do something fun, but the [chord] changes are clear.'

She does 'Do It Again' again and again. 'Remember that, that's a cute little ending,' she says and giggles again.

'Spacey,' he says.

As they start working on 'Sweet and Low Down', Michael says, 'You want to have a handkerchief like a lieder singer.'

'I don't know . . . ,' she says. 'Sing with me.'

He has a strong pop, Broadway style, while he plays a plunk-plunk accompaniment with brilliant articulation. 'It's going to be too high for you, when we go back into the uptempo reprise,' he tells her about a certain passage. 'I can either stay where I am . . .' and he plays high notes. Then, 'It's too high. I have to get back into the lower key.'

'Is this just me and you?' she asks him, referring to a duo presentation for the concert.

'This is just me and you,' he says. 'If you want to sing over the piano solo, do whatever you want to do.'

'Right now I just want to get it into my brain,' she says breathlessly. She isn't thinking about embellishment yet. She starts working on singing the word *electricity*.

'So,' Michael says, 'It's two bars . . . My advice is . . . "That's sweet and low down" – beat-beat . . .'

'It's a cute little tune,' she says.

He suggests, 'That's sweet and low low low,' playing and singing a rising scale, with Broadway-show pizzazz.

She says, 'That's too abrupt.'

Michael advises her about 'Sweet and Low Down', 'You sing this in a motherly way. You're giving advice here.'

She sings in a beautiful, ethereal voice and says, 'Let me get this on the tape.'

'Do you want to do one more version of "The Man I Love" on this tape?' he asks.

They work on the melody he had written for the introduction to 'The Man I Love'. Then he asks her about the song, 'Do you want to sing it the way it was written, or do you want to sing? . . .' and he plays a bit.

She said, 'Why don't I just go through it.' She noodled her way through the front.

At one point, she thought he was playing some higher notes than she was singing for a passage, and he said, no, he was playing below her, and when she sang the passage again, her reason for her question became clear. She suddenly soars to a very high note, up from her contralto register, and then she sinks gracefully back whence she had sprung, demonstrating perfectly her ability to make a listener cry or shudder with joy.

Michael would later reflect, 'Even as someone involved in the music with her, I was suddenly startled when she took a phrase in a direction that made my heart stop. I gasped at her ideas. I couldn't believe she was going so far out to the edge of the possible and miraculously bringing it off. She was a prima donna.'

She performed 'the Gershwin thing', as she called it, with Michael on Tuesday at the Dorothy Chandler Auditorium with the Los Angeles Philharmonic and her trio, with arrangements by Marty Paich and Michael. Her glorious voice sounded deeper, richer, more resonant and expressive than it ever had. She exuded control, changing keys in the middle of the word *shining* in 'A Foggy Day', lifting her encore song into the realm of the sublime. Sassy's reviews were superb. And the press compared Michael, as a pianist and conductor, with Leonard Bernstein. A reviewer for a UCLA newspaper wrote that her voice was as distinctive as the clarinet solo in 'An American in Paris'. Her sound had lost none of its softness and naturalness; she had given none of her power over to time. The CBS recording won her a Grammy nomination. Sassy's Kool Jazz Festival concert that year featured a taste of her Gershwin album in deference to CBS, which was covering her bills, she announced from the stage of Carnegie Hall. She was dressed in a tent-like dress the colour of orange sherbet. She ended with her a cappella masterpiece, 'The Lord's Prayer', and elicited a standing ovation.

She appeared at a ceremony at Atlanta's Clark College where Dizzy Gillespie was awarded an honorary doctorate at a jazz festival, and then she sang in Atlantic City in July; she performed on a National Public Radio show aired on 29 September that celebrated the fifth anniversary of NPR's 'Jazz Alive!' series. And under less than ideal conditions in October, in a large, poorly ventilated hall, she delivered a seventy-five-minute-long performance for an audience of 2,500 people in the

Stephens College Assembly Hall in Columbia, Missouri, with Butch Lacey on piano. Andy Simpkins the bassist, and Harold Jones on drums, repeating herself, repeating her repertoire, all the while investing the songs with the illusion of freshness. She repeated her jokes about being Della Reese and coming onstage looking like Lena Horne and going off bathed in perspiration like Sarah Vaughan. She had acquired an air of comical spontaneity, and she let it go at that.

She could charm an audience to the quick with her palaver about a mere glass of water. If the ice melted, she would tell an audience that she hated warm water, but she would let bygones be bygones with the missing ice and drink any old wonderful water during the show. Water glasses, stools and handkerchiefs became effective props to support a bit of small talk from her. 'May you live forever,' she once toasted a Wolf Trap audience with a glass of water, miming a tipsy woman, assuring the audience that she never drank when she worked, although she had probably had her share of Cognac before going onstage, 'and may I never die.' Her musicians marvelled that she drank ice water, something that no other singer could do and still sing. She was comfortable with her format, under the pressure of travelling, at her age, with her girth, in her physical condition, and with her psychological outlook from the years of having carried on in spite of everything.

For the Stephens College performance, she arrived in Kansas City at 5 a.m. on a Friday and travelled to Columbia by car for two and a half hours. Transformed over the years from a wallflower to a crowd-pleaser, she sat down at the piano to play for her encore at Stephens, as she had done in many other places. 'When I was seven, I wanted to play piano. And then,' she smiled, threw her arms out, and delivered her usual line: 'I discovered I was a jazz singer.' She played parts of well-known classical pieces. From Missouri, she flew to California for a recording session with Billy Eckstine in October 1982, and spent the rest of the month performing in California and in Houston and Dallas, Texas, then went to Italy and England.

In November she appeared at Dangerfield's in New York, where Billy Eckstine also performed in the 1980s; she sat on a stool and confided to the audience that she was afraid she would fall off the small stage if she stood up and walked around on it in her usual style. She was at her sweetest at such times. Writing letters to friends to thank them, in her very regular, neat handwriting, for favours they had done and for compliments they had paid her, she waxed chatty, informal and very generous, calling her friends 'you guys', kid-style, and wishing them 'all the good things', health, happiness, love and money, and God's blessings.

In 1983 she finally won her first Grammy for the Gershwin album. Carl Schroeder remembered the couple of times when he had been working for her and she had been nominated for Grammys. He had been shocked by her losses. Robert Richards later said, 'She thought the Gershwin album was one of her best.' She had rehearsed painstakingly with Michael Tilson Thomas, had listened to everything he said, and then she had performed in her own way. 'She felt that she had produced the one album that represented everything she could communicate in person. To listen to that album [she felt] was as exciting as seeing her in person. And the album let her combine all her popular, classical, operatic, and jazz background in one presentation,' Robert Richards said.

When the album had been released the previous summer, she had been performing at Avery Fisher Hall in New York City. Robert Richards went to see her backstage after the performance. She whispered to him, 'Come with me,' and she led him into a bathroom, where she locked the door and asked, 'What do you think of it?' He said, 'It's fabulous. How do you like it?' She shouted, '*Aaaaaaaaaaaaaaaaaaah!*'

The George Gershwin Songbook, which she had recorded for Mercury, was reissued in 1984 to celebrate her sixtieth birthday.

Gene Lees, a well-known writer about jazz, in love with Sassy's singing, immersed himself in an art music project, a suite, *The Planet Is Alive: Let It Live*, based on the poems of Karol Wojtyla, later Pope John Paul II. Sassy sang the hymn 'Let It Live' and other songs at a concert in Düsseldorf, West Germany, conducted by Lalo Schifrin, with arrangements and orchestrations by Francy Boland, and seventy instrumentalists, a blend of prominent American jazz musicians and European classical and jazz players, and a chorus. The strength of her soft voice elevated the work and justified Gene Lees's fervent belief that the whole piece should be released as an album. Though it was broadcast on television to an appreciative European audience, Lees couldn't induce a major American record company to issue the digitally recorded performance, which he eventually distributed through his own small company, Jazzletter, in Ojai, California. The tape retains the thunderous applause following the emotional finale with Sassy's rich, rousing voice ringing out, the highlight of the whole work.

She was also filmed in concert at the Monterey Jazz Festival with

Mike Wofford, Andy Simpkins, and Harold Jones in 1984,* where she sang 'That's All', 'Time After Time', 'I've Got the World on a String', 'The Island', and the inevitable 'Send in the Clowns'. On a video, one sees and hears her singing 'sure of my lines' in a rich confident voice, then affecting a surprised look to dramatise the words 'no one is there . . . Where are the clowns . . . quick . . . send in the clowns, there ought to be clowns . . . don't bother, they're here'. It's a video with nearly everything for which Sassy had become famous – the vocal acrobatics, the playfulness, a sight of the pretty ankles and feet as she perched on a stool, and above all the gorgeous voice which could never adequately be analysed or explained and would be most appreciated in performance, *in action*, for an audience.

She sang at Carnegie Hall, at the Blue Note, at Waterloo Village near Stanhope, New Jersey, everywhere earning reviews that said her voice was better than when she had begun her career. Now she was singing part of 'Misty' in a baritone voice, the rest in her higher register, creating a duet. She found the whole thing campy fun. George Gaffney, her pianist, was surprised to hear her get down to D-sharp below middle C – as low as he had ever known any woman to sing. Bob James, an accompanist in the 1960s, had thought she could go as low as C below middle C. In mid-1985, she became the 1,808th person to receive a star on the Hollywood Walk of Fame; Los Angeles Mayor Tom Bradley declared a 'Sarah Vaughan Day' in the city. Sassy celebrated with her mother and daughter, Debby.

During one jazz festival in New York, in the late 1980s, after the Kool Jazz Festival had been changed to the JVC Jazz Festival (named for the Japanese Victor Corporation), Billy Eckstine sang his set, Sassy sang hers, and they returned together to the stage to sing 'Remember', 'Dedicated to You', and 'Passing Strangers'. 'The atmosphere was loose and affectionate, the duets sweet and melodious. It was all a bit sloppy and obviously unrehearsed, but so what? It was a memorable few minutes of music,' wrote Peter Keepnews in the *New York Post*. Not all the critics were as sanguine about Billy Eckstine's vocal abilities in his seventies. But what he had lost in control of his vibrato, he had gained in the poignancy of his sound.

It was a period in the jazz world when several trends were becoming evident. Hundreds of young instrumentalists were building careers;

*Though the date on the video says 1984, the concert may actually have been filmed in another year, perhaps 1983. Larry Clothier, who worked for her for the entire year in 1984, recalls she did not play in Monterey that year.

jazz itself had become respected as a complex, internationally copied, often inspirational art form, far from its roots as the folk art of the black man's blues; colleges offered courses in jazz and in some cases granted degrees in jazz. But the public, not just jazz musicians mourning their friends, noticed that the legendary founders of New Orleans jazz, swing-era music, and all the stages and gradations of bebop, were dying. Dizzy Gillespie, about to turn seventy, kept reminding people of his age. A new era had begun.

Record companies, impressed by the success of CBS's recordings of a *wunderkind* trumpeter named Wynton Marsalis – with whom Sassy appeared in 1984 at a Boston Pops concert – kept signing youngsters to contracts. Record company executives opened their vaults and reissued the old jazz records that hadn't sold well during the reign of rock music. Polygram now owned the old Mercury masters of Sarah Vaughan's recordings and put out three boxes of seventeen LPs of Sassy's work from 1954 to 1959. Later, another box of her work done in the 1960s followed. Eventually everything recorded for Mercury appeared on compact disc.

Her songs with jazz groups for Mercury are effervescent treasures. Her voice in the 1950s was lighter, her embellishments more subtle and less obviously adventurous and dramatic than in the 1980s. Everybody in a position to criticise the recordings and publicise them loved them. CBS soon reissued its own far smaller collection. Musicraft, which had reissued its Sarah Vaughan material on LP, now brought out CDs. Pablo put out its CDs by the end of the 1980s, not very long after Sassy's contract with Norman Granz had ended. Only Mainstream, among Sassy's long-term contractors, delayed reissuing her work in the 1980s. Some Roulette recordings were reissued on CD. She was invited to sing the role of Bloody Mary for a CBS Masterworks record-ing of *South Pacific* with Jonathan Tunick conducting the London Sym-phony Orchestra done in London in January 1986. Sassy's earthy ver-sions of 'Bali Hai' and 'Happy Talk' stand out seductively from the operatic interpretations offered by the rest of the cast, which included Kiri Te Kanawa and José Carreras. She was startled to hear that Gunther Schuller had called her the greatest living singer in the world, when she herself had decided that the best was Leontyne Price. 'It's one thing to have a beautiful voice. It is another to be a great musician. It is still another to be a great musician with a beautiful voice who can also compose,' he said during a lecture at the Smithsonian Institution. 'Hers is a perfect instrument, attached to a musician of superb instincts,

capable of expressing profound human experience, with a wholly original voice.'

Sassy kept on trouping. At the Riverbend Festival in Chattanooga,
Tennessee, in June 1987, she went onstage to tell her audience that she
had just fallen in the shower minutes before she was scheduled to sing.
Her knees hurt; she was limping. But she performed for an hour, sitting
on a stool next to the piano. The audience gave her a standing ovation.
The next year, she became the fifty-sixth person to be inducted into
the American Jazz Hall of Fame, a joint project of the New Jersey Jazz
Society and Rutgers University's Institute of Jazz Studies in Newark.

By that time, she had appeared on several videos, one a CBS-Fox
release of the making of the album *South Pacific*, another called 'Sass
and Brass' with Dizzy Gillespie, Maynard Ferguson, Herbie Hancock,
and many other jazz stars, some of whom she had known for years
and whom she kissed delightedly on camera.

2

SEVENTEEN

Send in the Clowns

Drummer Harold Jones had become friendly with Waymon Reed during their days together in the Basie band. Furthermore, Harold had grown up with Andy Simpkins in Richmond, Indiana, where they had helped Jones's father wash, polish, and simonise cars for his business in the family's backyard. For the rest of their lives, Harold and Andy liked to tell the tale on themselves about their days in the car-washing business, when Andy used to get the plum jobs, such as polishing the chrome. Both had then enjoyed long, notable careers in jazz and established home bases on the West Coast. Harold went to work with Sassy's group during 1980, after Andy had already been travelling for a year with Sassy. 'Waymon told her to get me,' Harold said. He and Andy managed to have cordial relations with Waymon. Andy kept himself aloof from the couple's problems. 'Sassy and I totally related musically. We clicked immediately in our musical concept. I focused on the music,' he reflected later about how he maintained his balance with music.

'Sarah Vaughan was exactly the kind of person her nicknames suggested: Sassy and the Divine One,' Harold said. He knew that she was proud of her daughter, Debby, whom he recalled had won a beauty contest in Los Angeles, had been a cheerleader for the Los Angeles Raiders owned by Al Davis, and had decided to become an actress. Debby liked to stay home and go to rock concerts with her friends, but as she grew a little older and realised that her mother was one of the great singers of the world, Debby liked being included on the tours. Sassy loved having her daughter along and kept her close to her side. Many times, Harold and the others in the group ran interference for Sassy and Debby when people tried to invade their privacy. Even maids in the hotels liked to go into their rooms to look around. Andy Simpkins thought that Sassy was like a little 'sis' sometimes, just as Billy Eckstine had thought. Sassy could be a giggly little girl – and a 'sailor', too.

After Waymon was gone from Sassy's group, Mike Wofford, the pianist, met Andy Simpkins and Harold Jones on the road and found out that Sassy was looking for a new pianist.* Wofford was free at the beginning of 1983; he called Sassy's office and immediately had a job again. Though Mike Wofford was under the impression that Sassy stepped up the pace of her touring, resting primarily for the year-end holidays, everyone else – Simpkins and Lake, among others – recalled that she travelled only about six or seven months of the year. For Wofford, who had been recommended to Sassy the first time by Roy McCurdy, the second time around with Sassy, after Waymon Reed was gone, was very pleasant. All the good things about working with Sassy came to the fore again.

'She was one of the greatest jazz artists on any instrument,' Wofford said. Simpkins was amazed at the number of times he and the others in the group were exhausted from travelling and working, while Sassy remained fit and strong. 'What's the matter with you guys?' she often asked. 'Come on.' With no sleep, after difficult trips, she went right to work and sounded and behaved as if she felt fresh. 'I never heard her complain once about the weather, or about feeling depressed, or about her voice not being quite right. She never apologised to audiences for her having a cold, or if her throat didn't feel good, as so many singers did,' Wofford said. 'She was an old-school professional. She never made excuses. The only things that bothered her were bad lighting or sound systems. She was always on time; she never needed anyone to hold a curtain for her unless something happened beyond her control.'

She wasn't difficult with musicians, in Wofford's experience. 'She wasn't really a prima donna. If she ended up riding in a jeep when she had expected a limousine, she never caused a scene,' Mike recalled of his experience with her. 'She never whined about conditions and never felt sorry for herself.' Wofford admired her for all those reasons. 'It was unusual for people of her stature and under the special stresses of her career to go through life without a serious ego disorder,' he said. 'From what I understand, she came from a background where she

---

*George Gaffney had already played for Sassy and left once at this time. Throughout the 1980s, he entered and left her group and came back a handful of times.

became tough at a pretty young age. She didn't complain – never complained or whined, never,' he said, about her hard past or present experiences. Furthermore, 'If anyone tried to cater to her, that's one of the things that made her mad,' Wofford recalled. One reason that Harold Jones worked so well with Sassy, he said, was that he could be friendly with her and still keep a respectful distance between them.

Mike Wofford never saw her practise, vocalise, or warm up. The group would rehearse occasionally on the road or at her house in Hidden Hills, as he remembered, when she was changing material or introducing something new. Andy Simpkins especially enjoyed the rehearsals when they introduced new songs; Sassy would work on a new song she liked until it was in fine shape. Then it was forgotten about; it never got into her shows. Andy, too, was puzzled by her repetitions of her songs.

When they rehearsed in Hidden Hills, Sassy's mother was always cooking. Debby was around, going through all the usual things that teenage kids go through. Sassy was a typical doting mother, Mike thought. Whenever he showed up at the house for a rehearsal, Sassy was usually working at her sewing machine. That was the homebody side of Sassy, 'her other side', as Mike thought of it.

Even though the group sometimes didn't change the repertoire at all for months, subtle elements of the show changed. The tempo for a song could change from night to night. Sassy sometimes felt very well one night and changed the length of a song, opening it up and doing many extra choruses. Even though she was singing the same songs, she didn't want to play them the same way twice. Sassy loved it when musicians changed her music. It became part of Mike's job to try new things. But he had to be very clear in his own mind about what he was doing, because she responded to everything the musicians played, and she could roll right over a musician. Often she told Mike, 'Great,' after he tried something new. That kind of interplay let the musicians bounce off each other, not just accompany her. She was so sure of herself that nobody could throw her off balance. But if a musician was wrong, he had better watch out. She would let him know about it quickly. Andy Simpkins was once amazed by Sassy's ear. He was playing a rented bass which wouldn't stay in tune. Hearing it out of tune and wanting to save her good bassist the embarrassment of soloing with a terrible instrument, she sang along out of tune with him. All the while, she maintained a sixth sense about whether someone in an audience was taping her performances illegally. When that happened, she became furious.

Mike said, 'I don't think that anybody had real warm first meetings with her; she did not have a real charming personality. But every now and then I'd see little flashes of what lay under that stuff. It happened more than once, when I was with her. Just little subtle things that would pass. There was a lot of feeling but – whether it was her background or not – she couldn't let that show. Never let herself be in that position of not being a tough guy. Experience had probably taught her to keep her guard up,' he surmised.

George Wein thought that as the years passed, Sassy stopped trusting people. 'She trusted people, and that trust was violated. People took advantage of her.' Charlie Lake agreed: 'She didn't trust people.' And Harold Jones thought that racial tensions persisted. 'People didn't take it for granted that the black woman in the hotel lobby was occupying the penthouse,' he said.

It's possible that she had never really trusted people; she certainly became more forthright in her reactions, more demanding about her goals, and less dreamy and hopeful in her expectations. *Aggressive* was a word that some people used to describe her. *Temperamental* sufficed for them, too. Though she kept in touch constantly with a coterie of friends, she had been so disappointed by her personal experiences that she was less willing to take risks with most new people anymore.

Despite a long career that had brought her fame and wealth, Sassy still had lived a lifetime in Ella Fitzgerald's shadow. However, by the 1980s, Sassy's more frequent appearances and continuing adventurousness helped her sidestep comparisons to the other singer. Nevertheless Ella had still won more awards, and her girlish voice and infectious, rhythmic genius had brought her greater international notoriety. It was easy for the public to understand Ella Fitzgerald. As much as Sassy and Ella admired each other, Sassy privately suffered some feelings of disappointment about Ella's great popularity, many of Sassy's friends thought. (Pianist George Gaffney knew that Sassy, with her competitive spirit, also measured her achievements against the enormous financial success of Tom Jones and other singers who earned millions of dollars.) Mike Wofford recalled an Ella incident that occurred while he was travelling with Sassy to Bermuda for a performance in 1983. A press conference preceded one show, with television cameras and local rookie reporters on hand. One young woman reporter piped up, 'Miss Vaughan, do you really know Ella Fitzgerald?' It was such a weird question that Sassy couldn't help it; she started laughing. 'Yes, girl, I really do know Ella,' she replied.

By the 1980s, George Wein, producer of the Kool Jazz Festival, was paying Sassy $25,000 to $30,000 and even sometimes $35,000 a concert. Sassy discovered that he was paying Ella Fitzgerald more and wanted to know why. Wein explained that he booked Sassy for more concerts a year than he did Ella, the elder singer; Ella was only working about ten concerts a year by that time. So in the end, he told Sassy, she earned far more money from him than Ella did. He didn't know if that answer satisfied Sassy. Sassy made a formal recording with Ella for the first time in their lives in 1989 – the last recording Sassy would ever make – when they sang a brief, swinging duet on the introduction to 'Birdland' for a Quincy Jones all-star production, *Back on the Block*.

George Wein knew from some of Sassy's confrontations with his staff that she occasionally took a dim view of arrangements he made for her, and she said some grim things that upset him. He felt that he was a fan and a friend of the musicians he was employing, and for a long time he couldn't understand why confrontations always arose over money. Sassy, he thought, regarded him as The Man, someone who was just taking advantage of her. Often she became temperamental. Once she walked off a stage in Sweden because a concert promoter had not provided the monitors Sassy and Wein had contracted for. Wein could remember a time when Sassy hadn't used monitors at all and thoroughly seduced her audiences anyway. She really never needed monitors. He and Sassy had become prosperous and famous and found themselves at loggerheads at times. But when negotiations turned out to her liking, Wein said, she was the sweetest woman in the world to deal with.

Sassy's attitude towards her managers wasn't always so solicitous, either. She led Harry Addesso on a merry chase sometimes when he wanted her to do something she was in no mood to do. She had no interest in letting the press interview her because she saw that her concerts were sold out; she didn't see any reason to keep interview appointments for articles.

Her next manager, Milt Ebbins, by then in his seventies and a very professional, experienced manager, didn't stay with her for very long. However, Andy Simpkins thought Sassy respected and trusted Milt Ebbins; he was a fatherly type in whom anyone could confide. Even so, she wanted to try to stay in charge herself by then. When she tired of having her photographs taken for a *Down Beat* story in 1986, she yelled to Milt, who was standing nearby, 'Milt! Don't you ever do this to me again. Never! If you do, I'll never live to be old.' Her daughter, Debby, eventually reflected that Sassy acquired so much experience when it came to the management of her career that her husbands and many other people connected with her found it difficult to accept how strong she was. Rather like a force of nature, Sassy overwhelmed even the very concert halls where she performed.

She had less miraculous results when she tried to exert her will over the nuts and bolts in the offstage mechanism of her group. Andy Simpkins, for example, needed a hard case for his bass when he joined her group and faced the rugged trips on the itinerary. Sassy had a big, heavy, unwieldy case, so he decided to have a smaller, lighter case made that he could help in handling. When she saw it, the woman who had once borrowed her carfare to the Apollo Theatre to win an amateur contest said to him, 'If you're going to bring your own trunk out, you're going to pay for it yourself.' Dumbfounded, Andy replied, 'Why? This case will make it easier on everyone.' One of her business people at the time convinced her to absorb the expense.

But then she could be mightily generous. One Mother's Day, when she took a vacation in Barbados, she felt so guilty about not staying at home with her mother that she sent Pumpkin and another friend from New Jersey to Hidden Hills to take Ada Vaughan out to dinner. Sassy was so grateful to her friends that she paid for the plane fares and even for the dinners, though Pumpkin had wanted to treat Ada himself.

Sassy took vacations away from her family, usually going on cruises to the Caribbean with Robert Richards. Sassy liked to sit quietly on deck, reading and listening to music. She would give her cigarettes to Robert, whom she mischievously called 'Richard', asking him for a cigarette at dinnertime and then perhaps for another one later at night. Simpkins had the impression that she smoked less by the time he was working for her. She also tried to cut down on her drinking. Even though she indisputably loved Cognac (she hated champagne), she seldom had a drink and never took cocaine on vacation; a vacation meant a vacation from everything, according to Robert. Sometimes the two of them would get off the ship and take a taxi into towns on the islands where they stopped, but Sassy had no desire to look around. She always said, 'This looks like the last one. Let's go back to the ship.' So without shopping or walking around, she and 'Richard' returned to the cocoon of the ship.

Sometimes he went with her and a few more friends to a house she frequently rented in Barbados, where they lived very quietly for some weeks. Breakfast was at nine o'clock sharp, drinks were at 7 p.m. and dinner was served at 7.30. After dinner, they usually watched rented films, or listened to music or went out to a club to have a drink and listen to local music. The music bored her after an hour. The inevitable invitation for her to sing always came, and she always left at that time. Sassy sometimes would stay alone in her room all day in Barbados, listening to music, perhaps sewing or reading. She was much quieter in her habits now than in the old days.

Mundell Lowe, who occasionally saw her in Los Angeles, always told her where he was playing and asked her to come by. She often answered that she was heading to Barbados. 'I've got to go south and do my thing, to heal up,' she told him. At the time, Mundell thought she might be tired, even bored; he was disappointed that she was treading an artistically narrow path and that 'she clung to a limited repertoire out of the vast store of songs in her books'. Later, he would say, 'I suspect that Sassy had never been truly comfortable onstage. It had always been a tense situation for her. Performing took a lot out of her.' He could remember the days in the 1970s, when Sassy, Carmen McRae and Al Jarreau had stopped at the Trees, a club where Mundell played in Studio City; the three singers had sat in with him. Sassy sang anything that was played; if she didn't know the lyrics, she made up syllables. 'That's how flexible she could be when she was sitting in,' he said.

Pumpkin said, 'If I were to be absolutely candid, I'd have to say that she felt lonesome and disappointed at times,' in the 1980s, after the marriage to Waymon. She never confided her feelings about her marriages, her alliances and their endings, but he sensed the truth beneath the surface she presented. But clearly she didn't want to be bothered or pestered with problems. She would say, 'Don't ask me,' when someone tried to consult her about something apart from music, and then she would end up saying, 'Why did you do that?' when something she hadn't wanted to discuss became a *fait accompli* she didn't like. 'She just wanted to be euphoric,' Andy Simpkins decided; that was a key to understanding Sassy in the 1980s. 'She was enjoying her life,' he said. People had to learn that they couldn't box her in; if they let her do what she wanted to, then everything was great. Harold Jones said, 'Her only real problem was she needed her privacy.'

Marian McPartland, who invited Sassy to be a guest on her Peabody Award-winning 'Piano Jazz' show on National Public Radio, wanted Sassy to play several songs on the piano, but Marian let Sassy just sing – 'I prefer that,' Sassy said. They talked about old times they had shared as young women in the nightclubs of Chicago, and they talked about making mistakes in performances. 'I make boo-boos,' Sassy said. 'I know how to get out of them, and the audience loves it.'

'You learn something different [when you make a mistake],' Marian agreed.

'You just don't remember what you learned when you come off,' joked Sassy. She didn't mind making mistakes, she explained, because, she said, 'Music is not perfect. When it's perfect, it's too . . . it's not right.' She phrased her conversation exactly as she did the lyrics of her songs, emphasising a few words, pausing, going on to one word, elongating a vowel, pausing, and then on to a group of words. As she talked candidly about how the previous night she had stayed too long to have drinks with friends in her dressing room at the Blue Note in New York, a hint of shyness, a hesitancy, came into her voice. 'I should have gone home,' she said. From time to time, she giggled nervously.

As soon as she walked into a nightclub, she began to smoke and drink again. She ate excessive amounts, and her metabolism dealt with the meals eaten at odd hours less and less well. Luciano Pavarotti, visiting her backstage one night, was shocked to find her smoking in her dressing room. 'You smoke?' he said incredulously. 'Yes, I smoke,' she said, laughing a little. George Wein would recall she spent a great deal of money on her partying and all the things she indulged in for fun.

Returning to Brazil in 1987 to make an album, *Brazilian Romance*, for CBS, she was confronted by unusual music, new lyrics difficult to memorise, and a musical concept that was foreign to her taste. Guitarist, singer, composer and arranger Dori Caymmi, who was working for Sergio Mendes, the album's producer, became aware of tensions between Sassy and Mendes. Sassy wanted an acoustic album, because she had a purist view of what jazz should be, and Mendes wanted a contemporary-sounding album with electronic instruments. She wanted to use her trio and some Brazilian percussion players. Mendes's concept for the album included more liberties with jazz than Sassy wanted to take. Caymmi thought that Sassy felt sick during the recording sessions. Sometimes she arrived late and left early, because she felt nauseated. She told Caymmi that she was worried about being able to sing his song, 'Photograph', because the music was difficult and the words were new to her. In retrospect, Dori thought that Sassy had been correct; the record should have been more Brazilian; the guitars, which didn't sound right to her, placed the album too deeply into the harder-sounding pop or rock-and-roll style. A guitarist such as George Benson would have been more to her liking and better for the album.

After the recording sessions ended, she appeared at a festival in Rio de Janeiro, where she told everyone that she was angry and unhappy about the album. Actually is is very successful from a listener's point of view. Her soft contralto was perfectly suited to the subtle nasalities and guttural suggestiveness of the Portuguese language. And a song called 'It's Simple' wasn't simple musically. None of the songs were of the sort that most pop, rock, blues, or even jazz singers could handle, no matter how accomplished they were in their individual fields. Only a musician of Sassy's stature could hear the modulations in keys and many other complex elements in the background music on the album. Sassy's voice is the centre of attraction all the time; it overrides the rhythms, the electronics, and anything else to which she was unaccustomed or which could have upset her. But she made a bad impression on the people in the Brazilian studio. Dori had thought that she had been difficult to work with, 'a tough lady', he always remembered, even though he came to admire the musical direction she had tried to assert.

She often tried to persuade Michael Tilson Thomas to do an album with her in Brazil. 'It's fun,' she told him, hoping to persuade this musician for whom she had so much respect. 'You go to the studio, you have coffee, you go back to the studio, you have more coffee, you break for lunch, and during lunchtime, some guys in the band made a funny new percussion instrument once, with a live cricket in it, and you put that next to the microphone, and it says "queek queek". You're in the studio until about 10 p.m., and you feel terrific. It's the same thing all over again the next day. Oh, what a life.' But Michael was working so hard that he never got a chance to make an album with her in Brazil.

One night in 1989, Sassy was performing in a nightclub in the valley in California, when she saw Harold Levy, then Mickey Rooney's manager and lawyer, in the company of comedian Martha Raye. Sassy approached Levy to manage her and, on brief acquaintance, they began to work together. He made plans for Sassy's future, including a project with Quincy Jones. To many of Sassy's friends, Levy seemed to be managing Sassy and her business affairs well. Andy Simpkins became fond of Levy, who appeared to be bright, sharp and sensitive to creative people. He kept Sassy and her group as busy as ever. At the Grammy Awards on 22 February she received her second Grammy, a Lifetime Achievement Award, at the Shrine Auditorium in Los Angeles.

In April 1989 she was booked to sing with her trio at the Tri C Jazz Fest at Cuyahoga Community College in Cleveland, Ohio. Clark Terry, Louis Bellson and Milt Hinton were scheduled to play at the same festival with the Cleveland Jazz Orchestra and to jam with Sassy, too. Sassy arrived on a red-eye flight from California and went to her hotel with Harold Levy in tow. She called the festival producer because the hotel had no room for her. A young woman, Katie Neubauer, who was helping with festival arrangements behind the scenes, was dispatched to straighten out the problem for Sassy. Katie found the diva lying down on a couch in the lobby at 10 a.m. Katie apologised profusely and trembled as she said, 'Miss Vaughan, I'm so sorry.' Harold Levy said, 'I'm appalled.' Katie was thinking the same thing, so she said, 'I'm not doing this on purpose.' Sassy seemed calm. Levy looked clean-cut, attractive and dressed in casual, sporty California fashion. 'Mr California', Katie thought of his polished, well-tended appearance. Immediately she called another hotel, which had a suite available. The limousine had left by then, so Katie acted as chauffeur with a little Toyota. Sassy seemed to take it in good humour, bantering and teasing, 'Cleveland, Ohio. I haven't been in Cleveland, Ohio, in twenty years, and now I know why. Is this a George Wein festival?'

The suite at the new hotel turned out to be quite pretty, and the staff rolled out the red carpet for her, so she was able to settle down and take a nap. The next evening before the show, Katie was wandering around backstage at the theatre when she smelled heady marijuana smoke. She followed the scent to Sassy's dressing room, where the star was also enjoying a glass of brandy. Sassy then walked onstage and gave a magnificent performance. Katie was amazed that Sassy could perform so well while under the influence of brandy and marijuana.

After the show, Sassy even socialised with people at a party, which was a fund-raiser for scholarships; guests paid about one hundred dollars a person to attend. Artists seldom went to the parties, although they were supposed to attend as attractions for the donors. But Sassy kept her word and arrived for the cocktail party. Harold Levy stayed at her elbow, appearing definitely in charge and ready to smooth out anything for Sassy. To Katie, the 'coolest thing' was that people could approach Sassy 'at a time when she felt a little spacey, without much energy left', and found her gracious enough to chat a little. Katie overheard Clark Terry say to Louis Bellson, 'I wish that I could do with my trumpet what that woman does with her voice.' Afterward, Sassy handed a big bouquet of roses to Katie, saying, 'I can't take these on the road.' Thrilled, Katie treasured the vase in which the flowers had been delivered long after the flowers had died.

If there was one unfailing impression that everyone had of Sassy during the 1980s, it was that she was in charge during appearances of any kind before the public. Confronted with Dick Cavett's question during a television talk show interview about whether she could live up to her old nickname, Sailor, Sassy grinned, completely at ease, candid and articulate, and said she could outcuss Popeye, the Sailor Man. Would she give Dick Cavett a sample? 'I most certainly will not,' she said with her very ladylike sweetness.

But she wasn't feeling very well, her trio members began to realise. Pianist George Gaffney mentioned in the PBS documentary about her that aired after she died that she had spent a long time, perhaps a year by 1989, denying to herself that something was wrong with her health. He had seen her walk through long hallways in airports and stop to lean on wall telephones and water fountains, while she struggled to catch her breath. Andy Simpkins, too, noticed that she walked slower than usual. At the time he didn't think much about it, but in retrospect he remembered it as a clue to her faltering health. Yet she had never showed a moment's shortness of breath on stages. She didn't confide in anyone about her uncharacteristic weakness.

In June 1989, John S. Wilson wrote a review of unalloyed admiration for Sassy at the JVC Jazz Festival. 'Miss Vaughan was the ultimate diva – commanding the stage and her audience, being kittenish and boisterous with comedy bits that she has been doing for years, repeating encores that have become permanently attached to her and still eliciting ovations for the richest voice jazz has ever had . . . Miss Vaughan . . . was in charge from the moment she stepped on stage to parade before her cheering admirers and then, finding her glass of water misplaced on a small table, she angrily wrestled the table to one side of the stage, knocking her microphone to the floor in the process. Then she calmly settled on a high stool and scatted her way through "Sweet Georgia Brown" in the rhythmic manner of the Harlem Globe Trotters. She unleashed her voice in a strong but carefully shaded treatment of "The Island", a song whose lyrics she particularly admires . . .'

That was the last review that John Wilson wrote about Sassy. George Wein, who produced the festival, began listening to her concert with a different opinion of her that night. Just before she had gone onstage, she had told him that she wasn't going to fly to Europe for a tour that involved between ten and fifteen concerts he had arranged for her. She suggested a reason might be something he had done about the schedule of her concerts in Europe. Then she went onstage and sang the first two songs in a fashion that surprised him; he didn't think she was in good voice. By the third song something happened. Wein didn't know what it was, 'and I'll never know', he would say later, but she summoned all the majesty of her gift and treated the audience to what

Wein believed was one of her great concerts. He had never heard her give a bad performance, only great and better ones. This was one of the best. As she had always done, 'she enhanced my reputation as an impresario', he said.

When she came offstage, Sassy explained to Wein why she had to cancel the concert tour in Europe. She was suffering from arthritis in her hand, she told him. He said, 'We have to have a doctor's note to protect us! We can't just cancel like that! People will sue us!' Within a week, Wein received a note from a doctor in Virginia, who said that she had to stay at home for treatment for arthritis in her hand. Wein never saw her after that night. Neither he nor any of her friends knew that she was really sick, and they later thought that she herself may not have known. Modina Davis, who talked with Sassy at Carnegie Hall after the JVC concert that summer, had no idea that Sassy wasn't feeling well. But Robert Richards had his first inkling after that concert, when Sassy turned to him backstage, patted her upper abdomen, and said, 'It hurts me to sing these days.'

Charlie Lake, who was working as a road manager for Dizzy Gillespie, knew that Dizzy was supposed to play at many of the same concerts as Sassy in Europe that summer. Instead Dizzy played with the Claude Bolling band in Nice; Stan Getz took Sassy's place at another concert. And Wein managed to negotiate his way through the other obligations and present audiences with some good music. Nobody knew that Sassy wasn't simply being temperamental; her disputes through the years with George Wein had been no secret from her friends. Charlie Lake, recalling that she had backed out of performances before in her career, felt bad about her absence from the tour that summer. He knew that her trio had thought as late as the night before the plane left New York that it was going to fly to Europe. Charlie felt she had disappointed the musicians she was scheduled to play with. Everyone was so used to her phenomenal physical strength that no one could believe she might really feel sick. Furthermore, she had booked other engagements for the summer, and she kept those dates. They made her cancellation of the European tour seem capricious.

Later that summer, Robert Richards had a phone call from a friend in San Francisco who said that he had heard Sassy sing there; she sounded wonderful, but her hand was bandaged. What was the matter with it? Robert Richards telephoned and asked Sassy what was wrong with her arm. She said, 'I sprained it.' A few weeks later, when he saw her in California, she said, 'I slammed it in a car door.' Robert thought the discrepancy was just another instance of Sassy's preference for keeping her personal business to herself. When she wanted to tell him about something, she did; otherwise she simply kept her mouth shut. For the twenty years he had known her, that was the way she had always been.

In the fall, Sassy toured Japan, played in Blues Alley, a Washington DC club, and arrived in New York for a week's engagement for $60,000 at the Blue Note. Her arm was still bandaged. Her wrist had become so swollen that she couldn't even sign her name, Harold Jones noticed. She had seen a doctor in Washington DC and some tests had been done, but Jones didn't know the details. She still had no problem with breathing when she sang, as far as Jones knew. But she didn't feel well enough to show up for the first night of her engagement at the Blue Note. According to one friend, that day she had received the grim results of the tests done in Washington. So she knew the truth that she had lung cancer. Even so, she faced having to go out on a stage and entertain people from Wednesday through Saturday nights. Offstage, she made a lot of phone calls; a few people who worked at the Blue Note thought she seemed very upset. One night, Clifton Smalls, who had travelled with her in the Hines band and now lived in Brooklyn, showed up at the club and headed upstairs to her dressing room. Made aware that he was on his way, Sassy let out a hoot and a holler – 'Clifford!' – not forgetting for a second to tease him with the name she had invented for him. He wondered if the entire club audience and passers-by on the street had heard her. They hugged and kissed; Cliff confided that he had glaucoma, which made life so difficult, but his son helped him get around. Sassy sympathised and commiserated with him, 'I have glaucoma, too.' She didn't bother telling him why her hand was bandaged.

She didn't feel well enough to work for the last sets of the week on Sunday. Larry Clothier and Carmen McRae had flown from Savannah, Georgia, where Carmen had been working, to go to the Blue Note and hear Sassy that night. Carmen was booked to perform in the club the following week. She was too tired to go to hear Sassy, so Larry, Carmen's manager since the mid-1980s, went without her. Larry learned that Sassy had gone to the club Sunday afternoon, stayed for a while, and then left before she was supposed to sing. Nobody who worked at the Blue Note knew exactly what was wrong with her, but Sal Haries, the general manager, suspected it was serious; she had been behaving so erratically. Robert Richards went to her hotel and, along with some other close friends, learned she had lung cancer.

Sassy never sang in public again. During the next few months,

Richards visited her in Hidden Hills; from there they took a car trip. She was receiving chemotherapy treatments and feeling sick and in pain, he knew. She said, 'I'd like to go broke again, and this time I'd like to spend all the money myself.' He found her ironic humour very funny, as she had meant it to be. She wasn't weeping for herself. Listening to a recording of the gospel group Take Six, she commented to him, 'Isn't that a beautiful way to pray?'

Carmen McRae also visited Sassy in Hidden Hills and could see that Sassy was in severe pain. But Sassy didn't tell Carmen that she had cancer. Pumpkin visited her, too. Billy Eckstine often spoke with her on the telephone, but he was so upset by her illness that he couldn't bring himself to see with his own eyes that she was dying. Interviewed for the PBS documentary about Sassy, Eckstine, appearing fragile himself in 1991, said that she had 'cussed' him out for saying he was going to visit and then never arriving. 'I remembered her the way I wanted to,' he explained.

Michael Tilson Thomas had another project in mind for the two of them, and he called her during the last part of 1989 and left a message; he couldn't get through to her directly. A message came back to his office that Sassy sent her love and wanted to work with him, but she wasn't feeling up to it; she would get back to him soon. During those months, Sassy was shuttling back and forth between her house and the hospital, with Debby at her side; when Sassy stayed in the hospital, Debby slept in the hospital, too. Sassy's weight went down to about one hundred pounds. 'At least I won't have to diet when I go back on the road,' Sassy told Robert Richards. But she knew she was never going back on the road. When Johnnie Garry telephoned her, she told him that she had just seen Jake, her father. She celebrated her sixty-sixth birthday on 27 March 1990.

Modina Davis called Sassy in the middle of March. Sassy told her that she was supposed to record a Brazilian fusion album with Quincy Jones for his label, Qwest. 'I'm going to do it even if I have to do it right from this bed,' Sassy told her. When Harold Levy went to visit her in hospital, she sang a few bars for him. Her voice astonished him, Levy told Andy Simpkins; it was still beautiful. Then she decided she didn't want to stay in the hospital anymore. 'I want to go home! Take me home!' she cried out. Debby took Sassy home that night in an ambulance. Working as an actress under the name Paris Vaughan, Debby was featured in a television movie on the night of 4 April 1990, the forty-sixth anniversary of the day Sassy officially joined the Earl Hines band. Sassy died while watching the film.

★ ★ ★

Michael Tilson Thomas was working in Europe, where he had become principal conductor for the London Symphony Orchestra; word of Sarah Vaughan's death reached him there. The news caught most of the jazz world by surprise. New York's jazz radio stations began marathon playing sessions of her recordings. Her voice reigned on the airways for days; listeners had a chance to appreciate the full impact of her glorious instrument. Jazz musicians were unnerved to realise that one of their greatest singers, still at the peak of her powers, had been lost. Among the hundreds of newspapers and magazines that paid her tribute, *Spin* magazine published an article by Spencer Harrington that said, ' . . . she had no peer among the jazz singers of her generation, except perhaps for Ella Fitzgerald, who once called her "the greatest singing talent in the world".' He recounted she had once told Leonard Feather, 'It sure is a nice feeling to know that people will remember you after you've gone – that you'll manage to be a little bit of history.'

Two ceremonies were arranged, the first a funeral at the First Mount Zion Baptist Church in Newark, New Jersey, where Ada still maintained her membership. Sassy's recording of 'Ave Maria' was played. Leontyne Price, Sassy's idol, sent a message that Sassy had gone to 'the place where the music came from'. Preacher Wells came to the funeral. So did Marshall Fisher, who had avoided contact with Sassy for over a decade. Marshall had married a Japanese pianist, whom he lived with in New York; she confided in a friend that Marshall had been terribly upset by Sassy's death. 'He had cared about her all along, though he didn't want to be with her,' Larry Clothier said. Sassy was buried in Glendale Cemetery in Bloomfield, New Jersey.

Ada Vaughan was so stunned by her loss that she didn't recognise a musician who had played in one of Sassy's trios. A shaken, frail Billy Eckstine told reporters that 'God must have needed a lead singer'. Eckstine had been very sick the previous year; Sassy had worried about him and told Robert Richards repeatedly, 'He has lost his vibrato, he has lost his vibrato, and I've tried to tell him how to get it back, but he doesn't listen to me, he won't listen to me!' Now he had his vibrato back but he had lost her.

Sassy's assistants in later life, who filled the role that Modina Davis had handled in the 1950s, as friends and Girl Fridays, helped Ada and Paris Vaughan to plan the New Jersey funeral. Then Quincy Jones called numerous musicians and other entertainers – Dori Caymmi for one – to contribute their talents to a West Coast memorial service to be held at Forest Lawn Cemetery. Preacher went to that service too; so did many of Sassy's friends and admirers, among them Rosemary Clooney, Nell Carter and Joni Mitchell.

During the filming of the PBS tribute, it was difficult for all the musicians involved to talk about her; she had been so special to them – a figurehead of jazz. But for Billy Eckstine, especially, the project was an ordeal. Joe Williams, who took part in the documentary, thought Billy 'might not make it . . . I was surprised, because I had always known Billy as a tough guy,' Joe said. Friends greeting Billy when he toured England saw that he was still grieving for Sassy.

In 1991 Carmen McRae released an album called *A Tribute to Sarah*. Included among the songs associated with Sassy is an exceptionally touching song written by Carroll Coates about her going to heaven, where 'Lady', Billie Holiday, wanted to pass the word through other singers to Sassy that 'Lady' sang lead. And Sassy said to Bessie Smith, 'This is heaven, indeed. I'm new here, you lead.' Carmen had always been the message-bearer; when she sang the fanciful, uplifting song at the end of every performance in clubs and in concerts during the year after Sassy died, Carmen brought people to the verge of tears with her eloquence. She celebrated the modest, shy, vulnerable side of her old friend who had wrought miracles for American music:

> *Sarah!*
> *Who on earth could replace that sound*
> *so renowned!*
> *Sarah!*
> *She was 'Queen of the hill'!*
> *Sarah!*
> *She could soar like a symphony!*
> *And do more with a melody*
> *Than a hip whippoorwill!*

Interviewed on radio by John Tegler, Carmen told him, 'It was a hard album in regard to finding songs strictly Sarah's, because Sarah recorded every song in the world, but they didn't necessarily belong to her. "Send in the Clowns" was one of her big songs. "Misty", "Tenderley". I did "Poor Butterfly" mainly because I have a tape of Sarah singing that song, which to me was the greatest vocal interpretation of any song I ever heard in my life. I had recorded it long before . . . but it was like I had never even touched it, and on the album I didn't touch Sarah.'

* ★ *

Eventually Harold Levy and Paris Vaughan came to an acrimonious parting of the ways over the management of Sassy's estate. During 1991 Paris and Levy became adversaries in court in California. Paris took over as administrator for her mother's estate in Levy's place. The trouble was near resolution by the spring of 1992. Robert Richards thought that Sarah Vaughan would not have been surprised at the tension surrounding the management of her money and would have said, 'I sing, I just sing.'

A Discographical
Survey of
Sarah Vaughan

This section is a comprehensive survey, which doesn't purport to be a complete discography of Sarah Vaughan's work on records and compact discs.

Sarah recorded first for the tiny Deluxe and Continental labels in December 1944, then signed a contract with Musicraft, for which she made a number of recordings during the mid-1940s. Her earliest recordings are available on reissues, some just reminted on CDs, some on out-of-print LPs found in golden-oldie record stores, and of the reissues, some are bootlegs – illegal albums copied from legal issues or reissues.

Sarah recorded on a contract for CBS Records from 1949 to 1953, and in the 1980s she renewed her working relations with CBS Records and made more albums, one of them the vaunted *Gershwin Live!* album. In the 1980s, CBS also reissued her early work in a collection called *The Divine Sarah Vaughan: The Columbia Years*, including such Vaughan classics as the song 'Black Coffee'. After leaving CBS in 1953, she signed with Mercury for the period 1954 through 1959, and she also recorded for Mercury in the 1960s. Some of those records are available on out-of-print LPs. Polygram has reissued all or nearly all of her Mercury work in boxed collections of LPs and CDs called *The Complete Sarah Vaughan on Mercury, Volumes I through IV*.

In spring 1960, she started a recording contract with Roulette, which lasted until early 1963. In 1990, two dozen of her recordings for that label were reissued by Capitol/EMI as *The Roulette Years*, and another fourteen records came out as *The Singles Sessions* under the aegis of Capitol/EMI. In the late 1960s, Sarah didn't have a recording contract. The reasons for her spotty recording career in the 1960s and at times in the 1970s and 1980s are an integral part of her life story. By 1970, she was recording with her old colleague, Robert Shad, who had worked on her Mercury recordings and then started his own label, Mainstream. She stayed with Shad's label until the mid-1970s.

She began recording for Pablo in 1978 and continued with that label under the direction of jazz concert impresario Norman Granz, Pablo's owner and producer, until 1982, when she started working with CBS Records on several projects. On 9 April 1981 Atlantic Records released her album, *Sarah Vaughan Sings Songs of the Beatles*. Atlantic, which purchased the master of that record for its label, has no definite information on the recording date but has some reason to believe it might have been done in 1977 – a date confirmed by Sarah's British discographer Denis Brown and also by her friend Larry Clothier, manager of Carmen McRae. In the 1980s, Sarah recorded a duet, 'Blue', with Barry Manilow on his Arista album *2 A.M. Paradise Cafe*. Some Pablo recordings have been reissued by Fantasy. In general, all legal issues and reissues since 1980 have proper discographical data included in the liner notes.

Her first recording was made with Billy Eckstine, with whom she later recorded critically acclaimed duets. Dizzy Gillespie and Charlie Parker played for Sarah's early recordings under her own name. She was a recording artist for nearly fifteen years before she had a million-record seller – with a pop tune, 'Broken Hearted Melody'. For the Mainstream label, she made her first recording of 'Send in the Clowns', given to her by Mainstream's founder, Bob Shad. The song became Sarah's signature song in her late career and helped attract thousands of people, not necessarily jazz fans, to her concerts for the rest of her life. In retrospect, one can say that Sarah Vaughan had no bad years in her recording career, except for the years in which she made few or no recordings.

Some little labels (such as Memoir) have been duly licensed through the years to reissue Sarah's work. Other little labels have not been authorised, and jazz authorities and recording-world executives know which ones they are.

Discographies of Sarah Vaughan's recording career are *Sixty Years of Recorded Jazz* by Walter Bruyninckx, privately published by the author (address: Lange Nieuwstraat, 2800 Mechelen, Belgium), and *A Discography: The First 40 Years* by Denis Brown (second edition, Birmingham, England, 1987), which was published in the US by the Greenwood Press of Westport, Connecticut, in 1991. The Polygram collection contains a full listing of musicians with whom Sarah worked on her Mercury recordings. The Vintage Jazz Classics tribute album in memory of Sarah Vaughan was issued with details about the musicians involved. EMI and Capitol/EMI reissues of Sarah's work on Roulette also contain discographical details. Mainstream's recordings have discographical data in the original issues. According to Denis Brown, a projected reissue of Mainstream recordings would contain some previously unreleased cuts. In the late 1980s, Musicraft rereleased all of Sarah's recordings, with the exception of three tracks.

Phil Schaap, the noted discographer and jazz historian, has been able to supply information and refinement of material in existing discographies, and he has added his expertise to this survey.

This survey also includes information available from recording companies, primarily the larger companies whose issues are the easiest to obtain at the present time. Information has been derived from liner notes on albums in and out of print, licensed and unlicensed; and from published discographies, particularly the Bruyninckx; from advice and corrections so kindly offered by Denis Brown; and also from the discography published with *To Be or Not to Bop*, the memoirs of Dizzy Gillespie written with Al Fraser.

In this survey, the instruments are abbreviated as follows: trumpet (tp), trombone (tb), bass trombone (b-tb), soprano saxophone (s-sax), alto saxophone (as), tenor saxophone (ts), baritone saxophone (bar), clarinet (cl), flute (fl), flugelhorn (flghn), french horn (frhn), piano (p), bass (b), drums (d), guitar (g), violin (viol), vibraharp or vibraphone (vibes), tuba (tba). Other instruments are noted as they occur on records.

Sarah sings with:
Billy Eckstine and His Orchestra: Dizzy Gillespie, Shorty McConnell, Gail Brockman, Marion 'Boonie' Hazel (tp), Gerald Valentine, Taswell Baird, Howard Scott, Chips Outcalt (tb), John Jackson, Bill Frazer (as), Dexter Gordon, Gene Ammons (ts), Leo Parker (bar), John Malachi (p), Tommy Potter (b), Art Blakey (d), Connie Wainwright (g), New York City, 5 December 1944, on the Deluxe label.
    'I'll Wait and Pray'

Sarah Vaughan and Her All-Stars. This was Sarah's first recording under her own name, for which Leonard Feather, acting as producer, was offered twenty dollars for Sarah's work. With Dizzy Gillespie (tp, p), Aaron Sachs (cl), Georgie Auld (ts), Leonard Feather (p), Jack Lesberg (b), Morey Feld (d), Chuck Wayne (g). New York City, 31 December 1944, on the Continental label.
    'Signing Off'
    'Interlude' (first recording of 'Night in Tunisia')
    'No Smokes Blues' (two issued takes)
    'East of the Sun' (Dizzy Gillespie, p, not Leonard Feather)

Dizzy Gillespie All-Star Quintet: with Gillespie (tp), Charlie Parker (as),

Al Haig (p), Curly Russell (b), Sid Catlett (d). New York City, 11 May 1945, on the Guild label.
'Lover Man'

Dizzy Gillespie (tp), Charlie Parker (as), Flip Phillips (ts), Nat Jaffe (p), Curly Russell (b), Max Roach (d), Bill De Arango (g). New York City, 25 May 1945.
'What More Can a Woman Do?'
'I'd Rather Have a Memory Than a Dream' (Tadd Dameron for Jaffe)
'Mean to Me' (Jaffe back, p)

Stuff Smith Trio: Smith (viol), Freddie Jefferson (p), Pete Glover (d). New York City, 1 October 1945, on the Musicraft label.
'Time and Again'
The above data for this entry comes from Denis Brown. According to jazz historian Phil Schaap, Musicraft's owner, Albert Marx, haggled over the price to be paid Sarah – ten dollars or fifteen dollars. Liner notes for the 1990 CD reissue of the song suggest Marx agreed to pay her ten dollars, then heard her sing in rehearsal, and immediately invited her to sign a contract. And Stuff Smith wasn't offered one.

John Kirby band: Clarence Brereton (tp), Buster Bailey (cl), Russell Procope (as), Billy Kyle (p), John Kirby (b), Bill Beason (d). New York City, 9 January 1946, on the Crown label.
'I'm Scared'
'You Go to My Head'
'I Can Make You Love Me'
'It Might as Well Be Spring'
(Data for this entry comes from Denis Brown.)

Tony Scott and His Down Beat Septet: Scott (as, cl), Dizzy Gillespie (tp), Trummy Young (tb), Ben Webster (ts), Jimmy Jones (p), Gene Ramey (b), Ed Nicholson (d). New York City, 6 March 1946, on the Gotham label.
'All Too Soon'
(Data for this entry comes from Denis Brown.)

Dicky Wells's Big Seven: George Treadwell (tp), Dicky Wells (tb), Budd Johnson (ts), Cecil Scott (bar), Jimmy Jones (p), Al McKibbon (b), Jimmy Crawford (d). New York City, 21 March 1946.
'We're Through'
(Data for this entry comes from Denis Brown.)

Georgie Auld Orchestra: Al Aaron, Danny Blue, Art House, Al Porcino (tp), Tracy Allen, Mike Datz, Rudy de Luca (tb), Georgie Auld (s-sax), Lou Prisby, Gene Zononi (as), Al Cohn, Irv Roth (ts), Serge Chaloff (bar), Roy Kral (p), Barry Galbraith (g), Ed Cunningham (b), Art Mardigan (d). New York City, 30 April 1946, on the Musicraft label.
    'A Hundred Years from Today' (arranged by Tadd Dameron)
(Data for this entry for a recording done for Musicraft comes from Denis Brown and Phil Schaap.)

All the following records, unless otherwise noted, and until Sarah's Columbia contract began, were done for Musicraft. Albert Marx's small company went out of business at least for a while in the late 1940s, possibly during or as a result of the second recording strike called by the American Federation of Musicians. Sarah's recordings for Musicraft – some already noted and some to follow here – have been reissued by Marx and also by bootlegging companies.

Freddie Webster (tp), Leroy Harris (as), Lee Parker (bar), Bud Powell (p), Ted Sturgis (b), Kenny Clarke (d), plus string section, plus Hank Ross (cl). New York City, 7 May 1946. (This was conducted by Tadd Dameron, who wrote and arranged 'If You Could See Me Now'.)
    'My Kinda Love'
    'I Can Make You Love Me If You'll Let Me'
    'If You Could See Me Now'
    'You're Not the Kind'

Georgie Auld Orchestra: Neal Hefti, Al Porcino, Sonny Rich, George Schwartz (tp), Mike Datz, Gus Dixon, Johnny Mandel (tb), Georgie Auld (as), Gene Zanoni, Sam Zittman (as), Al Cohn, Irv Roth (ts), Serge Chaloff (bar), Harvey Leonard (p), Joe Pillicane (p), Art Mardigan (d). New York City, 14 June 1946.
    'You're Blasé' (arranged by Al Cohn)
(Data for the above entry comes from Denis Brown.)

Eddie Davis Quartet: Eddie 'Lockjaw' Davis (ts), unknown rhythm section, probably in rehearsal at the Spotlite Club or a Fifty-second Street Club. New York City, June 1946, released on the Swedish Hi-Fly label.
    'Don't Blame Me'

George Treadwell (tp, leader), Al Gibson (cl, as), George 'Big Nick' Nicholas (ts), Eddie de Verteuill (bar, as), Jimmy Jones (p), Al McKibbon (b), William Barker (d), Jimmy Smith (g). New York City, 18 July 1946.

'I'm Through with Love'
'Everything I Have Is Yours'
'Body and Soul'
'I've Got a Crush on You'

Teddy Wilson Octet: Buck Clayton (tp), Scoville Browne (as), Don Byas (ts), George James (bar), Wilson (p), Billy Taylor Sr (b), J. C. Heard (d), Remo Palmier (g). New York City, 19 August 1946.
'Penthouse Serenade'
'Don't Worry 'Bout Me'

Teddy Wilson Quartet: Charlie Ventura (ts), Wilson (p), Remo Palmier (g), Billy Taylor Sr (b). New York City, 19 November 1946.
'Time After Time'
'September Song'
(Data for the above entry comes from Denis Brown.)

George Treadwell (tp, leader), E. V. Perry, Roger Jones, Hal Mitchell, Jesse Drakes (tp), Ed Burke, Dickie Harris, Donald Coles (tb), Rupert Cole, Scoville Browne (as), Budd Johnson, Lowell Hastings (ts), Eddie de Verteuill (bar), Jimmy Jones (p), Al McKibbon (b), J. C. Heard (d), arranged by Bill Doggett. New York City, 2 July 1947.
'I Cover the Waterfront'
'Ghost of a Chance'
'Tenderly'
'Don't Blame Me'
(Denis Brown has a very different personnel line-up for this date, but the above line-up was remembered by trumpeter Hal Mitchell. The musicians at the session thought that 'Tenderly' would be the 'dud', Mitchell recalled, but it turned out to be a hit.)

Ted Dale Orchestra: no details about personnel available. New York City, 10 October 1947.
'The Lord's Prayer'
'Sometimes I Feel Like a Motherless Child'
'I Can't Get Started'
'Trouble Is a Man'

Lennie Tristano (p), Billy Bauer (g), Tommy Potter (b), Buddy Rich (d). New York City, 8 November 1947, 'Bands for Bonds' broadcast, not Musicraft.
'Everything I Have Is Yours'

(Note: Data for the above entry comes from Denis Brown, who adds that it was released on the English Spotlite label.)

Ted Dale Orchestra: Sam Musiker (cl), unknown flghn, fl, strings, Nicholas Tagg (p), Tony Mottola, Al Casey (g), Mack Shopnick (b), Cozy Cole (d), Ted Dale, arranger. New York City, 8 November 1947.
    'Love Me or Leave Me'
    'I'll Wait and Pray'
    'I Get a Kick Out of You'
    'The Man I Love'
    'I'm Gonna Sit Right Down and Write Myself a Letter'
    'The One I Love Belongs to Somebody Else'
    'Button Up Your Overcoat'
    'I Feel So Smoochie'
    'Blue Grass' (This track may have never existed. Data for it is uncertain.)

Richard Maltby and His Studio Orchestra: no personnel details available. New York City, 27 December 1947, according to Bruyninckx; 29 November according to Brown. Phil Schaap says it was recorded with the Ted Dale Orchestra on 10 October 1947.
    'It's You or No One'
    'It's Magic' (Sarah's first hit record in 1947, it sold only 25,000 copies, according to some sources, but other authoritative sources say her sales and profits were far higher. A reason might have been profit from sales to jukebox operators, who bought enormous numbers of the recordings.)
    'I Can't Get Started'

Jimmy Jones (p), Al McKibbon (b), Kenny Clarke (d), John Collins (g). New York City, 29 December 1947. (Jones was the contractor and musical director on this date, according to Schaap.)
    'What a Diff'rence a Day Makes'
    'Gentleman Friend'
    'Once in a While'
    'How Am I to Know' (Data for this track has not been confirmed.)

With Earl Rodgers Choir and unknown orchestra. New York City, 8 April 1948.
    'Nature Boy'
    'I'm Glad There Is You'
(Brown's spelling is Earle.)

With Jimmy Jones (p), Buddy Rich (d), from a television appearance. New

York City, 13 December 1948, issued on Joyce. (This information comes from Schaap.)

With unknown accompaniment. New York City, late 1948, on a V-disc.
'Black Coffee'
(This information comes from Bruyninckx. Brown lists the V-Disc recording as identical with the Columbia recording done with the Joe Lippman Orchestra on 20 January 1949.)

With Harry Sosnick and His Orchestra: studio orchestra musicians including strings and woodwinds, 1949.
'Tonight I Shall Sleep'
'While You Are Gone'
(This has been reissued on *The Sarah Vaughan Memorial Album* by Vintage – catalogue number VJC-1015-2 for the CD, 1991. All details about personnel, label, place, and exact date are unknown. The recording of this live performance is not referred to by Bruyninckx. Brown notes it as a recording done circa 1949.)

With Joe Lippman, conductor and arranger for the CBS Studio Orchestra: includes strings and harp, saxophones, trumpets, trombones, piano, bass, and drums, with such musicians as Jimmy Maxwell (tp), Henry W. Rowland (p), Bob Haggart (b), and Norris 'Bunny' Shawker (d). New York City, 10 January 1949.
'Black Coffee'
'As You Desire Me'
'Bianca'
(Bruyninckx and Brown say 20 January. The above date and personnel information comes from CBS liner notes, with full repertoire from Bruyninckx and Brown. Brown says that Rowland's first name is Bill.)

With Joe Lippman, conductor: same instrumentation, same rhythm section as preceding entry except for Terry Snyder (d). New York City, 25 January 1949.
'While You Are Gone'
'Tonight I Shall Sleep'
'That Lucky Old Sun'

With unknown rhythm section, in live performances. Probably New York City, 1948–49, not for Columbia but released on the Ozone label. (This information comes from Schaap, contradicting other sources.)
'Street of Dreams'

'Love Me or Leave Me'
'Body and Soul'

With unknown accompaniment. Los Angeles, 6 May 1949.
'Tonight I Shall Sleep'
'That Lucky Old Sun'
(Denis Brown says the above entry was done with the Joe Lippman Orchestra in Los Angeles, 6 May 1949. Schaap agrees.)

With Jimmy Jones (p) and other personnel. Los Angeles, May 1949.
'Everything I Have Is Yours'
'I Get a Kick Out of You'
'Tenderly'

With Joe Lippman, conductor and arranger: unknown strings, Jimmy Jones (p), Jack Lesberg (b), Bunny Shawker (d), Al Caiola (g), and others including Art Drellinger, Irv Horwitz, Sid Cooper, Hymie Schertzer (saxes), and a vocal group. New York City, 7 July 1949.
'Just Friends'
'Give Me a Song with a Beautiful Melody'
'Make Believe'
'You Taught Me to Love Again'

With Hugo Winterhalter, conductor and arranger, and the CBS Studio Orchestra, with Jimmy Jones (p), Bob Haggart (b), Terry Snyder (d), Tony Mottola (g), and such horn players as Billy Butterfield and Jimmy Maxwell in the trumpet section. New York City, 28 September 1949, except for 'Lonely Girl' on 25 September.
'I Cried for You'
'You Say You Care'
'Fool's Paradise'
'Lonely Girl'

With Joe Lippman, conductor and arranger, Billy Butterfield, Taft Jordan (tp), Will Bradley (tb), Toots Mondello, Hymie Schertzer (as), Art Drellinger, George Kelly (ts), Stan Webb (bar), Jimmy Jones (p), Eddie Safranski (b), William 'Cozy' Coles (d), Al Caiola (g). New York City, 21 December 1949.
'You're Mine, You' (arranged by Tadd Dameron)
'I'm Crazy to Love You'
'Summertime'
'The Nearness of You'

With Billy Eckstine in a vocal duet, Toots Mondello, Bernard Kaufmann (cl, fl), Art Drellinger, Hank Ross (cl, bass-cl, ts), unknown strings, Jimmy Jones (p), Sid Weiss (b), Bunny Shawker (d). New York City, 21 December 1949.
(Denis Brown cites 22 December as the recording date.)
    'Dedicated to You'
    'You're All I Need'
    'I Love You'
    'Every Day'
(These recordings were released on the MGM label.)

With Jimmy Jones (p). In concert at Carnegie Hall, New York City, 25 December 1949.
    'Once in a While'
    'Mean to Me'
(These recordings were done for the Voice of America, according to Brown.)

With Bob Cusumano, John Carroll, Bernie Privin (tp), Jack Satterfield, John D'Agostino (tb), Bill Versaci, Paul Ricci, Tom Parshley, Harry Terrill, G. Tudor (saxes), Bernie Leighton (p), Frank Carroll (b), Terry Snyder (d), Art Ryerson (g). New York City, 4 May 1950.
    'Our Very Own'
    'Don't Be Afraid'
(Denis Brown says this was the Norman Leyden orchestra.)

George Treadwell and His All-Stars: Miles Davis (tp), Budd Johnson (ts), Benny Green (tb), Tony Scott (cl), Jimmy Jones (p), Billy Taylor Jr (b), J. C. Heard (d), Freddie Green (g). Recorded at the Apollo Theatre, New York City, 18 May 1950.
    'Ain't Misbehavin''
    'Goodnight, My Love'
    'Can't Get out of This Mood'
    'It Might as Well Be Spring' (delete Budd Johnson, Benny Green, Freddie Green)

George Treadwell and His All-Stars: Miles Davis (tp), Budd Johnson (ts), Benny Green (tb), Tony Scott (cl), Jimmy Jones (p), Billy Taylor Jr (b), J. C. Heard (d), Mundell Lowe (elec.-g). Recorded in a studio at 729 Seventh Avenue, New York City, 19 May 1950.
    'Mean to Me'
    'Come Rain or Come Shine'

'Nice Work If You Can Get It'
'East of the Sun (and West of the Moon)'

Norman Leyden, conductor and arranger: CBS Studio Orchestra, Bud Powell (p), Frank Carroll (b), Terry Snyder (d), Mundell Lowe (g), eleven others on brass and reeds, including Jimmy Maxwell (tp). New York City, 27 July 1950.
    'Thinking of You'
    'I Love the Guy'

Stan Getz Band: Stan Fishelson, Al Porcino, Idrees Suliman (tp), Johnny Mandell (b-tp), Stan Getz, Zoot Sims, Don Lamphere (ts), Gerry Mulligan (bar), Billy Taylor (p), Tommy Potter (b), Roy Haynes (d). Recorded live onstage by Al Porcino at the Apollo Theatre, New York City, 19 August 1950.
    'My Gentleman Friend'
    'You're All I Need'
    'I Cried for You' (with Vaughan, another musician, and Charlie Parker (as), 23 August 1950. This entry's date comes from Schaap.)

Norman Leyden and His Orchestra: personnel not available. 5 September 1950. (Bruyninckx says Mitch Miller and His Orchestra, with Stan Freeman, p.)
    'Perdido'
    'Whippa Whippa Woo'

Norman Leyden, conductor and arranger, and his Studio Orchestra: with Jimmy Jones (p), Frank Carroll (b), Bunny Shawker (d), Mundell Lowe (g), Jose Luis Mangual (bongo). New York City, 6 December 1950. (Bruyninckx doesn't include Leyden and his orchestra but cites the same rhythm section.)
    'I'll Know'
    'De Gas Pipe She's Leaking, Joe'

Norman Leyden and His Orchestra: ten strings, harp, Billy Taylor (chimes), Frank Carroll (b). New York City, 17 January 1951.
    'Ave Maria'
    'City Called Heaven'
(Note: This could be Billy Taylor Sr or his son, Billy Jr both bassists, or Billy Taylor, the contemporary pianist, composer, and educator.)

Percy Faith, conductor and arranger, and his CBS Studio Orchestra:

strings, Stan Freeman (p), Frank Carroll (b), Terry Snyder (d), Art Ryerson (g). New York City, 4 April 1951.
    'Deep Purple'
    'These Things I Offer You'
(Denis Brown says 'Vanity' and 'My Reverie' were recorded and rejected in this session.)

Paul Weston, conductor and arranger, and his CBS Studio Orchestra: Milton Raskin (p), John Ryan (b), Nick Fatool (d), George Van Eps (g); Ziggy Elman played in the trumpet section of this large orchestra, along with ten others on brass and reeds. New York City, 1 June 1951.
    'My Reverie'
    'After Hours'
    'Vanity'
    'Out of Breath'

Percy Faith, conductor and arranger, and his CBS Studio Orchestra: strings, Stan Freeman (p), Frank Carroll (b), Phil Kraus (d, vibes), Art Ryerson (g). New York City, 19 September 1951.
    'Pinky'
    'Just a Moment More'
    'I Ran All the Way Home'
    'A Miracle Happened'

A trio, possibly including Jimmy Jones (p). In concert at Ann Arbor, Michigan, 15 November 1951.
    'I Ran All the Way Home'
(Issued on Vintage's *Sarah Vaughan Memorial Album*, 1991.)

Duke Ellington and His Orchestra: Duke Ellington (p, arranger) and personnel based on his band's line-up at the time – Clark Terry, Willie Cook, Francis Williams, Ray Nance, Dick Vance (tp), Juan Tizol, Britt Woodman, Quentin Jackson (tb), Jimmy Hamilton, Russell Procope, Willie Smith, Paul Gonsalves, Harry Carney (reeds, with Hamilton especially known for cl, Procope for as, cl, and Gonsalves for ts, Smith for as, Carney for bar. Probable bass and drums same as above. In concert at Ann Arbor, Michigan, 15 November 1951. (From the Vintage tribute album.)
    'Mean to Me' (incomplete)
    'Perdido'

Nat King Cole, in a vocal duet, same concert as above.
    'Love You Madly'

(The Vintage Jazz Classics liner notes say this performance never had a commercial issue; it was done outside the purview of Sarah's formal career and also outside Cole's commercial career for Capitol.)

Percy Faith, conductor and arranger, and his CBS Studio Orchestra: Robert Kitsis (p), Frank Carroll (b), Phil Kraus (d), Art Ryerson (g). New York City, 19 March 1952.
    'Street of Dreams'
    'Time to Go'
    'Corner to Corner'
    'If Someone Had Told Me'

Unknown accompaniment. Broadcast from Birdland jazz club, New York City, 22 March 1952.
    'Vanity'
    'Mean to Me'
    'Tenderly'
    'Perdido'
(Denis Brown includes 'Once in a While' among the songs and says her accompaniment was probably Lou Stein [p], Al Hall or Joe Benjamin [b], an unknown drummer, and Wild Bill Davis, organist.)

Chris Griffin, Red Solomon, J. Milazzo (tp), L. Altpeter, R. Dupont, John D'Agostino (tb), Bernie Kaufman, Al Freistat, Bill Versaci, T. Gompers, Harold Freedman (saxes), strings, Lou Stein (p), Frank Carroll (b), Terry Snyder (d), Art Ryerson (g). New York City, 28 July 1952. (This was apparently a CBS Studio Orchestra.)
    'Say You'll Wait for Me'
    'Sinner or Saint'
    'My Tormented Heart'
    'Mighty Lonesome Feeling'
(Denis Brown says this was the Percy Faith Orchestra, with Gus Griffith, not Chris Griffin.)

Unknown rhythm section. Broadcast from Birdland jazz club, New York, 8 August 1952.
    'Once in a While'
    'I Cried for You'
    'Street of Dreams'
    'Perdido'
    'I Ran All the Way Home'
    'Time to Go'

(Denis Brown places the recorded broadcast from Birdland on 23 August 1952.)

No details, issued only on small labels.
'You're Mine, You'
'The Nearness of You'
'You're Not the Kind'
'These Things I Offer You'
'Perdido'
(The above five songs, recorded with an unknown big band, are placed in either 1951 and 1952, according to Denis Brown.)

Will Bradley, Jack Satterfield, Al Godlis (tb), strings, Lou Stein (p), Frank Carroll (b), Terry Snyder (d), Art Ryerson (g). New York City, 30 December 1952. (This was apparently a CBS Studio Orchestra. According to Denis Brown, Percy Faith was the orchestra leader.)
'I Confess'
'Lover's Quarrel'
'Time After Time'

Percy Faith, arranger and conductor, and the CBS Studio Orchestra: Louis Stein (p), Frank Carroll (b), Terry Snyder (d), Art Ryerson (g). New York City, 5 January 1953.
'Linger Awhile'
'Spring Will Be a Little Late This Year'
'A Blues Serenade'
'Oo Whatcha Doin' to Me?'

Unknown accompaniment. Broadcast from the Appllo Theatre, New York City, 29 April 1953.
'Street of Dreams'

Unknown accompaniment. From Birdland jazz club, New York City, 5 September 1953.
'Body and Soul'
'Nice Work If You Can Get It'
'Everything I Have Is Yours'
'Summertime'
'Linger Awhile'
'East of the Sun'
(Denis Brown lists Sarah's trio of John Malachi [p], Joe Benjamin [b], and Roy Haynes [d] as accompanists for the above session.)

Bob Simmens Group: no personnel details. Broadcast on Armed Forces Radio Service, New York City, circa 1953.
'For You'
'Bianca'
'As You Desire Me'
'I Cried for You'
(This group is cited by Bruyninckx and Brown. Details about all the broadcasts cited above come from the Bruyninckx discography, with additional information supplied by Brown where noted.)

The Complete Sarah Vaughan on Mercury, Volumes I, II, III and IV, begins here, covering the years 1954 through 1959 on volumes I through III, all recorded in New York City unless otherwise noted, and 1963 through 1967 on Volume IV. Information is derived from booklets accompanying the collected LPs for Volumes I, II and III, and the CDs for Volume IV. Those booklets specify catalogue numbers and takes (the numbers for the versions included from Sarah's recording sessions) and note whether the record was ever issued before. This survey simply gives the names of the songs and musicians. The discography written for Sarah Vaughan by Walter Bruyninckx is used for comparison, corroboration and sometimes augmentation.

Volume I: 1954–1956 – 'Great Jazz Years'

Richard Hayman and His Studio Orchestra 10 February 1954.
'I Still Believe in You'
'My Funny Valentine'
'My One and Only Love'
'Come Along with Me'

Don Costa and His Studio Orchestra 29 March 1954.
'Imagination'
'It's Easy to Remember'
'And This Is My Beloved'
'Easy Come, Easy Go Lover'

John Malachi (p), Joe Benjamin (b), Roy Haynes (d) 2 April 1954.
'Lover Man'
'Shulie a Bop'
'Polka Dots and Moonbeams'
'Body and Soul'
'They Can't Take That Away from Me'
'Prelude to a Kiss'

'You Hit the Spot'
'If I Knew Then What I Know Now'

Hugo Peretti and His Studio Orchestra 6 July 1954.
'Old Love'
'Old Devil Moon'
'Exactly Like You'
'Saturday'

24 September 1954.
'Idle Gossip'
'Make Yourself Comfortable'

20–21 October 1954.
'Oh Yeah'
'I'm in the Mood for Love'
'I Don't Know Why'
'Let's Put out the Lights'
'Waltzing Down the Aisle'
'It's Magic'
'Honey'

Circa November–December 1954.
'How Important Can It Be?'
'The Touch of Your Lips'
''S Wonderful'
'Tenderly'

Jimmy Jones (p), Joe Benjamin (b), Roy Haynes (d). Carnegie Hall, 25 September 1954.
'Saturday'
'Time'
'Tenderly'
'Don't Blame Me'
'Polka Dots and Moonbeams'

Count Basie Band: Thad Jones, Reunald Jones, Wendell Culley, Joe Newman (tp), Bill Hughes, Henry Coker, Benny Powell (tb), Marshall Royal (as, cl), Ernie Wilkins, Frank Foster (ts), Frank Wess (ts, fl), Charlie Fowlkes (bar), Jimmy Jones (p), Joe Benjamin (b), Roy Haynes (d). Carnegie Hall, 25 September 1954.
Medley of 'I Ain't Mad At You' and 'Summertime'

'Old Devil Moon'
''S Wonderful'
'It's Easy to Remember'
'East of the Sun'
'How Important Can It Be?'
'Old Devil Moon'
'Make Yourself Comfortable'
(Details of the Carnegie Hall recordings are derived from the Bruyninckx discography and not included in *The Complete Sarah Vaughan on Mercury* albums.)

Clifford Brown (tp), Herbie Mann (fl), Paul Quinichette (ts), Jimmy Jones (p), Joe Benjamin (b), Roy Haynes (d), Ernie Wilkins (leader, arranger). 16 December 1954.
    'September Song'
    'Lullaby of Birdland' (two takes)
    'I'm Glad There Is You'
    'You're Not the Kind'

18 December 1954.
    'Jim'
    'He's My Guy'
    'April in Paris'
    'It's Crazy'
    'Embraceable You'

Hugo Peretti and His Studio Orchestra 17 March 1955.
    'Whatever Lola Wants'

20 March 1955.
    'Slowly with Feeling'
    'Experience Unnecessary'

9 August 1955.
    'Fabulous Character'
    'Johnny, Be Smart'
    'Hey, Naughty Papa'

10 October 1955.
    'The Other Woman'
    'Never'
    'C'est la Vie'

Mid–October 1955.
 'Paradise'
 'Time on My Hands'
 'Gimme a Little Kiss'

22 October 1955.
 'Mr Wonderful'
 'You Ought to Have a Wife'

Ernie Wilkins and His Studio Orchestra: Wilkins, Ernie Royal, Bernie Glow (tp), J. J. Johnson, Kai Winding (tb), Julian 'Cannonball' Adderley, Sam Marowitz (as), Jerome Richardson (fl, ts), Jimmy Jones (p), Turk Van Lake (g), Joe Benjamin (b), Roy Haynes (d), 25 October 1955.
 'Sometimes I'm Happy'
 'I'll Never Smile Again'
 'Don't Be on the Outside'
 'It Shouldn't Happen to a Dream'

26 October 1955.
 'An Occasional Man'
 'Soon'
 'Cherokee'
 'Maybe'

27 October 1955.
 'Why Can't I?'
 'How High the Moon'
 'Over the Rainbow'
 'Oh, My'

Hal Mooney and His Studio Orchestra 1 April 1956.
 'The Boy Next Door'
 'Shake Down the Stars'
 'I'm Afraid the Masquerade Is Over'
 'Lush Life'
 'A Sinner Kissed an Angel'
 'Old Folks'
 'The House I Live In'
 'I'm the Girl'

2 April 1956.
 'Hot and Cold Runnin' Tears'

'The Edge of the Sea'
'I've Got Some Crying to Do'
'That's Not the Kind of Love I Want'
'Old Love' (Brown says date is 6 July 1954.)

8 April 1956.
  'My Romance'
  'Lonely Woman'
  'Only You Can Say'
  'I Loved Him'

Hugo Peretti and His Studio Orchestra 21 June 1956.
  'It Happened Again'
  'I Wanna Play House'

Volume II: 1956–1957 – 'Sings Great American Songs'

Hal Mooney and His Studio Orchestra 29 October 1956.
  'You're My Everything'
  'Autumn in New York'
  'My Darling, My Darling'
  'Little Girl Blue'
  'Bewitched'
  'Dancing in the Dark'

30 October 1956.
  'Can't We Be Friends?'
  'All the Things You Are'
  'It Never Entered My Mind'
  'Homework'
  'They Say It's Wonderful'
  'The Touch of Your Hand'

31 October 1956.
  'My Heart Stood Still'
  'Let's Take an Old-Fashioned Walk'
  'My Ship'
  'A Tree in the Park'
  'A Ship Without a Sail'
  'He's Only Wonderful'

1 November 1956.
    'But Not for Me'
    'Poor Butterfly'
    'Love Is a Random Thing'
    'If I Loved You'
    'September Song'
    'Lost in the Stars'

2 November 1956.
    'If This Isn't Love'
    'It's Delovely'
    'It's Love'
    'Lucky in Love'
    'It's Got To Be Love'
    'Comes Love'

Mid-November 1956.
    'The Bashful Matador'
    'Leave It to Love'
    'Don't Let Me Love You'
    'The Second Time'

David Carroll and His Studio Orchestra 29 November 1956.
    'April Gave Me One More Day'
    'I've Got a New Heartache'
    'Don't Look at Me That Way'
    'The Banana Boat Song'

Jimmy Jones (p), Richard Davis (b), Roy Haynes (d), 14 February 1957.
    'Words Can't Describe'
    'Pennies from Heaven'
    'All of Me'
    'I Cried for You'
    'Linger Awhile'

Hal Mooney and His Studio Orchestra: with strings, Jimmy Jones (p), 20 March 1957.
    'Someone to Watch Over Me'
    'A Foggy Day'
    'Bidin' My Time'
    'He Loves and She Loves'
    'Love Walked In'
    'Looking for a Boy'

'I've Got a Crush on You'
'Isn't It a Pity'
'Do It Again'
'How Long Has This Been Going On?'
'Aren't You Kinda Glad We Did?'
'The Man I Love'

21 March 1957.
    'Let's Call the Whole Thing Off'
    'They All Laughed'
    'Lorelei'
    'I'll Build a Stairway to Paradise'

24 April 1957.
    'Summertime'
    'Things Are Looking Up'
    'I Won't Say I Will'
    'Of Thee I Sing'
    'My One and Only'

Billy Eckstine, in a vocal duet, with Hal Mooney and His Studio Orchestra,
24 April 1957.
    'Isn't This a Lovely Day?'
    'Easter Parade'
    'Now It Can Be Told'

25 April 1957.
    'Alexander's Ragtime Band'
    'I've Got My Love to Keep Me Warm'
    'You're Just in Love'
    'My Man's Gone Now' (delete Eckstine)
    'Cheek to Cheek'
    'Remember'
    'Always'

26 April 1957.
    'Passing Strangers'
    'The Door Is Open'

Hal Mooney and His Studio Orchestra, 3 June 1957.
    'You'll Find Me There'
    'Please Mr Brown'

'Band of Angels'
'Slow Down'

Billy Eckstine, in a vocal duet, with Hal Mooney and His Studio Orchestra,
12 July 1957.
'Goodnight Kiss'
'No Limit'

Volume III: 1957–1959 – 'Great Show On Stage'

Jimmy Jones (p), Richard Davis (b), Roy Haynes (d). Recorded at Mister
Kelly's, Chicago, Illinois, 6 August 1957.
'September in the Rain'
'Willow Weep for Me'
'Just One of Those Things'
'Be Anything but Darling Be Mine'
'Thou Swell'
'Stairway to the Stars'
'Honeysuckle Rose'
'Just a Gigolo'
'How High the Moon'
'Dream'
'I'm Gonna Sit Right Down and Write Myself a Letter'
'It's Got to Be Love'

7 August 1957.
'Alone'
'It's Got to Be Love'

8 August 1957.
'If This Isn't Love'
'Embraceable You'
'Lucky in Love'
'Dancing in the Dark'
'Poor Butterfly'
'Sometimes I'm Happy'
'I Cover the Waterfront'

Hal Mooney and His Studio Orchestra, 29 October 1957.
'Sweet Affection'
'Meet Me Half Way'
'What's So Bad About It?'

11 November 1957.
   'Gone Again'
   'The Next Time Around'

26 November 1957.
   'That Old Black Magic'
   'I've Got the World on a String'
   'Hit the Road to Dreamland'

8 December 1957.
   'Friendly Enemies'
   'Are You Certain?'

Ray Ellis and His Studio Orchestra, November–December 1957.
   'Careless'

This discography follows the liner notes from Polygram for the complete Mercury collection of Sarah Vaughan recordings, but her accompanist, Ronnell Bright, who played for the Count Basie orchestra sessions with Sarah in 1958, remembers distinctly a different schedule for the recordings. They were done in either September or October 1958, over a period of a few days in a West Fifty-seventh Street studio on the same block with Carnegie Hall. The biography follows Ronnell Bright's information.

Count Basie Orchestra: Ronnell Bright (p) sitting in for Basie, Thad Jones (leader, tp), Wendell Culley, Snooky Young, Joe Newman (tp), Henry Coker, Al Grey, Benny Powell (tb), Marshall Royal (as, cl), Frank Wess (as, ts, fl), Frank Foster, Billy Mitchell (ts), Charlie Fowlkes (bar), Richard Davis (b), Sonny Payne (d), Freddie Green (g), 5 January 1958.
   'Stardust'
   'Doodlin''
   'Darn That Dream'

Ray Ellis Studio Orchestra, 7 January 1958.
   'Mary Contrary'
   'Separate Ways'
   'Broken Hearted Melody' (This was Sarah Vaughan's first gold record, rising to seventh place in the pop charts in late 1959 and selling over a million copies.)

Hal Mooney and His Studio Orchestra and Chorus, 29 March 1958.
   'Too Much Too Soon'

'Padre'
'Spin Little Bottle'

Members of the Count Basie Band, same personnel as on 5 January 1958;
15 December 1958.
'Smoke Gets in Your Eyes'

23 December 1958.
'Moonlight in Vermont'
'Cheek to Cheek'
'Missing You'
'Just One of Those Things'
'No 'Count Basie'

Thad Jones (tp), Wendell Culley (tp), Henry Coker (tb), Frank Wess (ts),
Ronnell Bright (p), Richard Davis (b), Roy Haynes (d). At the London
House, Chicago, Illinois, 7 March 1958.
'Detour Ahead'
'Three Little Words'
'Speak Low'
'Like Someone in Love'
'You'd Be So Nice to Come Home To'
'I'll String Along with You'
'All of You'
'Thanks for the Memory'

Quincy Jones, conductor and arranger, Zoot Sims, Jo and Marcel Hrasko,
William Boucaya (saxes), Michel Hausser (vibes), Ronnell Bright (p), Rich-
ard Davis (b), Pierre Michelot (b), Kenny Clarke (d), Pierre Cullaz (g),
with strings. Paris, France, 7 July 1958.
'Please Be Kind' (with Davis)
'The Midnight Sun Will Never Set' (with Davis)
'Live for Love' (with Davis)
'Misty' (with Davis)
'I'm Lost' (with Michelot)
'Love Me' (with Michelot)
'That's All' (with Michelot)

Quincy Jones, conductor and arranger, Maurice Vander, Ronnell Bright
(p), Richard Davis (b), Roger Paraboschi or Kansas Fields (d), with strings
and woodwinds. Paris, France, 12 July 1958.
'Day by Day'

'Gone with the Wind'
'I'll Close My Eyes'
'The Thrill Is Gone'

Hal Mooney and His Studio Orchestra. New York City, 26 September 1958.
'Cool Baby'
'Everything'
'I Ain't Hurtin''
'Disillusioned Heart'

Belford Hedricks, conductor and arranger, and his orchestra, 2 September 1959.
'I Should Care'
'For All We Know'
'My Ideal'
'You're My Baby'
'Smooth Operator'
'Maybe It's Because I Love You Too Much'
'Our Waltz'
'Never in a Million Years'
'Close to You'
'Eternally'

Later in the same year, date unknown.
'Some Other Spring'

Fred Norman, conductor and arranger, and his studio orchestra. Late 1959.
'Say It Isn't So'
'If You Are But a Dream'
'Maybe You'll Be There'
'All of a Sudden My Heart Sings'
'There Is No You'
'Missing You'
'Please'
'Funny'
'I've Got to Talk to My Heart'
'Out of This World'
'Last Night When We Were Young'
'Through a Long and Sleepless Night'

Belford Hendricks, conductor and arranger, and his studio orchestra. Late 1959.

'I'll Never Be the Same'
'Through the Years'

(Denis Brown lists a recording done in Europe circa 1960 and released on
European labels by Sarah with the Clark Terry quartet with Ronnell Bright
[p], Richard Davis [b], Roy Haynes [d], and Terry [tp, vocal].)
'Scat Blues'

Sarah Vaughan recorded, from spring 1960 through early 1963, for Roulette Records, owned by Morris Levy, a backer of Birdland. Selections
from her work for the label appear on *The Roulette Years*, a collection
reissued in 1991 by Capitol Records, licensed by EMI Records. The LP
and CD do not constitute her complete work for the label. And EMI
Records had no complete list of her Roulette work available for publication
as of 1992. The following recordings were released in 1991 by EMI Records
as *The Singles Sessions* on Roulette.

'My Dear Little Sweetheart' (with 'Ooh, What a Day', not on the
album, as the flip side of the single release)
'Serenata' (with 'Let's', not on the album, as the flip side of the single
release)

Los Angeles, October 1960, arranged by Billy May.
'The Green Leaves of Summer'
'Them There Eyes'
'Don't Go to Strangers'
'Love'

New York, January 1961, arranged by Joe Reisman.
'What's the Use?'
'Wallflower Waltz'
'True Believer'
'April'
'If Not For You'
'Oh, Lover'

February 1962, arranged by Quincy Jones.
'One Mint Julep'
'Mama, He Treats Your Daughter Mean'

The following information about all Sarah's recordings done for the Roulette label between 1960 and 1963 comes from Denis Brown. Bruyninckx

also has written a discography of the same period. In some cases, Brown and Bruyninckx data differ. Brown's seems generally the most up-to-date and complete. Recordings made by Sarah Vaughan for other labels are not included for the period here. In general, for a full listing of her recordings between 1960 and 1963 for all labels other than Roulette and for some personnel details involved in Roulette and other recordings, consult the Brown discography.

Jimmy Jones Orchestra: Harry 'Sweets' Edison (tp), Gerald Sanfino (fl, ts), Janet Soyer (harp), unknown strings, Ronnell Bright (p), Barry Galbraith (g), Richard Davis or George Duvivier (b), Percy Brice (d). New York City, April 19, 1960.
    'My Ideal"
    'Hands Across the Table'
    'You've Changed'
    'Crazy He Calls Me'
    'I'll Be Seeing You'
    'Stormy Weather'
    'The More I See You'
    'Star Eyes'
    'Trees'
    'Moons over Miami'
    'Dreamy'
    'Why Was I Born'

Joe Reisman Orchestra. New York City, May 5, 1960.
    'Serenata'
    'My Dear Little Sweetheart'
    'Let's'
    'Ooh, What a Day'

Count Basie Orchestra, with a duet with Joe Wiliams. New York City, July 19, 1960.
    'If I Were a Bell'
    'Teach Me Tonight'

Billy May Orchestra. Los Angeles, California, October 18, 1960.
    'Green Leaves of Summer'
    'Them There Eyes'
    'Don't Go to Strangers'
    'Love'

Jimmy Jones Orchestra. Harry 'Sweets' Edison (tp), October 12, 1960.
    'What Do You See in Her?'
    'Trouble Is a Man'
    'I'm Gonna Laugh You Right Out of My Life'
    'Every Time I See You'

Jimmy Jones Orchestra. Harry 'Sweets' Edison (tp), New York City, October 13, 1960.
    'When Your Lover Has Gone'
    'Ain't No Use'
    'Gloomy Sunday'
    'Somebody Else's Dream'

Jimmy Jones Orchestra. New York City, 19 October 1960.
    'Jump for Joy'
    'You Stepped Out of a Dream'
    'Wrap Your Troubles in Dreams'
    'Have You Met Miss Jones?'

Joe Reisman Orchestra. New York City, 5 January 1961.
    'What's the Use?'
    'Wallflower Waltz'
    'True Believer'

Joe Reisman Orchestra. New York City, 9 January 1961.
    'April'
    'If Not for You'
    'Oh, Lover'

Count Basie Orchestra. New York City, 10 January 1961.
    'You Go to My Head'
    'You Turned the Tables on Me'

11 January 1961.
    'The Gentleman Is a Dope'

12 January 1961.
    'Mean to Me'
    'Lover Man'
    'Alone'

13 January 1961 (the date listed according to Roulette's files).

'I Cried for You'
'Little Man You've Had a Busy Day'
'Until I Met You'
'There Are Such Things'
'Perdido'

Marty Manning Orchestra. New York City, June 1961.
'Untouchable'
'Sleepy'
'The Hills of Assisi'

Mundell Lowe (g), George Duvivier (b). New York City, July 1961.
'Just Squeeze Me'
'Body and Soul'
'Through the Years'

18 July 1961.
'After Hours'
'My Favourite Things'
'Great Day'
'Sophisticated Lady'
'Every Time We Say Goodbye'
'Ill Wind'
'In a Sentimental Mood'
'If Love Is Good to Me'
'Easy to Love'
'Vanity'
(Denis Brown includes 'Wonder Why' and not 'After Hours' for the 18
July 1961 date.)

Quincy Jones Orchestra. New York City, February 1962.
'The Best Is Yet to Come'
'Baubles, Bangles, and Beads'
'So Long'
'I Could Write a Book'
'Moonglow'
'Witchcraft'
'On Green Dolphin Street'
'Maria'
'The Second Time Around'
'Invitation'
'You're Mine You'

'Fly Me to the Moon'

Early February 1962.
'Baubles, Bangles, and Beads'
'One Mint Julep'
'Mama, He Treats Your Daughter Mean'

Don Costa Orchestra. New York City, 23–25 July 1962.
'I Remember You'
'I Fall in Love Too Easily'
'I Hadn't Anyone Till You'
'Glad to Be Unhappy'
'Oh, You Crazy Moon'
'Snowbound'
'Look to Your Heart'

27 July 1962 (probable date).
'Stella by Starlight'
'Blah, Blah, Blah'
'What's Good About Goodbye'
'Spring Can Really Hang You up the Most'

Barney Kessel (g), Joe Comfort (b). Los Angeles, California, 7 August 1962.
'I Understand'
'Key Largo'
'The Very Thought of You'
'Just Squeeze Me'
'When Sunny Gets Blue'
'Baby, Won't You Please Come Home'
'When Lights Are Low'
'All I Do Is Dream of You'
'Just in Time'
'All or Nothing at All'
'Goodnight, Sweetheart'

Benny Carter Orchestra. Los Angeles, California, August 1962 (probable date).
'Nobody Else But Me'
'Falling in Love with Love'
'I Believe in You'
'A Garden in the Rain'

'I'm Gonna Live 'Til I Die'
'I Can't Give You Anything but Love'
'After You've Gone'
'Moonlight on the Ganges'
'The Lady's in Love with You'
'The Trolley Song'
'Honeysuckle Rose'
'Great Day'

Marty Manning Orchestra, 13 February 1963.
'There'll Be Other Times'
'Don't Go to Strangers'
'Enchanted Wall'
'Call Me Irresponsible'

27 February 1963.
'Star Eyes'
'Do You Remember?'
'I'll Never Be the Same'
'I Was Telling Him About You'

5 March 1963.
'Icy Stone'
'As Long as He Needs Me'
'Once Upon a Summertime'
'Bewildered'
'Within Me I Know'

11 March 1963.
'Full Moon and Empty Arms'
'Ah, Sweet Mystery of Life'
'Because'
'Be My Love'
'Intermezzo'
'My Reverie'
'Moonlight Love'
'I Give to You'

Gerald Wilson Orchestra. Los Angeles, California, 29 May 1963.
'I Guess I'll Hang My Tears Out to Dry'
''Round Midnight'
'Midnight Sun'

'Easy Street'
'In Love in Vain'

31 May 1963.
'A Taste of Honey'
'Moanin''

6 June 1963.
'What Kind of Fool Am I?'
'The Good Life'

12 June 1963.
'Sermonette'
'The Gravy Waltz'
'Baby, Won't You Please Come Home'

Benny Carter Orchestra. Los Angeles, California, 13–16 June 1963.
'If I Had You'
'What'll I Do?'
'You're Driving Me Crazy'
'Always on My Mind'
'Solitude'
'I'll Never Be the Same'
'So Long, My Love'
'The Lonely Hours'
'These Foolish Things'
'Look for Me, I'll Be Around'
'Friendless'
'The Man I Love'

Lalo Schifrin Orchestra. Chicago, Illinois, late June 1963.
'More Than You Know'
'Something I Dreamed Last Night'
'Lazy Afternoon'
'I Didn't Know About You'
'I Got Rhythm'
'I Wish I Were in Love Again'
'This Can't Be Love'
'Just Married Today'
'Come Spring'
'Slowly'

Marty Manning Orchestra. July 1963.

''Til the End of Time'
'None But the Lonely Heart'
'If You Are But a Dream'
'Only'
'Experience Unnecessary'

Volume IV: 1963–1967

Quincy Jones, orchestra conductor. Copenhagen, Denmark, July 1963.
'He Never Mentioned Love'
'Gone'
'Right or Wrong'
'Show Me a Man'

Kirk Stuart (p), Charles 'Buster' Williams (b), Georges Hughes (d). Tivoli,
Copenhagen, Denmark, 18–21 July 1963.
'I Feel Pretty'
'Misty'
'What Is This Thing Called Love?'
'Lover Man'
'Sometimes I'm Happy'
'Won't You Come Home, Bill Bailey?'
'Tenderly'
'Sassy's Blues'
'Polka Dots and Moonbeams'
'I Cried for You'
'Poor Butterfly'
'I Could Write a Book'
'Time After Time'
'All of Me'
'I Hadn't Anyone Till You'
'I Can't Give You Anything But Love'
'I'll Be Seeing You'
'Maria'
'Day In, Day Out'
'Fly Me to the Moon'
'Baubles, Bangles, and Beads'
'The Lady's in Love with You'
'Honeysuckle Rose'
'The More I See You'
'Say It Isn't So'
'Black Coffee'

'Just One of Those Things'
'On Green Dolphin Street'
'Over the Rainbow'

Quincy Jones, orchestra leader, Robert Farnon, arranger and conductor, featuring the Svend Saaby Choir. Copenhagen, Denmark, 12 October 1963.

'Charade'
'It Could Happen to You'
'Blue Orchids'
'This Heart of Mine'
'Then I'll Be Tired Of You'
'Funny'
'My Colouring Book'
'How Beautiful Is the Night'
'Hey There'
'Deep Purple'
'I'll Be Around'
'The Days of Wine and Roses'

Quincy Jones, producer; details unknown. Los Angeles, California, 13–14 February 1964.

'How's the World Treating You'
'My Darling, My Darling'
'Bluesette'
'You Got It Made'
'Make Someone Happy'
'Sole Sole'

(Denis Brown adds another track to this session, 'The Other Half of Me'.)

Quincy Jones, producer, Richard Hixon, Billy Byers, Britt Woodman, Wayne Andre, Benny Powell (tb), Jerome Richardson (fl), Bob James (p), Barry Galbraith (g), George Duvivier (b), Bobby Donaldson (d), Willie Rodriques (perc), Lewis Eley, Emanuel Green, Charles Libove, Leo Kruczek, Tosha Samaroff, Gene Orloff, Bernard Eichen, Harry Lookofsky (viol), Frank Foster (arranger, director). New York City, 23 August 1964.

'Mr Luck'
'The Boy from Ipanema'

Similar personnel to preceding entry, except delete Woodman, Powell (tb), Duvivier (b), Galbraith (g), Rodriques (perc), and add Jose Mangual, Juan Cadavieco, Rafael Sierra (perc), 14 August 1964.

'Quiet Nights' (strings out, guitar added)
'Jive Samba'

Quincy Jones, producer, Kai Winding, Richard Hixon, Billy Byers, Wayne
Andre, Benny Powell (tb), Jerome Richardson (fl), Robert Rodriquez (b),
Bobby Donaldson, William Correa, Juan Cadavieco, Jose Mangual, Rafael
Sierra (perc), Lewis Eley, Emanuel Green, Charles Libove, Leo Kruczek,
Tosha Samaroff, Bernard Eichen, David Nadien, Harry Lookofsky (viol),
Frank Foster (arranger, conductor), 15 August 1964.
'A Taste of Honey'
'Shiny Stockings'
'Night Song'
'Stompin' at the Savoy'
'Fascinating Rhythm'
'The Moment of Truth'
'Tea for Two'

Same personnel as preceding entry, but delete Byers, add Bill Watrous
(tb). New York, 18 August 1964.
'Fever'
'Avalon'

Details unknown, 14 December 1964.
'We Almost Made It'

Details unknown, December 1964.
'How Soon'
'Dear Heart'
'Too Little Time'
'Dreamsville'
'Bye Bye' (theme from 'Peter Gunn')
'Moon River'
'(I Love You and) Don't You Forget It'
'Slow Hot Wind'
'It Had Better Be Tonight'

Quincy Jones, producer. Details unknown.
'Pawnbroker's Theme'

Details unknown, 10 October 1965.
'Darling'
'I'll Never Be Lonely Again'

'Habibi' (love song from 'Sallah')

Luchi De Jesus (arranger). Details unknown, 10 November 1965.
    'Make It Easy on Yourself'
    'What the World Needs Now Is Love'
    'I Know a Place'

11 November 1965.
    'Little Hands'
    'Yesterdays'
    'A Lover's Concerto'
    'He Touched Me'

12 November 1965.
    'If I Ruled the World'
    'Waltz For Debbie'
    'On a Clear Day You Can See Forever'
    'The First Thing Every Morning'

Luchi De Jesus (arranger), Bob James (arranger★), 7 April 1966.
    'Who Can I Turn To?'★
    'The Shadow of Your Smile'★
    'I Should Have Kissed Him More'
    'Call Me'

8 April 1966.
    'One, Two, Three'
    'Michelle'
    'Sneaking Up on You'

11 April 1966.
    'With These Hands'
    'Dominique's Discotheque'
    'Everybody Loves Somebody'
    'What Now My Love'
    'Love'

Details unknown. January 1967.
    'Jim'
    'The Man That Got Away'
    'My Man'
    'Happiness Is Just a Thing Called Joe'

'Trouble Is a Man'
'He's Funny That Way'
'For Every Man There's a Woman'
'I'm Just Wild About Harry'
'Danny Boy'
'Alfie'

Clark Terry, Charlie Shavers, Joe Newman, Freddie Hubbard (tp), J. J. Johnson, Kai Winding (tb), Phil Woods, Benny Golson (reeds), Bob James (p), plus a large orchestra. Thad Jones, Manny Albam, J. J. Johnson, Bob James (arrangers), 23 January 1967.
    'On the Other Side of the Tracks' (Johnson)
    'All Alone' (Jones)
    'I Want to Be Happy' (Jones)
    'S'posin'' (Albam)
    'I Had a Ball' (Johnson)

24 January 1967.
    'Take the "A" Train' (Johnson)
    'I Left My Heart in San Francisco' (Jones)
    'The Sweetest Sounds' (James)

Brown's discography includes some recordings done for labels such as Bell by Sarah in the late 1960s. Also, for April 1992, Scotti Bros Records scheduled the CD issue of Sarah Vaughan recorded live, with personnel as follows: Zoot Sims (ts), Clark Terry (tp), Jaki Byard (p), Milt Hinton (b), Alan Dawson (d). Live performance, New Orleans, Louisiana, June 1969.
    'I Cried for You'
    'Tenderly'
    'Time After Time'
    'Sometimes I'm Happy'
    'Misty'
    'Day In, Day Out'
    'Lover Man'
    'Bluesette'
    'All of Me'

University of Illinois Big Band, John Garvey (director), Benny Carter (arranger). New Orleans, Louisiana, June 1969.
    'The Lamp Is Low'
    'Watch What Happens'
    'There Will Never Be Another You'

Unknown chorus and New Orleans group. New Orleans, Louisiana, June 1969.
    'A Closer Walk with Thee'

The following recordings were made in the early 1970s for Mainstream Records, owned by Robert Shad. (In 1991, Mainstream's owners were planning to reissue all of Sarah's recordings done for the label, including some previously unreleased tracks, possibly on a new label, according to Brown.)

Ernie Wilkins Orchestra: Buddy Childers, Al Aarons, Gene Coe (tp), George Bohanon, Benny Powell (tb), Jerome Richardson, Bill Green, Jackie Kelso (reeds), Bill Mays (p), Joe Pass, Al Vescovo (g), Bob Magnusson (b), Earl Palmer (d), Alan Estes (perc), Jimmy Cobb (d). Los Angeles, California, 16–20 November 1971.
    'Imagine'
    'On Thinking It Over'
    'Inner City Blues'
    'Sweet Gingerbread Man'
    'Magical Connection'
    'That's the Way I Heard It Should Be'
    'Tomorrow City'
    'Universal Prisoner'
    'Trouble'
    'If Not for You'

Peter Matz, Michel Legrand, and Jack Elliott and Allyn Ferguson, arrangers and conductors. Originally issued on the album *Feelin' Good*, Sarah's third album for the label, 1972.
    'Alone Again Naturally' (Matz)
    'Easy Evil' (Matz)
    'When You Think of It' (Matz)
    'Take a Love Song' (Matz)
    'And the Feeling's Good' (Matz)
    'Promise Me' (Matz)
    'Rainy Days and Mondays' (Matz)
    'Deep in the Night' (Legrand)
    'Run to Me' (Elliott and Ferguson)
    'Greatest Show on Earth' (Elliott and Ferguson)
    'Just a Little Lovin'' (Elliott and Ferguson)

Michel Legrand, arranger and conductor on songs with an asterisk. A variety of arrangers are noted for the remaining songs. A double-LP set was released in 1974 as *Sarah Vaughan*; both records were recorded earlier than 1974 and released as single issues. Sessions with Legrand took place during 17–20 April 1972. According to Bruyninckx, personnel in the Legrand Orchestra included Buddy Childers, Chuck Findley, Conte Condoli, Gary Barone, Al Aarons (tp), Lloyd Ulyate, Charlie Loper, Frank Rosolino, Grover Mitchell, Bob Knight, George Roberts (tb), Tommy Johnson (tuba), Vince De Rosa, Bill Hinshaw, Art Maebe, George Price, Sinclair Lott, Ralph Pyle, Dick Perissi, Dick Macker (frhn), Bud Shank, Pete Christlieb, Jerome Richardson, Bob Cooper, Bill Hood, Bernie Fleischer (reeds), Dave Grusin, Mike Wofford, Artie Kane (keyboards), Ray Brown, Chuck Berghofer, Bob Magnusson (b), Chuck Rainey (elec-b), Shelly Manne, John Guerin (d), Larry Bunker (perc), Tom Tedesco (g).

'The Summer Knows'*
'What Are You Doing the Rest of Your Life?'*
'Once You've Been in Love'*
'Hands of Time (Brian's Song)'*
'I Was Born in Love with You'*
'I Will Say Goodbye'*
'Summer Me, Winter Me'*
'His Eyes, Her Eyes'*
'Pieces of Dreams'*
'Blue, Green, Gray, and Gone'*

'Send in the Clowns' (Paul Griffin, arranger). (This song was presented to Sarah by Bob Shad, and Sarah made her first recording of it for Mainstream. The album on which this song appeared, apart from its inclusion in the double-record set, was *Send in the Clowns* and included that song and the nine following songs, released in 1974 and possibly earlier, too. However, there is no mention of this song in the Bruyninckx discography for any recording sessions by Sarah for Mainstream. The following nine songs are also omitted from the Bruyninckx discography. But they are included in Brown, who also includes 'Send in the Clowns', for the recording date of 1974 in Los Angeles. However, it is likely that 'Send in the Clowns' was recorded in New York, because Sarah's friend Robert Richards in New York City talked with her on the day she recorded it.)

'Love Don't Live Here Anymore' (Gene Page)
'That'll Be Johnny' (Gene Page)
'Right in the Next Room' (Gene Page)
'I Need You More (Than Ever Now)' (Gene Page)
'On Thinking It Over' (Ernie Wilkins)
'Do Away with April' (Gene Page)

'Wave' (Michel Legrand)
'Got to See If I Can't Get Daddy to Come Back Home' (Gene Page)
'Frasier (the Sensuous Lion)' (Wade Marcus)

Carl Schroeder (p), John Cianelli (b), Jimmy Cobb (d). Recorded in concert for issue by Mainstream at the Sun Plaza Hotel, Tokyo, Japan, 24 September 1973.

'A Foggy Day'
'Poor Butterfly'
'The Lamp Is Low'
''Round Midnight'
'Willow Weep for Me'
'There Will Never Be Another You'
'Misty'
'Wave'
'Like Someone in Love'
'My Funny Valentine'
'All of Me'
'Love Story'
'Over the Rainbow'
'I Could Write a Book'
'The Nearness of You'
'I'll Remember April'
'Watch What Happens'
'Bye-Bye Blackbird'
'Rainy Days and Mondays'
'Sarah's Tune, Number One'
'On a Clear Day'
'I Remember You'
'I Cried for You'
'Tenderly'
'Summertime'
'The Blues'
'There Is No Greater Love'
'Tonight'

Jimmy Rowles Quintet: Al Aarons (tp), Teddy Edwards (ts), Rowles (p), Monte Budwig (b), Donald Bailey (d). Probably in Los Angeles, California, circa 1974.

'The Folks Who Live on the Hill' (without Aarons and Edwards)
'That Face'
'That Sunday'
'A House Is Not a Home'

'Frasier'
'Morning Star'
(Pianist Jimmy Rowles arranged four songs for the above album, which were not released: 'I Can't Escape from You', 'There's Danger in Your Eyes, Cherie', 'Too Late Now', and 'Bewitched'. Of the songs that were released, 'Morning Star' was written by Jimmy Rowles with lyrics by Johnny Mercer, though W. C. Handy was given credit – apparently by accident – for the composition. This information comes directly from Jimmy Rowles.)

Carl Schroeder (p), Bob Magnusson (b), Jimmy Cobb (d). Recorded for an album called *Jazz Jamboree*, according to Bruyninckx, in Warsaw, Poland, 24 October 1975, on the Pronit label.
    'On a Clear Day You Can See Forever'
    ''Round Midnight'
    'What Are You Doing the Rest of Your Life?'
    'Sassy's Blues'
    'They Long to Be Close to You'
    'A Foggy Day'
    'My Funny Valentine'
    'Tenderly'
    'Won't You Come Home, Bill Bailey?'
    'The Nearness of You'

Sarah Vaughan: Songs of the Beatles, with a large studio orchestra: Lee Ritenour, Dean Parks, Louis Shelton (g), Mike Lang (keyboards), Davis Hungate (p), Jeff Porcaro (perc, d), Bobbye Hall, Joe Porcaro, Steve Forman (perc), Steve Porcaro (synth), Toots Thielemans (harmonica), John Smith (ts), Bob Magnusson (b), Billy Thetford (leader), Perry Morgan, Jim Gilstrap (background singers), Sid Sharp (concertmaster, strings), Marty and David Paich (rhythm, horn, and strings arrangers). Daven Sound Studios, Universal City, California, 1977.
    'Get Back'
    'And I Love Her'
    'Eleanor Rigby'
    'Fool on the Hill'
    'You Never Give Me Your Money'
    'Come Together'
    'I Want You'
    'Blackbird'
    'Something'
    'Here, There and Everywhere'
    'The Long and Winding Road'

'Yesterday'
'Hey Jude'
'Honey' (unissued)
'Golden Slumbers' (unissued)
(Data on unissued songs come from Denis Brown.)

Denis Brown includes recordings of a Washington DC broadcast done on 6 March 1977, and live performances in June 1977 in the Ronnie Scott jazz club in London's Soho section, the latter with her trio – Carl Schroeder (p), Walter Booker (b) and Jimmy Cobb (d) – and released on the English Pye label as *Ronnie Scott Presents Sarah Vaughan, Volumes I and II.*

Various studio groups, with songs arranged by Edson Federico (p), in Rio de Janeiro, Brazil, on 31 October, 3, 4, 5 and 7 November, 1977. Aloysio de Oliveira, producer; Durval Ferreira, creative director, composer. In his review in the *Los Angeles Times* in 1978, Leonard Feather especially praised Antonio Carlos Jobim (keyboards, composer) on 'Triste'; Milton Nascimento (vocalist, g) on 'Courage'; lyrics by Ray Gilbert for Marcos Valle's 'If You Went Away'; Dori Caymmi's 'Roses and Roses'; Oscar Neves's 'I Live to Love You'; and composer Ferreira's song, 'The Day It Rained'. From Denis Brown come the following details:

Milton Nascimento (g, vocal), Jose Roberto Bertrami (Fender p), Novelli (elec-b), Nelson Angelo (elec-g), Roberto Silva (d), Danilo Caymmi, Paulo Jobim (fl), Chico Batera, Arivoldo (perc) on 'Courage', 'Bridges'.

Jose Roberto Bertrami (Fender p), Sergio Barroso or Claudio Bertrami (b), Helio Delmiro (g), Chico Batera, Ariovaldo (perc), Mauricio Einhorn (harmonica), Wilson Das Neves (d), Dori Caymmi (vocal) on 'Roses and Roses', 'A Little Tear', 'The Day It Rained', 'If You Went Away'.

Tom Jobim (Yamaha p), Jose Roberto Bertrami (Fender p), Helio Delmiro (g), Wilson Das Neves (d), Sergio Barroso (b), Chico Batera, Ariovaldo (perc) on 'Someone to Light Up My Life', 'Triste'.

One of the above groups on 'Vera Cruz', 'The Face I Love', 'Cantador'.

Pablo Records released the recording as *I Love Brazil.* It was nominated for a Grammy but didn't win.

The following recordings were done for Pablo Records between 1978 and 1982 in Hollywood, California, and later reissued by Fantasy Records.

Denis Brown includes in this era an album entitled *Milt Jackson and Count Basie and the Big Band, Vol. 2,* on which Sarah Vaughan scats with the saxophone section on the song 'For Lena and Lennie', arranged by Quincy Jones, recorded in Hollywood, California, 18 January 1978.

Oscar Peterson (p), Ray Brown (b), Louis Bellson (d), Joe Pass (g). Hollywood, California, 25 April 1978.
> 'I've Got the World on a String'
> 'Midnight Sun'
> 'How Long Has This Been Going On?'
> 'You're Blasé'
> 'Easy Living'
> 'More Than You Know'
> 'My Old Flame'
> 'Teach Me Tonight'
> 'Body and Soul'
> 'When Your Lover Has Gone'

Billy Byers, conductor and arranger on the big-band sides, with Waymon Reed (tp, flghn), J. J. Johnson (tb), Frank Foster, Zoot Sims (ts), Frank Wess (ts, fl), Jimmy Rowles (p) in Hollywood, California, Mike Wofford (p) in New York, Joe Pass (g) in Hollywood, Bucky Pizzarelli (g) in New York, Andy Simpkins (b), Grady Tate (d). Issued as the album *Sarah Vaughan: Duke Ellington Song Book One*, Hollywood, California, 15 and 16 August 1979.
> 'I'm Just a Lucky So and So' (solo by Reed)
> 'Solitude' (solo by Johnson)
> 'I Didn't Know About You'
> 'All Too Soon' (solo by Wess)
> 'Sophisticated Lady' (solo by Wess)
> 'Day Dream' (solos by Reed and Sims)

New York City, 12 and 13 September 1979.
> 'In a Sentimental Mood'
> 'I Let a Song Go Out of My Heart' (solo by Foster)
> 'Lush Life'
> 'In a Mellow Tone' (solo by Foster)

Waymon Reed (tp, flghn), Frank Wess (fl), Eddie 'Cleanhead' Vinson (as, vocal), Mike Wofford, Jimmy Rowles, Lloyd Glenn (p), Andy Simpkins, Bill Walker (b), Grady Tate, Charles Randell, Roy McCurdy (d), Joe Pass, Bucky Pizzarelli, Pee Wee Crayton (g). Hollywood, California, 15 and 16 August 1979, and New York City, 12 and 13 September 1979. Issued as *Sarah Vaughan: Duke Ellington Song Book Two*.

'Chelsea Bridge' (solo by McCurdy)
'What Am I Here For?' (solo by Rowles)
'Tonight I Shall Sleep' (solo by Pizzarelli)
'Rocks in My Bed' (solos by Glenn, Crayton, Walker, Randell)
'I Got It Bad and That Ain't Good' (solo by Pizzarelli)
'Everything But You' (Vaughan with Wofford and Pass)
'Mood Indigo' (solo by McCurdy)
'It Don't Mean a Thing (If It Ain't Got That Swing)' (solo by Pizzarelli)
'Prelude to a Kiss'
'I Ain't Got Nothing But the Blues'
'Black Butterfly' (solo by Pizzarelli)
(Both above albums were originally called *A Celebration of Duke*.)

Helio Delmiro (g), Andy Simpkins (b), Grady Tate (d), Wilson Das Neves (perc), arranged by Edison Federico. Rio de Janeiro, Brazil, 1–5 October 1979.

'Dindi' (issued on *The Best of Sarah Vaughan* in 1983)
'Bonita' (this and all the rest were issued on *Copacabana*)
'Double Rainbow'
'Copacabana'
'To Say Goodbye'
'Gentle Rain'
'Dreamer'
'Tete'
'The Smiling Hour'

Count Basie Orchestra: Sam Nestico, conductor and arranger except where noted, Sonny Cohn, Frank Szabo, Willie Cook, Bob Summers, Dale Carley (tp), Mitchell 'Booty' Wood, Bill Hughes, Dennis Wilson, Grover Mitchell (tb), Kenny Hing, Eric Dixon, Bobby Plater, Danny Turner, Johnny Williams (saxes), George Gaffney (p), Andy Simpkins (b), Harold Jones (d), Freddie Green (g). Hollywood, California, 16 and 18 February 1981. (Schaap says the bassist and drummer were possibly, respectively, Cleveland Eaton and Greg Field.)

'I Gotta Right to Sing the Blues' (solo by Wood)
'Just Friends'
'If You Could See Me Now' (arranged by Allyn Ferguson)
'Ill Wind'
'When Your Lover Has Gone'
'Send in the Clowns'
'I Hadn't Anyone Till You'
'All the Things You Are' (solo by Hing, arranged by Allyn Ferguson)

'Indian Summer'
'From This Moment On'

Sir Roland Hanna (p), Andy Simpkins (b), Harold Jones (d), Joe Pass (g). Hollywood, California, 1 and 2 March 1982. Issued as *Crazy and Mixed Up*.
'I Didn't Know What Time It Was'
'That's All'
'Autumn Leaves'
'Love Dance'
'The Island'
'Seasons'
'In Love in Vain'
'You Are Too Beautiful'

George Gaffney (p), Andy Simpkins (b), Harold Jones (d), with Michael Tilson Thomas and the Los Angeles Philharmonic Orchestra, arranged by Marty Paich. Recorded live in Los Angeles, California, for the album *Gershwin Live!*, 1982, for CBS Records.
'Overture: Porgy and Bess'
Medley: 'Summertime'/'It Ain't Necessarily So'/'I Loves You, Porgy'
Medley: 'But Not for Me'/'Love Is Here to Stay'/'Embraceable You'
'Someone to Watch Over Me'
'Sweet and Low Down'
'Fascinating Rhythm'
'Do It Again'
'My Man's Gone Now'
'The Man I Love'
Medley: 'Nice Work If You Can Get It'/'They Can't Take That Away from Me'/''S Wonderful'/'Sewanee'/'Strike Up the Band'
Encore: 'I've Got a Crush on You'/'A Foggy Day'
Sarah Vaughan won a Grammy for this album.

With Barry Manilow, in a duet on his album *2 A.M. Paradise Cafe*, on the Arista label. Los Angeles, California, 1984. Gerry Mulligan (bar), Bill Mays (p, Rhodes), George Duvivier (b), Shelly Manne (d), Mundell Lowe (g).
'Blue'

Denis Brown includes a recording entitled *The Planet Is Alive, Let It Live* by Sarah with a large studio orchestra conducted by Lalo Schifrin in Düsseldorf, West Germany, 30 June 1984, with Francy Boland, arranger, done for Jazzletter Records, PO Box 240, Ojai, California 93023. The music was composed by the Italians Tito Fontana and Sante Palumbo for Italian translations of poems written in Polish by Karol Wytola as a young student priest before he became Pope John Paul II. American writer Gene Lees wrote English versions of the six poems sung by Sarah. The record was released by Lees on his own label as *The Planet Is Alive . . . Let It Live!* underscoring the breadth of Sarah's musical reach. Major record labels had refused the project.

London Symphony Orchestra, directed by Jonathan Tunick. London, England, 27–31 January 1986, for CBS Records.
    'Happy Talk'
    'Bali Ha'i'

Milton Nascimento (vocalist, composer), George Duke (keyboards), Alphonso Johnson (b), Dan Huff (g), Dori Caymmi (g, arranger, composer), Carlos Vega (d), Paulinho DaCosta (perc), Hubert Laws (fl), Tom Scott (lyricon, ts), Ernie Watts (as), Marcio Montarroyos (tp, flghn), Chuck Domanico (b), Siedah Garrett, Gracinha Leporace, and Kate Markowitz (background vocals), and twenty-four string players (violins, violi, celli, harp), produced and composed by Sergio Mendes. New York City and Detroit, Michigan, January–February 1987, except for Milton Nascimento recorded in Rio de Janeiro, Brazil, for CBS Records. (This discography follows the album's liner notes, but Dori Caymmi says the album was recorded in Rio de Janeiro. It's possible that parts of the album, called *Brazilian Romance* were redone or recorded in several locations.)
    'Make This City Ours Tonight' (solos by Scott, Montarroyos)
    'Romance' (solo by Montarroyos)
    'Love and Passion' (with Milton Nascimento in a vocal duet; solo by Scott)
    'So Many Stars'
    'Photograph' (with Chuck Domanico, b)
    'Nothing Will Be as It Was' (solo by Ernie Watts)
    'It's Simple'
    'Obsession' (solo by Laws)
    'Wanting More'
    'Your Smile'

Denis Brown includes recordings of Christmas carols done by Sarah Vaughan with the Mormon Tabernacle Choir and Utah Symphony Orchestra for Hallmark Cards, Summer 1988. The time and place for Sarah's contribution to the recordings, which may have been recorded separately from the orchestra, are unknown.

Quincy Jones group, *Back on the Block*, Qwest Records, Los Angeles, California, 1989.

'Wee B. Dooinit' (Acapella Party)
'Jazz Corner of the World' (introduction to 'Birdland'), 'Birdland'

Final Notes

The following three groups of recordings made in the early 1960s have been situated together at the end of this survey, not interspersed with other recordings in chronological order, because the continuity of Sarah's recordings for her major contracts would be broken. These next recordings became commercially available on the CD issued as a tribute to Sarah Vaughan by Vintage Jazz Classics in 1990. They don't appear to be available from any other source.

Joe Williams, in a vocal duet, accompanied by the Count Basie Orchestra: Count Basie (p), Sonny Cohn, Thad Jones, Joe Newman, Snooky Young (tp), Henry Coker, Al Grey, Benny Powell (tb), Marshall Royal, Frank Wess, Frank Foster, Billy Mitchell, Charlie Fowlkes (reeds), Eddie Jones (b), Sonny Payne (d), Freddie Green (g). Madison Square Garden Jazz Festival, 2 June 1960.

'Teach Me Tonight'

Ronnell Bright (p), Richard Davis (b), Percy Brice (d). Madison Square Garden Jazz Festival, 2 June 1960.

'What Is This Thing Called Love?'
'Gone with the Wind'
'All of Me'
'Don't Blame Me'
'Just One of Those Things'
'Misty'
'Sometimes I'm Happy'

Ronnell Bright (p), Richard Davis (b), Percy Brice (d), Woody Herman (cl) where indicated. Probably New York City, circa 1961 or 1962.

'Day In, Day Out'
'But Not for Me' (with Herman)
'The More I See You'
'Green Dolphin Street' (with Herman)
'Just One of Those Things' (with Herman)
'I'll Be Seeing You'
'I Cried for You' (with Herman)
'Poor Butterfly'

As examples of out-of-print albums on little record labels found in stores specialising in old records, Sarah's work was available in 1991 in the following forms, without discographical details:

On the Top Line label, licensed by Charly Records, 156/166 Ilderton Road, London SE15 1NT, England, was an album containing the following songs: 'Thanks for the Memories', 'Start Believing in Me', 'My Funny Valentine', 'A Foggy Day', 'Send in the Clowns', 'Three Little Words', 'Like Someone in Love', 'Detour Ahead', 'You May Not Be an Angel', 'If You Could See Me Now'.

On Trip Records, Springboard International Records, 8295 Sunset Boulevard, Los Angeles, California 90046, some early monophonic records were reissued by licensing agreement with Mercury. One of them made up the album *Sarah Vaughan Sings Great Songs from Hit Shows*, and though that wasn't seen among the out-of-print Trip albums available in 1991, the Memoir label's Mercury-licensed issue of that album was for sale.

On Spinorama, Premier Albums, 356 West 40th Street, New York 18, New York, an album so old that the zip code hadn't been changed to 10018 yet, with 'East of the Sun', 'What More Can a Woman Do?', 'No Smoke Blues', 'I'd Rather Have a Memory Than a Dream', 'Mean to Me', 'Love Was Just an Interlude', 'Tribute to Sarah', 'Signing Off' – obviously reissues of some of her very early recordings.

On Bell Records, 1650 Broadway, New York 19, New York, another very old LP of reissues: 'The One I Love Belongs to Somebody Else', 'Love Me or Leave Me', '100 Years from Today', 'Penthouse Serenade', 'Everything I Have Is Yours', 'Lover Man', 'I'm Through with Love', 'Don't Worry 'Bout Me', 'September Song', 'Gentleman Friend', 'I Feel So Smoochie', 'Trouble Is a Man'.

Films Sarah also sang on the soundtrack LPs for several films, which are documented in Denis Brown's discography. The films are *Murder, Inc*; *Bob & Carol & Ted & Alice*, for which she sang an aria from Handel's *Messiah*, arranged by Quincy Jones; *Sharkey's Machine*, on which Sarah sings the love theme for the film by herself and a duet, 'Before You', with Joe Williams, issued by Warner Brothers Records in 1981; and *Cactus Flower*. Her performances of 'A Time for Love Is Anytime' for *Cactus Flower* and of an aria from Handel's *Messiah* for *Bob & Carol & Ted & Alice* are included only on the LPs, not in the films.

Grammy Awards Sarah Vaughan received one Grammy award from the

National Academy of Recording Arts and Sciences in 1982 for Best Jazz Vocal Performance for *Gershwin Live!* a CBS Records album done with Michael Tilson Thomas. She received her second Grammy as a Lifetime Achievement Award on 22 February 1989. At the Grammy Awards ceremony at the Shrine Auditorium in Los Angeles, she sang 'So Many Stars'.

She was nominated for Grammys and didn't win in 1959 for 'Broken Hearted Melody' on Mercury; in 1976 for her album done live in Japan for Mainstream; in 1978 for *How Long Has This Been Going On?* for Pablo; in 1979 for *I Love Brazil* for Pablo; in 1980 for *The Duke Ellington Songbook* for Pablo; in 1983 for *Crazy and Mixed Up* for Pablo; and in 1985 for 'Blue', a duet with Barry Manilow on his album, *2 A.M. Paradise Cafe*, for Arista.

Other Awards and Honours In 1980, a plaque in her honour was installed in the sidewalk on Swing Street (West 52nd Street between Fifth and Sixth avenues) – in front of the CBS Building.

For a performance on television on 9 May 1981, Sarah won an Emmy in the category of Individual Achievement – Special Class.

In 1985, she became the 1,808th person to be awarded a star on Hollywood's Walk of the Stars.

In 1988, she entered the Jazz Hall of Fame in New Jersey.

In addition to her early successes in the polls in *Down Beat* (1947 through 1952) and *Metronome* (1948 through 1953), and in *Billboard* magazine polls as the best female singer and the Esquire New Star Award in the 1940s, she placed first again in *Down Beat* in 1973 and from 1975 through 1979. In 1978, she won the award as best female singer in *Jazz Journal* magazine published in London, England.

Videography

The following videos and films have been used for reference for this biography.

Listen to the Sun, produced and directed by Thomas C. Guy Jr.

A video under the auspices of the *Montreux Jazz Festival* in Switzerland was filmed of Sarah Vaughan in concert in a festival.

Sarah Vaughan Live from Monterey, Sony, 1984, at the Monterey Jazz Festival, with Sarah's trio – Mike Wofford, piano; Andy Simpkins, bass; Harold Jones, drums – with guest Joe Williams; also pianist Hank Jones, drummer Shelly Manne, trombonist George Bohanon, trumpeter Clark Terry, guitarist Mundell Lowe, and clarinettist Eiji Kitamuru.

Sarah Vaughan: The Divine One, produced by Toby Byron and Richard Saylor, directed by Matthew Seig, as part of the *American Masters* series on the Public Broadcasting System.

Sass and Brass, HBO Video, 1986, filmed in New Orleans, with Sarah's trio – George Gaffney, piano; Andy Simpkins, bass; and Harold Jones, drums – and trumpeters Don Cherry, Maynard Ferguson, Dizzy Gillespie, Al Hirt, Chuck Mangione, and pianist Herbie Hancock, bassist Ron Carter, and drummer Billy Higgins.

Bibliography

Sources of information for this book, apart from interviews with people who knew Sarah Vaughan throughout her career, have been newspapers, magazines, liner notes for recordings, and books. Sarah Vaughan's life, though never treated in a biography about her, has been an integral part of the jazz world since the mid-1940s; her career path paralleled and crossed everyone else's in jazz. She has been mentioned in countless biographies and histories of contemporary jazz. Among them have been: *American Singers* by Whitney Balliett (Oxford University Press, New York and Oxford, 1990); *Amateur Night at the Apollo*, by Ralph Cooper (Harper and Row and Consort, New York, 1991); *American Women in Jazz* by Sally Placksin (Wideview Books, New York, 1980); *Four Lives in the Bebop Business* by A. B. Spellman (Limelight Editions, New York, 1985); *Good Morning Blues: The Autobiography of Count Basie*, as told to Albert Murray (Random House, New York, 1985); *Inside Bebop*, reprinted as *Inside Jazz*, by Leonard Feather (Da Capo Press, New York 1979); *Jazz: America's Classical Music* by Grover Sales (Prentice-Hall, Englewood Cliffs, New Jersey, 1984); *Jazz Portraits* by Len Lyons and Don Perlo (William Morrow, New York, 1989); *Jazz Singing* by Will Friedwald (Charles Scribner's Sons, New York, 1990); *Louis' Children* by Leslie Gourse (William Morrow, New York, 1984); *Mabel Mercer: A Life* by James Haskins (Atheneum, New York, 1987); *Miles: The Autobiography* by Miles Davis with Quincy Troupe (Simon and Schuster, New York, 1989); *Oscar Peterson: The Will to Swing* by Gene Lees (Prima Publishing and Communications, Rocklin, California, 1988); *Rhythm-a-Ning* by Gary Giddins (Oxford University Press, New York, 1985); *Showtime at the Apollo* by Ted Fox (Holt, Rinehart and Winston, 1983, and Owl Books, 1985, New York); *Singers and the Song* by Gene Lees (Oxford University Press, New York, 1987); *Talking Jazz* by Max Jones (W. W. Norton, New York, 1988); *To Be or Not to*

Bop by Dizzy Gillespie with Al Fraser (Doubleday & Company, Garden City, New York, 1979, and Da Capo Press, New York, 1985); *The Best of the Music Makers* by George T. Simon and Friends (Doubleday & Company, Garden City, New York, 1979); *The Big Bands* by George T. Simon, 4th ed. (William Morrow and Company, New York, 1980); *The Great American Popular Singers* by Henry Pleasants (Simon and Schuster, New York, 1974); *The Jazz Scene* by W. Royal Stokes (Oxford University Press, New York, 1991); *The World of Earl Hines* by Stanley Dance (Charles Scribner's Sons, New York, 1977).

In short, Sarah Vaughan infuses the jazz literature, because the art of jazz is infused with her voice. Every experienced writer about jazz has had the occasion and inspiration to write about her, whether in newspaper articles, in magazines, in liner notes, or for television. Dan Morgenstern, of Rutgers University's Institute of Jazz Studies, Chip Deffas, Gene Santoro, Mitchell Seidel, George Kanzler Jr, John S. Wilson, Martin Williams, Gunther Schuller, Gene Lees, Nat Hentoff – book writers, critics, jazz historians, journalists, periodicals writers – have confronted the jazz force of Sarah Vaughan in their work. Morgenstern was the writer for an excellent video biography of Vaughan aired on PBS on 29 July 1991. Canadian and British journalists, whose works have come to my attention, have also expanded my understanding of Sarah's impact on her audiences abroad.

Books used specifically and directly as references for this biography are *Current Biography* (H. W. Wilson Company, New York, November 1957 and April 1980); *Sarah Vaughan, a Discography* compiled by Denis Brown (Greenwood Press, New York, 1991); *Top Pop Singles, 1955–1990*, published in 1991, and *Pop Memories, 1890–1954*, both by Joel Whitburn (Record Research, Menomonee Falls, Wisconsin, 1986).

Stan Britt, a British interviewer, has written liner notes for *The Singles Sessions*, a Roulette collection of Sarah's reissued work; Gene Lees wrote the liner notes for the Columbia Records collection of *The Divine Sarah Vaughan, 1949–1953*; that is just one aspect of his work with and about Sarah. See the discographical survey in this book for the information about the recording released by his own company. Dan Morgenstern, of Rutgers University's Institute of Jazz Studies, wrote the liner notes for *The Complete Sarah Vaughan on Mercury*.

Special thanks to Roberto Medina, director of the morgue at the *New York Times*, and to the Institute of Jazz Studies at Rutgers for making files available to me for research. Polygram, Mercury, Columbia, Roulette and Pablo also aided me immeasurably with their recordings. All the most important labels for which Sarah recorded assisted me with research materials in one way or another.

The following newspapers and periodicals have been referred to specifically in my book on Sarah Vaughan: *Newsweek, Time, Billboard, Washington Post, Metronome, New York Daily News, Chicago Sun, Village Voice, Down Beat.* England's *Melody Maker, Ebony,* the *Times* of London, *Los Angeles Times, Toronto Telegram, Toronto Globe and Mail, Toronto Star, New York City World Telegram and Sun,* the *Newark Sunday News,* the *Newark Star-Ledger, New York Times, Variety, Saturday Review, New York Daily Mirror, New York Post, Black American, Spin* and *Tan Confessions.* The following wire services have been referred to specifically, too: *Associated Press, NNPA,* the National Negro Press Association, a wire service based in Washington DC and *ANP,* the Associated Negro Press, a wire service based in Chicago.

Rights and
Permissions

Index